Winning Major Business

Winning Major Business

Concepts, caveats and practical approaches
to marketing and selling
projects, programmes and major products (PPPs)
to institutional purchasers world-wide

Current best practice and a step beyond

by Alex Weiss and Stephen Willson

with cartoons by Matt Pearce

Greenfield Publishing

**This book is dedicated to our wives, Lynda and Alex,
for their forbearance during its writing and publication.**

First published in Great Britain in 1994 by
Greenfield Publishing
P. O. Box 12,
Kenilworth,
Warwickshire, CV8 1ZS

Copyright © Alex Weiss and Stephen Willson 1994
All rights reserved

Typeset, 10.8 on 12.8 Times New Roman

Printed and bound in Great Britain by
Bell & Bain Limited, Glasgow

British Library Cataloguing in Publication Data

Weiss, Alexander Peter William
Winning Major Business: Concepts, Caveats and Practical Approaches to Marketing and Selling Projects, Programmes and Major Products to Institutional Purchasers Worldwide - Current Best Practice and a Step Beyond
I. Title II. Willson, Stephen John
III. Pearce, Matt
658.8

ISBN 0-9523328-0-9

Acknowledgements

We wish to thank our many former colleagues who, during discussions over a number of years on the wide range of subjects covered in this book, illuminated the issues and gave us helpful insights into many of the challenges facing the capital goods industry.

Particular thanks needs to be given to those who helped to check the final text, both for contents, and for typographical errors. These include the specialist help given by Paul Calderwood, who checked Chapter 11 on Promotion Strategy and Public Relations and John Garside, who reviewed the Commercial chapter. Both gave helpful comment and advice. Bob Judge read the whole manuscript and, in particular, the chapter on Finance. He made a number of invaluable comments. Lynda Weiss checked the entire text for clarity and typographical errors and she and Tom Weiss also provided many useful suggestions to make the book more readable

Inevitably, some of our material has come from sources that have already been published. Notable are the texts by Igor Ansoff, the matrix by the Boston Consulting Group, the work of Kenichi Ohmae on strategies for competitive advantage, Don G Reinertsen's data from new product killers, and concepts from Strategic Selling by Miller & Heiman. The sources of the nine segment model and the Rush Job Calendar are unknown to the authors, who wish to thank the originators and also apologise in advance if any other names have been missed from this list. The omission is entirely unintentional.

Contents

Introduction   v

An important notice
Why we wrote the book and how to use it
Key definitions
Relating the book to the capital goods industry
An overview of book contents

PART 1   HOW TO WIN BUSINESS   1

Chapter 1   The purchase process and assessing customers   3

Institutional purchases
The purchase process
Potential customers
Special selling situations

Chapter 2   Business development   14

Customers and opportunities
Teaming and collaboration
Influencing the specification
Bid decisions
Customer sources of value and expectations
Sales, capture and exploitation plans.

Chapter 3   The tender process   39

Win strategies
Pricing
Bids and their evaluation
Negotiating
Keeping it sold

Chapter 4 Bid management   66

Bidding
Proposals
Bid and proposal reviews

Chapter 5 The sales function and sales management   83

The selling function and sales executives
The selling process
Managing sales departments
Managing sales staff
Information systems

Chapter 6 International selling   121

Approaching overseas markets
Export sales management
Overseas representation
Export rules and tools

PART 2   BUSINESS STRATEGY AND MARKETING   151

Chapter 7 Strategic planning and segmentation   153

Planning
Business charters and mission statements
Routes to growth
Segmentation
Competition

Chapter 8 Market research   175

Approaches
Market sizes
Gathering data
Results

Chapter 9 PPP strategy   183

Issues and perceptions
Life cycles
Barriers to entry
Customer sources of value

Chapter 10 PPP planning and development   205

PPP plans
Developing new PPPs
Financial issues

Chapter 11 Promotion strategy and public relations   220

Strategic issues
Press relations and lobbying
Exhibitions
Literature and audio-visual
Advertising

PART 3   SUPPORTING FUNCTIONS   239

Chapter 12 Relating to the commercial function   241

Contracting and key contract issues
Export concerns
Financial issues
Other types of contract

Chapter 13 Relating to the financial function   257

Financial goals
Definitions
Pricing
International issues

Chapter 14 Relating to the project/programme management function   263

Management & managers
Subcontracting
Overseas contracts
After sales support

Appendix A Glossary of terms   269

Appendix B   Bibliography   273

Index   275

Order Form

LIST OF ILLUSTRATIONS

Fig 1. Strategic planning.
Fig 2. Marketing model.
Fig 3. Sales model.
Fig 4. Concerns of purchase influencers.
Fig 5. A customer family tree.
Fig 6. The selling process.
Fig 7. Bid/no-bid form.
Fig 8. Bid factors.
Fig 9. The bid process.
Fig 10. Customer concerns.
Fig 11. Value, cost & competitive factors.
Fig 12. Learning curves.
Fig 13. Capture plan.
Fig 14. Price estimate summary.
Fig 15. Software pricing.
Fig 16. Overhead recovery.
Fig 17. Errors in costing.
Fig 18. Rush job calendar.
Fig 19. Weighted points scale evaluation.
Fig 20. Value to price ratios.
Fig 21. Number of pages in proposals.
Fig 22. Form of proposals.
Fig 23. Storyboard.
Fig 24. Proposal reviews.
Fig 25. Bid review checklist.
Fig 26. Account management form.
Fig 27. Areas of customer influence.
Fig 28. The sales funnel.
Fig 29. Ratholing.
Fig 30. Sales control meeting agenda.
Fig 31. Bid/no-bid form.
Fig 32. Price/technical compliance.
Fig 33. Bid initiation form.
Fig 34. Number of bids per year.
Fig 35. Bid win analysis.
Fig 36. Bid loss analysis.
Fig 37. Visit report.
Fig 38. Prospect recording.
Fig 39. Recruitment checklist.
Fig 40. Commission levels.
Fig 41. Key financial issues.
Fig 42. Different planning approaches.
Fig 43. The Ansoff matrix.
Fig 44. The Willson/Ansoff matrix.
Fig 45. Nine ways to segment customers.
Fig 46. Segmentation & market strategies.
Fig 47. Cost of & profit from serving markets.
Fig 48. Market definitions.
Fig 49. Sources of data.
Fig 50. Positioning.
Fig 51. Competitor assessment.
Fig 52. PPP attractiveness.
Fig 53. Life cycle sales pattern.
Fig 54. The Boston matrix.
Fig 55. PPP life extension.
Fig 56. Demand/technology curve.
Fig 57. Switching costs.
Fig 58. Value, price & cost comparison.
Fig 59. Cost saving & differentiation.
Fig 60. Presenting PPP plan financial data.
Fig 61. Five categories of purchasers.
Fig 62. Sales & cash flow.
Fig 63. Impact of development problems on profit.
Fig 64. Technological maturity/customer experience.
Fig 65. Approaches to innovation.
Fig 66. Break even point.
Fig 67. Right mix of public relations.
Fig 68. The message varies during the PPP life.
Fig 69. Use of PR tools.
Fig 70. Some INCOTERMS.
Fig 71. Profit, capital turnover & ROI.
Fig 72. Checks before teaming.

Introduction:

Important notice · Why we wrote the book · Use of the book · Key definitions · The PPP's: Projects, Programmes & Major Products · The PPP environment · Alternatives and options · Project/programme management · Sales & marketing · Relating the book to PPP industry · Overview of book contents

Important notice

We have long felt the need for a book on industrial marketing and selling in the projects, programmes and major products field, and this book is the result. We have written it in a modular fashion in order to facilitate its use as a reference document. **It is, however, essential that even the skimming reader should first read the introduction, in order to understand a few key definitions and abbreviations selected for use throughout the book.** At the beginning of each part of the book, we have written a short summary, together with a list of chapters and, at the beginning of each chapter, a list of the topics covered. At the end of the book, there is a glossary of terms and a comprehensive index. We hope that you, the reader, will easily find the part of the book which deals with any topic of particular interest to you.

Why we wrote the book

For years, the provision of training for sales and marketing staff in the projects, programmes and major products environment has involved attending courses or reading books designed for those involved in selling consumer goods - anything from cigarettes to soap powder. Those selling major capital items find it very difficult to relate to such training. The result is that most people in this specialist field face the slow process of learning, either on the job, or from others with more experience than themselves. Knowledge is thus sparse and formal documentation all but non-existent.

After years working as practitioners, we became involved in developing a series of customised training courses aimed towards those selling programmes, projects and major products to governments and other bureaucratic customers. In the absence of any succinct term, we have christened the offerings PPPs, pronounced "three peas," as a convenient shorthand term. This term covers anything from nuclear power stations to office blocks, from chemical complexes to telephone exchanges, from satellites to fleets of new airliners, and from new motorways to bridges and tunnels.

We hope that by recognising the difference between the two markets, this book will provide useful guidance to sales and marketing staff, irrespective of their level of experience. It will provide them with practical advice in the competitive area of winning major business. It will, in addition, help those in other functions, such as commercial, project/programme management and finance, who are involved in helping to win contracts. It will also give a useful insight for those aspiring to or actually employed in general management, who will need a good understanding of how a company should respond to market drivers and the processes of winning new business. It is a book that, as the twentieth century draws to a close, is long overdue. It is a condensation of what is known, together with a number of new concepts. Through the act of writing it down and the use of diagrams, it should progress the state of the art.

Use of the book

We see this book being used in a number of ways. First, it will provide an essential reference book on all aspects of selling and marketing. Second, it will act as a vital reminder for those with experience of the subject, as well as filling gaps in their knowledge. Thirdly, it will form the basis of an excellent vehicle for instruction and is certain to prompt internal discussion. Finally it will assist in the generation or improvement of the many proformae which are so vital to the effective operation of any sales and marketing function.

Key definitions

There are a number of key terms that need definition right at the start. We are not saying that these are the only definitions, just that they are the ones used throughout this book. Without this clarity of definition, successful communication is precluded. Where we have quoted actual financial values, these are the values at the time the book was written unless otherwise stated.

The PPP's: Projects, Programmes and Major Products

One of the main difficulties, which we came up against at the start of the book, is the definition of what is being marketed and sold. Are the offerings projects or programmes, systems or products, hardware or software or even services? Perhaps it is indeed a mixture of a number of these. We conclude that it is all of them and that a single acronym is needed for use throughout. Thus was born PPP. So, in whichever major industry you, the reader, are employed, we hope that the term PPP can apply to your offerings and that you will be happy to associate with the term.

Some PPPs are virtually standard, others are custom-built to suit the purchaser. All are complex, of high monetary value and difficult to market and sell. The customers are equally different from the families in the consumer market. They tend to be faceless, hard to identify and multifaceted; bureaucratic institutions with complex purchasing processes and lengthy timescales. Trying to discover who makes the actual purchase decision is like trying to get water out of a stone. The purchasers are large organisations, almost always large companies or government departments.

The PPP environment

The PPP environment is different from the classical concept of fast moving consumer goods sales and marketing. The value of the offering is high and the volume low, when compared with those of consumer markets. Contracts are signed, rather than orders placed. Often delivery timescales are measured in years, occasionally tens of years. "Closing" by asking for the order, the mainstay and focus of much consumer goods sales activity and training, is thus inappropriate. Major interaction with the customer community is common during implementation of a PPP and delivery varies from handover of a turnkey project to shipment from the factory. The supplier and customer in PPPs often share a mutual destiny; failure can be disastrous for both.

Two interesting examples of catastrophic failures of PPPs were widely reported in the UK press in the early nineteen nineties and it is not, perhaps, surprising that both were in the information technology field. The first was the Stock Exchange's computer system, designed to implement paperless share dealing. The system had to be abandoned and a new start made. A similar fate was inflicted on the London Ambulance Brigade's new computerised system which, as well as causing chaos on its first day in use, apparently never performed satisfactorily and was quickly discarded in favour of the old manual slips of paper. In both cases, senior executives lost their jobs and, in the latter case, lives were possibly lost as well, as a result of the slow response of ambulances to emergency calls; measured in hours on the first day.

Alternatives and Options

Few PPPs are purchased which exactly match every single requirement in the tender specification. It is becoming increasingly common to acquire alternative, lower cost solutions. This leads to the need for an understanding of the difference between an alternative and an option. The former is, in effect, a second bid; an alternative to the main bid, which may provide an acceptable solution to the requirement in the tender specification. An option, on the other hand, is something that may or may not be needed, but which in some way enhances the performance or utility of the basic PPP.

Project/programme management

The person responsible for implementing the PPP, and ensuring that the customer gets what the contract specifies, can be known by a number of titles. Two of the most common are the project manager and the programme manager. For the purposes of this book, the abbreviation PM is used to describe this important function. Having said that, different companies and different industries use the two words in contradictory ways. For example, with the production of a major product, the person with overall responsibility for seeing that a specific number is built each month may be called the programme or the project manager. Similarly, the manager responsible for the design and development of a company's new range of PPPs may also use such titles. However, to repeat, we have defined the PM as the person accountable to the customer for the implementation of the PPP.

Sales and marketing

The terms sales and marketing, which vary widely from company to company, also need definition. In the context of this book, "sales" is the activity of following up qualified leads and turning them into contracts. "Marketing" involves deciding what to sell, where to sell it and obtaining and qualifying leads. Traditionally, in the PPP industry context, it also includes promotion in the public relations sense. These are not the only definitions possible of the two terms sales and marketing, but for consistency they are used in this way throughout the book.

The word sales director is generally used to describe the director responsible for selling, though we recognise that titles such as business development director, marketing director or even sales and marketing director are often employed in PPP companies for such a role. Furthermore, in the PPP arena, it is noticeable that the conventional consumer goods split of marketing and sales is rarely found. To reflect the reality of how the function is usually organised in the PPP environment, the first part of the book looks at the selling process, while the second part deals with business strategy including marketing.

As we have already mentioned, there are many differences between classic consumer marketing and PPP marketing. We recognise that the so-called four Ps of the marketing mix, a well proven product marketing philosophy, do not provide a good way of looking at PPP marketing.

1. **P**roduct strategy including definition of what is to be offered.
2. **P**rice Strategy.
3. **P**romotion strategy.
4. **P**lace (Distribution strategy.)

Not only do the four Ps not fit comfortably into the PPP approach to the marketplace but, in addition, marketeers in a PPP environment will almost always wish to add a fifth P:

5. **P**olitics and lobbying strategy

For these reasons, we have dealt with the subject matter in a different way and structured it in the sections on PPP development, pricing, promotion and public relations, and overseas representation respectively. The last mentioned section covers the use of representatives, agents and distributors. For practical convenience, we use the single term representative throughout.

At times throughout the book we may appear to have taken a patronising view of customers. This is not what we intended. The ideal view that the customer is always right needs to be the driver for all company employees, particularly those in the sales and marketing function. However, in winning new business, sales executives need to recognise and use the shortcomings of customers. It is this latter point that we wish to highlight.

Relating the book to PPP industry

In considering the relationship between this book and the real world of PPP industry and its customers, it is interesting to look at a model of the way in which the marketing and selling challenges are met by typical PPP companies. The intention is not to encourage a particular organisational structure, but rather to illustrate a way in which actions are carried out. Certainly, although strategic planning, marketing and sales are split into three, this is rarely found organisationally in PPP companies. Whilst details will change, both from company to company and also from industry to industry, readers should have little difficulty in adapting the model to their own organisations and market situations. By comparing this model of their company with the contents of this book, a clear map should emerge which will help readers to access the parts of the book that are relevant to their needs. The three parts of the model are strategic planning, marketing and sales.

Strategic planning

Any business faces a number of external and internal factors that affect the way in which it operates. The external factors include such influences as the political, economic, legal, social, regulatory and technological situations and predicted changes generally resulting from competitive rivalry. A marketing audit will reveal internal changes and cover such items as the Company's business charter, finances, capacity, key resource availability, core competencies and the PPP capability. Customer needs and perceptions, as well as the competitive situation, will influence the present and future position of the Company in the marketplace.

A situation analysis of these factors leads to a business concept definition, which together with examination of a number of past and current factors results in a market assessment, the three outputs of which are the business strategy, the market strategy and the PPP strategy. Investments, acquisitions, joint ventures, licencing policies and disposals are all a part of business strategy. On the market side, the size and trend of market segments, market shares and growth are all of concern. The PPP strategy will include the approach to new developments and make or buy policies.

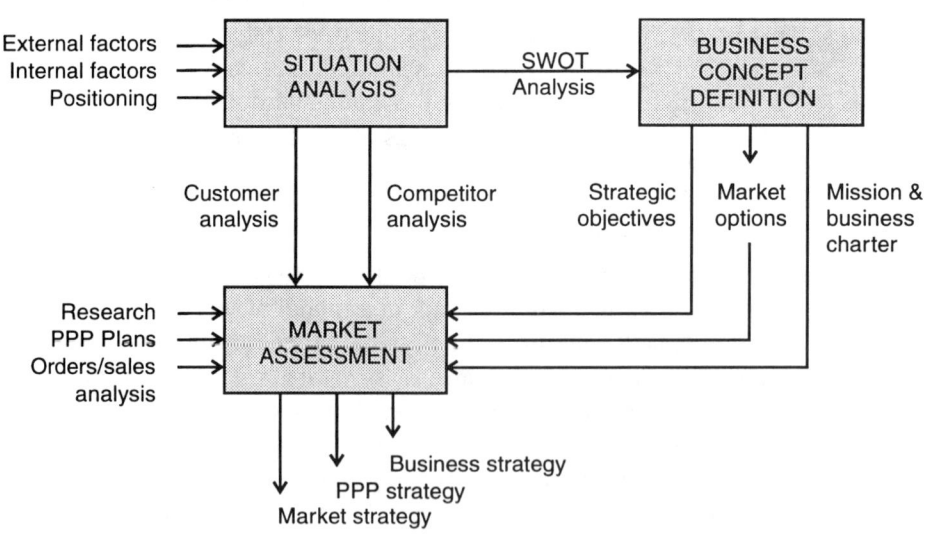

Figure 1. Strategic planning business model

Marketing

Marketing takes inputs from two sources. Strategic planning provides the business, PPP and market strategies. The marketplace provides the various new opportunities and customer needs, together with competitor data and a range of market intelligence. Marketing analysis is then carried out and includes examining feed back via marketing metrics.

The outputs of the analysis are marketing plans, PPP plans and selected opportunities, as well as a number of tactical requirements. These include budget objectives, investment plans and bid criteria; the last dependant on forward load and resource availability. All of these factors need consideration in marketing implementation, which will provide qualified leads and information about the situation in the various markets of interest. The other function carried out here is promotion and public relations, including such activities as advertising, audio-visual work, exhibitions, literature preparation, mailshots, lobbying and press relations.

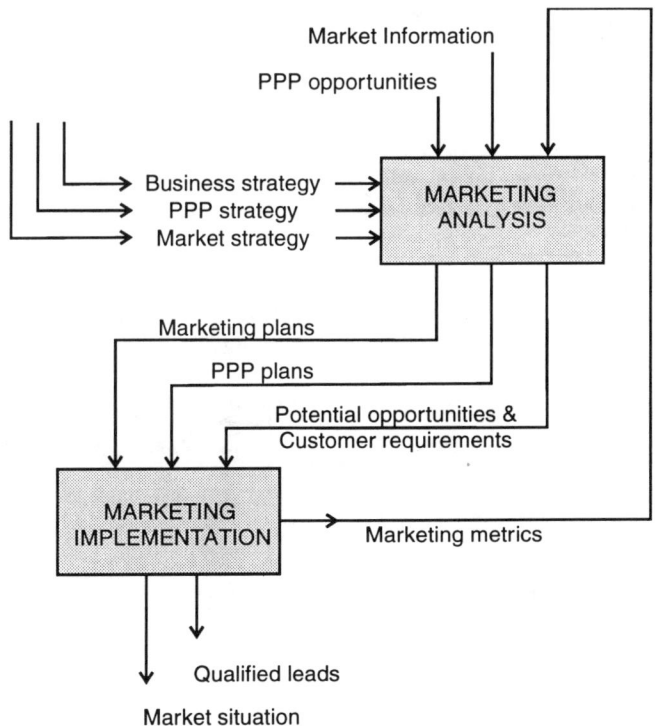

Figure 2. A PPP marketing model

Sales

Qualified leads and enquiries, including requests for proposals, quotations and tenders, together with other market intelligence such as contract awards, are analysed in conjunction with bid criteria and details of the Company's sales performance. The requirement for collaboration, with the need for confidentiality and teaming agreements, is also considered at this stage. Sales implementation examines prospects and forecasts, positive bid decisions and their associated bid initiation forms (BIFs). The most important outputs are win strategies, capture plans and the winning of contracts for new business, which may require equipment trials or demonstrations. Order intake forecasts and intelligence from the market place, including new PPPs being offered and other competitor data must not be forgotten. Finally, the derivation of sales metrics will allow further cost effectiveness analysis.

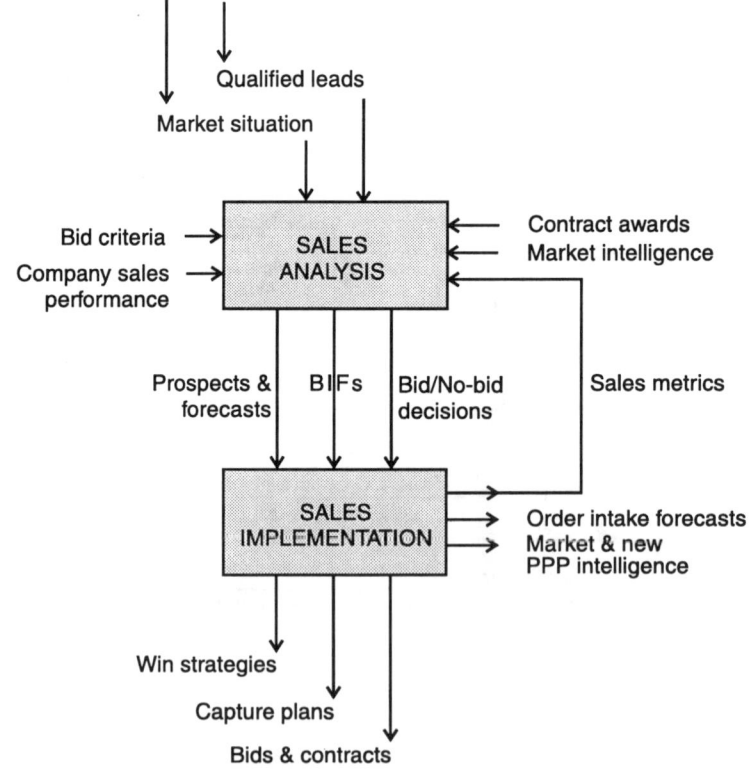

Figure 3. A model for PPP selling

Overview of book contents

We have purposely divided this book into three parts. The first part deals with the selling process, or how to win business from the customer. It starts by looking at the home market and later considers the differences when dealing with overseas markets. Major chapters cover the purchase process and assessing the customer, business development, the tender process, bid management and proposals, the sales function, sales management and international selling.

The second part of the book deals with business strategy and marketing, or how to get to the point where PPPs can be offered to customers. It starts with a chapter on strategic planning and segmentation then moves into market research. Subsequent chapters cover PPP strategy, planning and development, ultimately progressing into promotion strategy and public relations.

The final part deals with the areas in which sales and marketing staff need to relate to the other support functions, such as commercial and finance, with a somewhat arbitrary division of the work carried out by the two functions, and project/programme management. The book concludes with two appendices; a glossary of terms and a short bibliography. Following a comprehensive index, there is a form for ordering further copies of this book.

PART 1:

HOW TO WIN BUSINESS

The purchase process & assessing the customer · Business development · The tender process · Bid management · Sales management · International selling

Part 1 of this book examines the winning of business for companies. It reviews the complete purchase process from the first indication of a need by a potential customer organisation to the award of a contract. It also looks at customers, how to assess them and their advisors, as well as how to deal with original equipment manufacturers, sister divisions and second hand sales. The second chapter considers the assessment of opportunities, deciding which ones warrant a bid and positioning for competitive advantage. Next, there is an examination of the tender process, concentrating on how to get into the winning position. Two chapters follow describing, respectively, how to manage the bidding process in order to produce winning tender submissions and how to manage a sales team in a PPP environment. Having looked first at the home market, Part 1 ends by considering the differences found when selling in export markets.

Chapter 1:

The Purchase Process & Assessing Customers

Institutional purchase roles · Typical government & institutional purchasers · Who influences customers · The stages of the purchase process · Contacting potential customers · Customer family trees · Budget approval limits · Dealing with Original Equipment Manufacturers · Engineering consultants · Sister divisions in the Company as customers · Second-hand sales

Institutional purchase roles

There are two key reasons for needing to understand the mechanisms through which projects, programmes and major products, the PPPs, are purchased. The first is in order to influence specific purchases in favour of the Company. The second is that understanding how such purchases are made often helps in the difficult tasks of segmentation and the selection of target markets.

Industrial purchases are distinct from consumer purchases because they are institutionally rather than individually centred. PPP purchases additionally differ in usually extending over longer time frames, due to their complexity, magnitude and long term impact on the purchaser's business. A further distinction can usefully be made between PPP purchases; whether they are planned, proactive or reactive. Each is likely to be championed from a different area of the customer organisation and have its own characteristics in terms of urgency, as well as its sources and degree of uncertainty.

While on the subject of the methods used in making PPP purchases, it is worth noting that in common with leadership styles, purchases may either be led autocratically, democratically, or indeed, given free reign. In this latter case, major players abdicate from being involved for one reason or another. This is often because of the perceived risk of being closely associated with a major decision that they consider may turn sour.

Penetrating and staying abreast of the specifics of the decision making process in any particular deal is a continuing challenge for the sales executive. The elements of central concern are who has the power to make the decision, what is the source of that power and who has the authority to take such a decision. These elements are likely to shift during the purchase process for three main reasons.

CONSUMER GOODS SELLING TECHNIQUES ARE RARELY APPROPRIATE IN THE PPP ARENA.

1. As customer internal staff positions change
2. From their own internal wranglings
3. Under the influence of the competition and other external influences.

It is critical to explore the customer organisation to identify and enter into open conversation with each of the influencers and thus affect their say on this purchase decision. Remember, if sufficiently motivated, any one of the influencers can put their foot down, say no and this negative will stick. The corollary is not, however, true. Only the decision maker(s) has that ability. In fact, in many purchasing processes, some members can make no positive input at all into the purchase decision, but still hold a power of veto. The classic "If we buy that, we're certain to have maintenance problems" can be a killer. It is also important to establish who in the customer community is championing the particular purchase and, if at all possible, to convert them into a champion for the Company's own PPP.

Each of these influencers will see varying amounts of value from different facets of the available offerings. These differences result from the diversity of their outlook. For example, if they are in operations and only concerned with cost, they

PURCHASE INFLUENCERS	CONCERNS
Buyers	Price reduction
Operations	Performance and technical solution
Installation	Least hassle
Maintenance	Reliability and life cycle costs
Logistics and Support	Best value from their budget, LCC
Finance	Cash, profit, ROI, NPV, payback period
Commercial Department	Contract conditions
Engineering Consultants	Value for money
Technical Experts	Technical solution
Internal Champions	Personal Value
End Users i.e. the customer's customer	Value for money and ease of use
Others: Political, standards setting bodies, policy makers, trade associations	Meet political and other requirements

Figure 4. The concerns of key purchase influencers are many and varied. Sales executives need to understand the reasons for them.

will not appreciate value accruing from increased revenue or reduced capital. A selection made at this level would be a cue to try to escalate the decision if the value of the Company's offering, in profit or investment terms, is not going to be appreciated. The aim should be to include those involved with making profit or even those concerned with the level of investment. Admittedly, such involvement is likely anyway with the majority of PPP purchases, owing to their size and impact. However, the point is worth bearing in mind. See also Page 29 on value.

As already noted, it is extremely rare for a single individual in government or institutional organisations to purchase a PPP. Usually, a committee undertakes the process of arriving at a purchase decision; the role of the members being identifiable with varying degrees of difficulty. It is not always clear who is the decision maker and a common comment by the chairman, notionally the decision maker, is "Well, can I take it that we are all happy with the choice of company X?" It is not uncommon, after such a decision has been made to find that, individually, most of the committee members would have preferred the offering of company Y. The name given to this flawed decision making is "group think."

Typical government and institutional purchasers

Users

The actual people involved in working with the PPP. Their influence can vary enormously and, in service industries, they can be quite remote from the purchasers. It can often require considerable thought to decide who is the user. Taking railway equipment as an example, is the user the operating company, the train crew or the passengers?

Buyers

Their power varies, usually depending on the complexity of the purchase. It may vary from being told what to purchase and on what terms, in the case of a major plant acquisition, to near total authority in the case of vehicle purchases.

Influencers

This grouping includes technical experts, specifiers, installers, maintainers, commercial and legal staff. It also includes independent consultants, often employed to give an outside view. In government ministries, retired staff often return in an advisory role and have significant influence as a result of their previous full time employment role.

Gatekeepers

Those producing industrial standards and legal requirements fall into this category; so do those in the customer's finance function. Usually a negative influence, such as the over protective secretary denying access to a key player, or the buyer failing to circulate a piece of technical information to the selection committee. An example of a positive role is when a member of the sales force is aware of a source of equipment used by the customer's competitor.

Deciders

These will probably never come to light. If the purchase is successful, everyone will claim credit, but if unsuccessful, no-one will take the blame. This reflex reveals why influencing the institutional purchase process is often likened to collecting fingerprints on a communal gun. In the event of error, no individual can be singled out for blame.

Politicians

Increasingly important in large government purchases, the list can run from the ministers involved through to a member of parliament with a local employment issue.

Different PPPs require different approaches to the various members of the customer community. These variations will depend on a number of factors and it is important that the sales executive assesses each carefully before making any serious approach to the customer.

- User technical ability and rate of staff turnover
- Purchase process
- Support and upgrade requirements
- Level of customer interest
- Existing infrastructure
- User interface (or is it a black box)
- Length of sales cycle (months, years or decades)
- Cultural interface and resistance to change (training requirements)

Furthermore, there is a need for care when deciding at what level to make the initial approach. Generally, starting at a senior level and working down is better than the reverse. It is also important to avoid bypassing the purchasing department and talking only to engineers.

Who influences customers

It is interesting to look at the large number of organisations, individuals and other factors that exert an influence on the purchasing decisions of customers acquiring PPPs. At one extreme there are governments, with their standards bodies, strategic industries, local manufacture preferences and acquisition rules covering, for example, foreign exchange, offset and barter. Next are prime contractors, who are at the top of the PPP tree and may have a significant, if not overriding, say about what is purchased. Then there are competitors and any consultants involved in the particular acquisition. Finally there is the Company selling team and its local representative, agent or distributor.

In fact, every employee in the Company has a selling role when in contact with potential customers. From the chief executive and the management team to the telephone operator and the security guard, each has the ability to influence the selection of the Company for a new piece of business. All will influence the customer to a greater or lesser degree and it is important that they all remember this if a contract is to be won.

The stages of the purchase process

The scope and type of interaction with the customer will be determined by the stage reached in the purchase process. The nature of what is being acquired will affect the process itself and will clearly be different for say a suspension bridge as opposed to a fleet of delivery vans. Repeat purchases, particularly where the organisational impact is low, are likely to follow the classic model.

- Identify the need
- Establish a specification
- Identify the solutions
- Evaluate the solutions
- Select a supplier

In certain parts of the PPP arena, the process is much more iterative and also far more time consuming. The customer may start with a possible solution, find that it exceeds available funds, find an alternative supplier or change the specification and so on. With many iterations, the danger arises of an outdated solution, which begets the temptation for the customer to rewrite the specification again. The process is further complicated by the stage of procurement, some or all of which may be used for any particular purchase.

- Pre-feasibility study
- Feasibility study
- Definition study
- Full scale development
- Low rate initial production
- Full production
- Field support

The letting of the contract for each of these stages, including the studies, will in turn usually involve the purchaser in all of the following activities.

- Compiling a bidders' list
- Putting the specification out to tender
- Evaluating the tenders
- Negotiating with the best two or three bidders
- Awarding the contract
- Post contract review

Each stage is subject to influence, not only by the contractor, but also by any competitors. The result is a process, which, for the largest type of PPPs, may easily take ten to fifteen years from start to production; a very long gestation period!

Contacting potential customers

There are several ways of communicating with potential customers; by telephone, by writing, or by visiting. A further subdivision of each of these three categories is possible. The telephone has two main uses. A telephone call is a good way of setting up a cold call to an individual in the customer community. With large, bureaucratic customers and a well-known supplier, this is often done secretary to secretary, or sales executive to secretary. Apart from that, it is best reserved for communication where the caller is personally known to the customer.

The letter is a better way of starting the cold calling process, but must be brief and to the point. Customers are busy people, who don't have time to read reams of paper. The letter requires a follow up very soon after its expected arrival. Faxes are suitable as follow on written communications between individuals known to each other, but less good for the initial approach, since they give the undesirable impression of pressurising the recipient.

The visit itself should never be a genuine cold call in the PPP business, since the caller won't be taken seriously. It might even appear presumptuous and it is almost certain that no-one of consequence will be available. Always make an appointment. Depending somewhat on the nature of the PPP and the number of customer staff likely to be present, a visit by one or two people is generally the right approach. Only use a sales team when the customer will be fielding a similar sized team.

It is noticeable that the size of team needed varies with time. Start with a small number, build up the size of the team and, toward the end, reduce the team size again. There needs to be great sensitivity in listening to the customer and interpreting the meaning of what is being said. Customers often give veiled messages and unless understood, it is easy for a contract to slip through one's fingers. Furthermore, it is not always appropriate to ask directly for clarification. In the closing stages, a one to one meeting with the customer will often reveal things that would never be said in an open meeting.

Customer family trees

The customer family tree is a map of the customer's organisation, vertically by seniority and horizontally by function. It must reflect the reality of who has authority and not just copy out the organisation chart. It is usually in a state of flux and therefore inaccurate, as well as overlooking the realities of people having been promoted to get them out of the way. It is important, in putting together a customer's family tree, that there are no gaps in the tree, particularly amongst those directly involved in the purchase process. The task of putting the tree together falls on the sales executive. It often requires significant work and discussion with members of other functions within the Company to establish all the parts of this jigsaw. A copy of the customer's internal telephone directory can be revealing. As an aside, a customer's reception staff and security guards, who are generally friendly and talkative, will know who is busy and, by inference, important.

The ability to relate to customers' organisations critically affects the chances of influencing their perception of a particular PPP. This implies a dual approach to the customer, in terms both of seniority and function, as well as the need to find

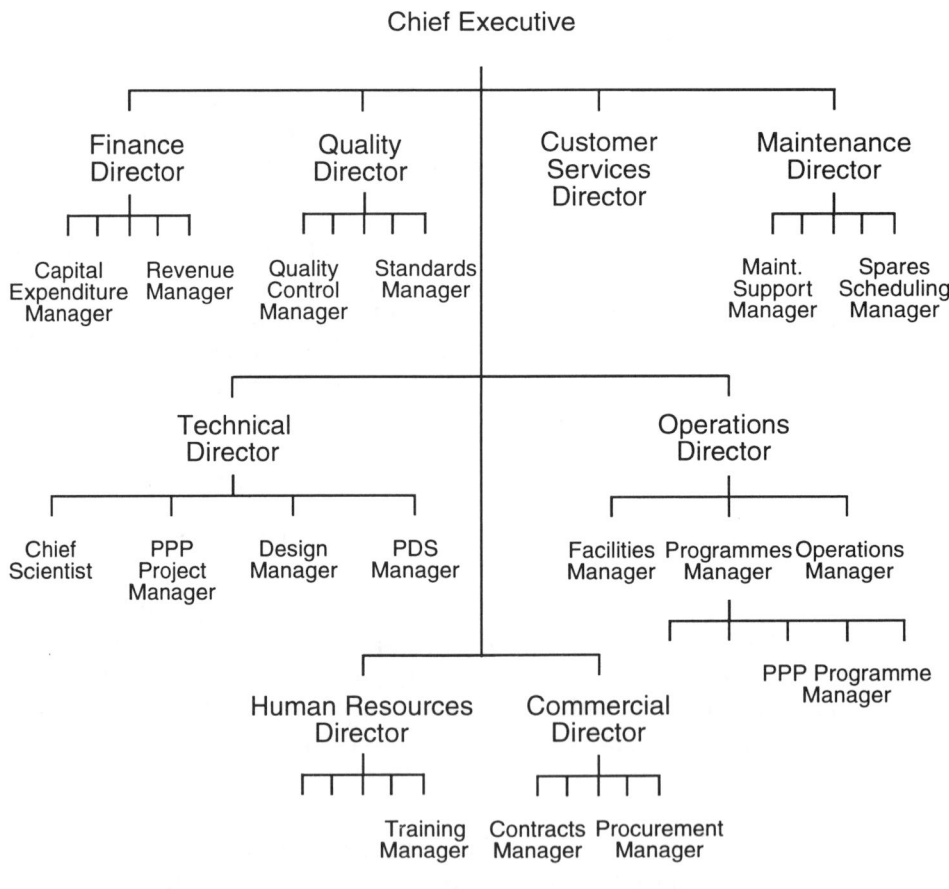

Figure 5. A typical customer family tree, showing some of the complexities likely to be experienced. Every reader will be familiar with this type of chart, but it is easy to miss people out or be misled by customer published charts.

personalities within the Company who can relate well to their opposite numbers. This is usually done by matching function and seniority, but often personal friendship, such as having gone to university together, or common interests, such as playing golf, can cut across the conventional boundaries to advantage.

Budget approval limits

It is of critical importance to determine each customer decision maker's level of authority to approve expenditure. Prices within individuals' authority levels will allow them to make decisions without referring them upwards. This can speed the decision making process but, more importantly, allow the sales team to target the right selection authority. One particular example of the benefits of such identification lies at the end of the customer's financial year, when significant sums of unspent cash may be available for immediate contracts. Unfortunately, pride can prevent questions about such cash being asked directly.

Dealing with Original Equipment Manufacturers (OEMs)

One of the more difficult problems in selling PPPs is when the customer is a prime contractor, rather than the final purchaser. Examples include selling ventilation systems to hotel construction companies and engines to ship builders. In all these cases, both the final purchaser and the prime contractor will have a view about the preferred supplier and both will need persuading that the Company's offering is the best one for the requirement.

A pull strategy can be particularly effective in such instances. Here the justification for a PPP is made to the end user buying it from the OEM. The OEM may not have the experience, sophisticated resources or commitment to make such a convincing case. However, the OEM still requires persuading of the advantages of the proposed PPP. Neglecting to take this two pronged approach can easily lead to failure, with the prime contractor saying to the final customer "It will be much more expensive if you insist on this supplier for the PPP" or conversely, the final purchaser saying "I know you've offered supplier X's PPP, but I insist on this other supplier's PPP because…" Usually, a single sales executive can deal with both entities, but occasionally, due to the difference in culture between the two purchasing organisations, the use of a pair of sales executives is the better approach. Of course, there then needs to be the closest working relationship between the two.

Engineering consultants

Because of the very complexity of PPPs, it is common for customers to employ consultants to assist them in their purchase and subsequent implementation. Perhaps the best established example of this is the architect in new building construction, where the total cost can be very high, as sums up to £1B spent on buildings like Canary Wharf testify. Perhaps more common is the engineering consultant, so frequently found in complex civil engineering projects, from the construction of a motorway to the building of a new chemical complex. In truth, some prime contractorship roles are more like those of an engineering consultant combined with the role of equipment purchaser.

Bear in mind that these consultancy companies are generally sophisticated organisations, with bright people who should not be underestimated. However, they may also have divergent interests and concerns from their client organisations. Most noticeable of these is their desire to show through their transactions that they justify their cost.

Engineering consultants need to be treated as if they were customers and, as with the case of prime-contractors, the two pronged selling approach is essential. Like prime contractors, both groups consider that they are employed by the final customer to keep subcontractors away and it is not uncommon for them to try to stop any contact with the customer. It is necessary to understand their position and dealt with it both sympathetically and firmly.

Sister divisions in the Company as customers

In the same way that civil war appears to be so much more savage than other forms of warfare, so selling to sister divisions is more fraught with problems than selling to any other customer. It is common to hear people say "We'd rather buy from anyone, in preference to one of our sister divisions." What is it that brings about this sad state of affairs? It usually starts with the fact that the sales team don't treat other divisions as if they were real customers. Do they get entertained as if they were customers? Usually they do not. Furthermore, what happens when the selling division's deliveries start to lag behind schedule? Deliveries to the sister division get diverted to a "real" customer.

The purchasing division's receipt of a quotation illustrates the other side of the coin. "Unless you reduce this quite unreasonable quote, we'll get **our** divisional manager to go to the chief executive and he'll order **your** divisional manager to give us a realistic price." Thus the hatred grows.

Company inter-divisional trading rules are often defined and try to ensure that the corporation doesn't take contingency on contingency nor profit on profit. Fine, unless a divisional manager's bonus depends on the level of profit the division achieves. In this case, an instruction will quickly go out not to waste resources on selling to sister divisions. Another possible corporate approach is to take all the profit at the integrating stage and distribute it subsequently.

By far the best solution is one where companies treat inter-divisional trading as an arm's length activity and sales staff look upon their sister divisions in an identical way to any other customer. Buying divisions must genuinely be able actually to make purchases outside the organisation. If this is only a superficial policy, then outside suppliers will quickly tire of quoting in what becomes obvious as a "no win" situation.

Second-hand sales

Companies are often tempted to sell second-hand equipment as if it were new. Such equipment has frequently only had minimal use, perhaps a trial or demonstration, subsequently being refurbished to an "as new" condition. What is essential is that no customer is ever offered such equipment as new, but a genuine statement made about its condition. Refurbished to an "as new" condition with a full or even extended warranty is quite acceptable, though any potential customer will also expect a discount for what is clearly a used item.

In many fields, the sale of genuinely second-hand equipment, offered as such, is becoming increasingly common. The trend is being driven not only by long equipment life but also by early obsolescence, matched to lack of funds, particularly for new technology. These cases bring into play all the techniques involved in selling new PPPs.

Affordability and supportability are usually the two key factors and these will need greater than usual attention in any proposal to sell a second-hand PPP to a customer. It is worth noting that many such sales result from a sales executive's genuine desire to help a customer and such an attitude should be encouraged, even when the sales executive has no solution to offer and has to point the customer to another second hand supplier.

Chapter 2:

Business Development

The Company's viewpoint · Qualifying & quantifying customers · Qualifying opportunities · Strategic issues · Wants & needs · Funding · Feasibility studies · Demonstration programmes · Skills/core competencies match · Technology needs · Teaming · Collaborative programmes · Competitive analysis · White papers · Specmanship · Unwitting bid decisions · Bid/no-bid decisions · Initial win strategies · Generating attractive alternatives · Customer sources of value · Producing & using value case · Cost, value & competition · Learning curves & customer expectations · Pricing strategies · Payback analysis · Sales plans · Capture plans · Project/programme management plans · Exploitation plans

The Company's viewpoint

Following examination of the customer community, its functioning and how to make initial contact, the business development or selling process will now be considered from a company's point of view. It is essential to recognise that once the tender documents arrive in the offices of the various bidding companies, the result of the competition is usually all but a foregone conclusion. The reason for this is that potential winning bidders will carefully position themselves during the pre-tender period in such a way as to ensure that their bids will be the lowest priced compliant ones.

It is therefore essential to formulate a capture plan after selection of a prospect as a serious one and to continue to update the plan during the progress of the prospect. The process starts with the identification of a worthwhile opportunity for a PPP and ends with the award of a contract. The plan needs to cover both internal factors, such as resource availability and core competencies, as well as external issues including the best ways to influence the contents of the specification and the likely competition. Page 35 gives further information on capture plans.

Qualifying and quantifying customers

From a vendor's perspective, one of the ways in which customers differ from one another is in the certainty of whether they will actually make the purchases that they talk about. Moreover, the length of the delay before they place any contract will also vary. Companies in the PPP business accept long and cumbersome purchase procedures, but some customers are far worse than others in this respect. The worst indulge in what can only be described as window shopping. It is therefore always important at the outset to rate every opportunity in terms of the probability of any contract being let and the likely time scale of any award. Only then should the Company's chances of winning be addressed.

Generally, quantifying customers is rather easier as, by the very nature of the PPP business, the number of customers is significantly smaller than in consumer markets. At the bottom end numerically, the Space business includes only a small minority of nations, whilst selling to every government in the world still keeps the number below 200. Bureaucratic organisations, such as local councils, police and emergency services number less than 100 in the UK. Industrial customers, though they may run into the thousands, still represent manageable quantity. Whatever the total number of customers, it is important to assess this figure with accuracy.

Qualifying opportunities

"How real is this prospect?" is the problem that haunts most sales directors. It is, fortunately, not usually too hard to arrive at a sensible judgement. Because the purchase of PPPs involves many people, a poll of views across those involved in the purchase process can quickly lead to a body of opinion. Many are those who wax lyrical about their requirement for a new PPP. A quick check with procurement may elicit that there are no funds available for it.

It is common practice in many PPP markets for companies to have to pre-qualify for inclusion on the bidder's list. This pre-qualification usually requires the submission of a document indicating the capabilities, experience and standards employed by the proposed supplier, together with copies of the annual accounts to prove that the company has the financial stability and staying power for the PPP business. Indeed, it is likely that any potential supplier will also have to satisfy a vendor approval process.

Strategic issues

It is easy to forget strategic factors in the rush to deal with short term issues. They concern major long term changes in the market place, of which there are some

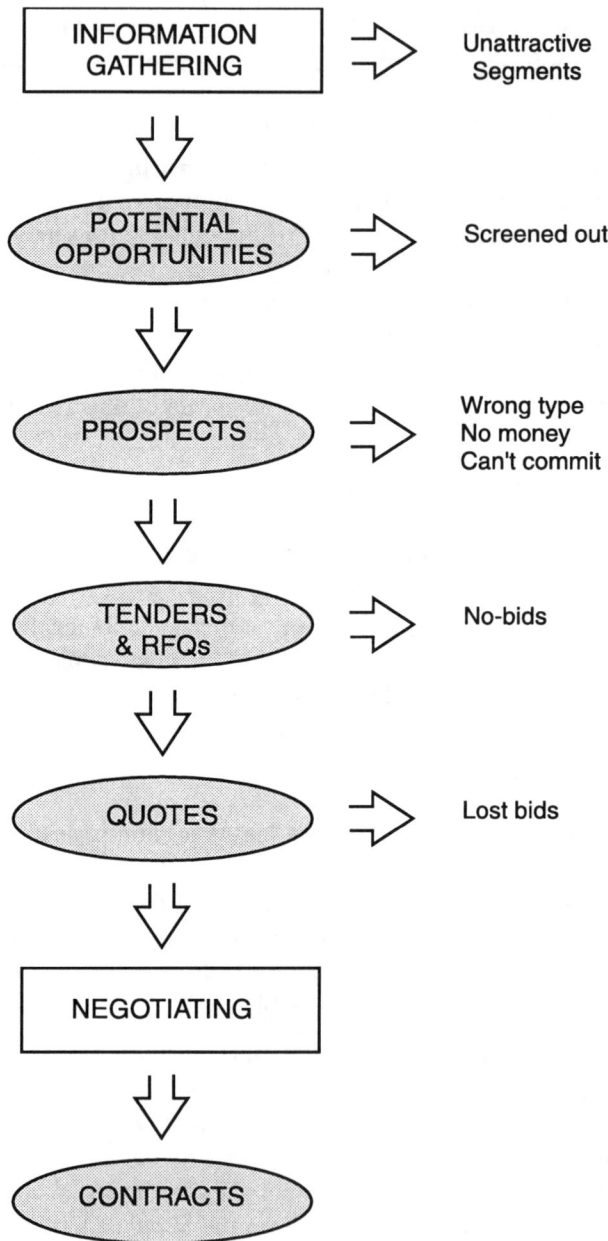

Figure 6. It is essential that all those involved in winning new business clearly understand the nature of the selling process.

recent interesting examples. These include the large cutback in defence spending by the industrialised nations following the collapse of the Soviet Union, the ever soaring price of labour in the industrialised nations with the consequent drive to automate and the growing impact of the environmental lobby not the least towards nuclear power generation. Whilst these are unlikely to impact on the day to day tactics of a company, they need remembering when deciding what type of business to bid for in the future.

Wants and needs

In looking for new opportunities, any company's activity will start with intelligence gathering, which will involve contact with the customer community, particularly the users and specifiers. An obsolescence review is often beneficial, with a scrutiny of customer equipment that may be due for replacement. In the complex PPP business, many customers will have their own technical establishments, or rely heavily on technical consultants, and close liaison should be maintained with these organisations. The aim should be to identify customer problems, particularly those hitherto unrecognised by the customer.

It is essential to establish if customers know what they actually want and whether the Company understands exactly what they require. It may even be necessary to go back a step and evaluate customer needs as opposed to wants. As an analogy, travel to many of the oil rich nations shows motorways from the airport to the city centre that would do justice to the most demanding Californian freeway need. Sadly, the traffic on such motorways is so light that a simple four lane highway would suffice into the foreseeable future.

In the early 1970's a bright sales executive was travelling in the Middle East. He recognised that with the fourfold increase in oil prices, the Arab Gulf States did not have the necessary aviation infrastructure, apart from the basic airfields, to deal with the increase in passenger traffic that would inevitably result from these states' new found wealth. The countries concerned were not even aware of the impending problem. He and his company developed an outline radar-based air traffic control network, stretching from Kuwait in the North to Oman in the South. He then proceeded to sell a large number of systems to the various countries involved, having first got them to recognise the need and then to establish the necessary budgets; there being plenty of oil revenues to provide the necessary funding.

Individuals in companies may see a piece of equipment and want it regardless of whether their own situation justifies such a purchase. A similar evaluation of a customer's needs can give a useful indication as to the solidity of the allocated budget and the way the budget will stand up to inquisition, which at some stage is almost certain to occur.

It is important to recognise the scope of the solution, which can vary from simple equipment supply to a complete turnkey solution. (The word turnkey is much misused and means the establishment of a PPP on, literally, a greenfield site and handing over the keys upon completion.) A question, often asked in the next few paragraphs, must follow. "Why should the customer choose our company's offering?"

Funding

Probably the single most important rule for anyone involved in selling is "No money, no sale!" Without funding for a PPP, all that a customer is doing is inviting a company to waste money in a futile bidding process. Would that the situation was always that clear! The problem, both with government institutions and with any large bureaucratic organisation, is that budgets can change, seemingly at a moment's notice. Thus selling a PPP will often involve helping the customer to keep the budget in place, not only before contract award, but equally afterwards.

This leads to two important issues. First, it is essential to establish who owns the budget. For example, does it belong to the city, the region or is it a national budget? Second, others in addition to direct competitors are a problem. Any supplier to a company's clientele is vying to obtain scarce finance and should, in that sense, be recognised as a competitor and treated as such. Furthermore, unless a sense of urgency exists, or can be created within the customer organisation, the opportunity is likely to devolve into the "nice to have" category and suffer consequent deferral.

Feasibility studies

It is not unusual, in the PPP business, for customers to identify a need, but then not know what it is they actually want, particularly if it is, for them, a rare type of purchase. This can lead to early feasibility studies being undertaken. Many a company has got itself into a winning position by internally funding some or all of this work, and submitting the results to the customer as an unsolicited proposal, together with a budgetary price.

Formal funded studies, carried out for the customer, can be of great value in enabling a company to create value cases for the various players in the customer organisation. Engineering consultants often carry out such studies on behalf of the customer. Thus, sales executives must ensure that these consultants have a clear knowledge of the application and benefits of the Company's offerings. Where a company carries out a paid study, it is essential to establish if a condition of undertaking such work is a ban from bidding to supply the PPP, when the time comes, in the interests of retaining vendor independence.

Demonstration programmes

It is not readily possible to demonstrate all PPPs, but for those which are suitable, the ground needs treading with the greatest care. Any live demonstration is a potential disaster just waiting to happen. The gremlins seem to recognise what is going on and conspire to cause the greatest possible equipment problems at the worst possible moment. A good point to start is to ask the rhetorical question "Why is there to be a demonstration?" Sometimes, the customer demands a "try before buy" approach, but equally often it is sales executives, who have put their feet in it by saying "We'd be pleased to give you a live demonstration." Until there are answers to several further questions, it is best to avoid this tactic.

- What competitive advantage can be gained?
- When will the demonstration be held?
- How will it be carried out?
- Is the equipment available?
- Are the people available?
- How much will the demonstration cost?

After acquiring the necessary information, a reasoned decision is possible, based on the potential worth to the Company of carrying out a demonstration. However, care needs taking in two important areas. The first is to ensure that the Company controls, as far as is possible, the attendees at the demonstration. Where it is to take place overseas, it is important to maintain control over the equipment to minimise the risk of someone taking it apart and reverse engineering it. A document known as a carnet must be obtained to allow temporary export and re-import of the equipment at the end of the demonstration. For sensitive technology, an export licence may also be needed.

Skills/core competencies match

It can be very tempting to bid for something that is not in the direct current line of business of the Company, even though it is with the same customer community. At the onset, always ask the question "What value can the Company add?" Opportunities can look particularly attractive because the full nature of the competition is less than totally clear. It is, therefore, vital to make a careful assessment of the Company's match of skills and its range of core competencies against those needed to bid and implement a new PPP. Any mismatch will need overcoming, either by growing new skills, by acquisition, or by teaming.

Technology needs

Increasing degrees of complexity and reducing numbers of captive markets mean that financial constraints are making it ever more difficult for companies to afford to invest in all the required technology for their markets. Consider those technologies that are key to the business, those which are basic to the industry and those which are particular to a given opportunity. Clearly, such a list is in descending order of importance and development resources and funding should be allocated accordingly. Where skills do not exist within the Company, the availability of and access to suitable technology will require examination. Teaming is generally the only option and these reasons are powerful drivers in selecting the right partner. Where such expertise is fundamental to success in the market place, the way the Company itself operates comes into question.

Teaming

It is essential to recognise that the need to form a team with another company is always a sign of weakness, because companies only seek partners if they lack some vital skill or ability themselves. Having said that, teaming can bring large short term benefits, not the least being the opportunity to win business that would not, otherwise, be accessible. It can also significantly reduce risk through the availability of the partner's expertise.

However, taking on larger overall contracts, regardless of the usual size of involvement by the Company, may incur larger risk through being jointly and severally liable for any contract resulting from a team bid. An assessment of possible teaming partners requires examination of the competitive strengths of the Company and those of the potential partners that may be available. At times, in the PPP business, political needs can be overriding and the choice of partner predicated by their nationality.

Before any serious discussions take place, a confidentiality agreement needs signing. The Company's ability to protect its expertise from an expansionist partner always requires consideration. On occasions, engineers are a route for the unwitting leakage of technical know-how. In particular, an assessment must be made of the clever bits in the design being offered. A decision should follow on which partner will undertake which parts and how to protect or assure access to the technology. There is further information about selecting team partners on page 264 and about confidentiality agreements on page 254.

Technology and funding needs can be important drivers and the reputation of any potential team mate and their impact on the customer will require careful evaluation. Never forget that a teaming arrangement may have business potential well beyond that of any immediate contract. British Aerospace's teaming with McDonnell Douglas in the 1970's to sell the Harrier to the US Marines as the AV8 led, nearly two decades later, to the sale of their Hawk training aircraft to the US Navy as the T45 Goshawk.

This type of relationship takes a lot of managing, as will be explained later. Suffice it to say for now that there are several instances of simultaneous teaming in one venture and competition between the same parties for another piece of business. A further danger to be avoided is having a partner pull out of a bid at the last moment to go it alone, leaving insufficient time for the Company to find an alternative solution.

Collaborative programmes

There is an increasing trend in Europe for governments to collaborate on major PPPs. Examples include Concorde and the Airbuses, nuclear fusion research, the Channel Tunnel and a number of military projects. Such PPPs have problems

INTERNATIONAL COLLABORATION CAN BE FRAUGHT WITH DIFFICULTIES.

peculiar to their very nature. Foremost are the communication difficulties, caused by different languages, as well as by time zone differences. In some cases, there are workshare rules, which seem to act more like a corset in restricting flexibility rather than in working in a beneficial manner. There will always be an increased cost base, which seems to mount disproportionally with an increase in the number of nations involved.

Generally, the contrasting technical requirements of the individual nations will always lead to compromise, whilst the political machinations can be difficult to deal with at best, and a pain at worst. Many people think that collaborative PPPs are less prone to cancellation as no nation likes to let down another by calling for cancellation. The down-side is that each nation may come under financial pressure at different times and this pressure may lead one nation to withdraw from what seems to be a viable programme, thus causing its collapse.

From the above, it might appear that there are few benefits and many snags in getting involved in collaborative programmes or even forming a team with another company. It is easy to overlook the advantages, which include winning business that would otherwise not be available and learning new skills from the partnership.

Competitive analysis

The question of which opportunities to tackle should naturally lead to a competitive analysis. This requires examination of which companies are likely to bid and, for each one, what is their rationale for involvement. An assessment should encompass their strengths and weaknesses, an analysis of their future strategy and how important this opportunity is to them. Finally, try to establish where the customer's sympathies lie and whether, particularly in an international bid, there are any political considerations that are likely to impact on the final outcome. Is the Company the preferred supplier and are there any switching costs? This is a filtering phase.

White papers

White papers, in the PPP context, have nothing to do with government white papers. They are statements, written by a supplier's sales or engineering staff, about issues that are important to one or more members of the customer organisation. Their topics and publication schedule both need careful thought. A white paper often requires the Company to undertake significant study work. The particular individual or group of people targeted for receipt of the white papers requires careful selection, both in terms of receptiveness to the paper and in terms of understanding of the issues addressed. White papers will impact on the Company's strategy for winning the bid, as well as on its competitive position. Thus, a feedback plan, giving information about the impact of each white paper on the customer is an essential element.

Specmanship

Perhaps the most common cry in the PPP business is "We lost it on price." This may appear to be so, but is rarely the root cause of the loss. Generally, the cheapest bid, in PPP business, is the one either where compliance involves the least change of an existing design, or where the most attractive alternative has been generated. As a result, it is clear that the battle to win the hearts of the customer's specification (spec) writers is a crucial one that requires a lot of careful thought and planning. A good knowledge of competitors' offerings can often lead to a small item in the spec forcing a competitor into an expensive change and, unfortunately, vice versa.

Specmanship is, perhaps, best illustrated by the arrival of a request for quotation. Experienced staff can tell which vendor had a hand in writing it. Key inclusions that suit the Company's offering, but will be expensive and awkward for the competition, arise in four main areas.

- Recognisable performance measurement points
- Specific features
- Standards
- Difficult environmental conditions

It is thus important to select performance measurement points that will fit with the customer's subsequent weighted scale evaluation, but which may be difficult for competitors to make or meet.

Another place to influence the specification is in the area of standards. Buildings that have to survive earthquakes and fly by wire systems that need to survive electromagnetic interference are both good examples where standards get called up in tender specifications. Companies involved in bidding for such requirements will usually have a significant involvement in the drafting of the standards and their later amendment. They usually have to argue vehemently for clauses that favour their particular technology or solutions.

All good sales executives will have "neutral" draft specifications, which they can give to the customer's spec writer to "help" with a difficult and tedious task. More enlightened customers are now issuing cardinal points specifications (CPS), which, instead of specifying every item down to the last nut and bolt, only define the key parameters. For example, a CPS for a desalination plant might only cover the number of litres per hour of water, its maximum salt content, the availability of the plant in percentage terms and the environmental conditions. There is no attempt to detail how the plant would operate, nor to give specifications for individual pieces of equipment within the plant. Such reaction may be a response to specmanship, but may also be driven by the resulting much reduced evaluation effort, with consequent cost and time savings.

Unwitting bid decisions

Once a customer enquiry arrives and discussions have started with a sales executive, there is an expectation by the customer that, when the time comes, the Company will make a bid. This assumption is often made by customers but may prove rash, particularly for vendors with well-run sales departments, where decisions on whether or not to bid are the subject of serious debate. In truth, a decision to bid should not be made until sufficient information is available to allow a reasonable value judgement. The difficulty is that no customer likes to hear that a potential supplier does not wish to bid and no sales executive likes to bear that bad news to the customer. Regardless, it is essential that anyone involved in early discussions with the customer is aware of this caveat and avoids phrases like "When we bid" using instead "If we decide to submit an offer."

This is probably a good place to mention the dangers of unintentionally committing the Company. Sales executives should always remember that they are speaking on behalf of the Company and that the dangers are likely to be more severe when writing on company letterhead; the customer then having written evidence of what was said. Until and unless the UK moves to the German practice of having all letters signed by two members of the Company for just this reason, extra care will always have to be taken.

Bid/no-bid decisions

The bid/no-bid form is a guide to help in deciding whether to pursue individual opportunities. It will probably need minor adjustments to suit particular industries and individual companies.

It divides into three parts. The first deals with the PPP opportunity, the second with the customer and their contracting record, the last with internal company issues. It is a tool of sales management and the sales director or manager should complete it in consort with the sales executive, rather than delegating it to the latter alone. It is critical to maintaining stability of resource needs and allocation, as will be seen when examining the sales funnel. More information on the sales funnel is available on page 92 and on the bid/no-bid form on page 99.

The scoring, on which the person completing the form will have to find a personal calibration, usually recommends a no-bid for scores under fifty per cent, a positive bid decision for results over sixty percent and further debate for results between these two figures. Use of the form is also a good way to avoid the pitfall of bidding for everything, as it allows comparison of scores and allocation of priorities. Avoid at all costs the mindset which says "If we don't bid we can't win" since the corollary does not apply. Nevertheless, the criteria behind bid/no-bid decisions need reassessment from time to time to reflect changes both with the customer community and internally in the Company.

Country:		PPP:	Customer:		Date:	
	Bid Factor	Negative 1 2	Neutral 3		Positive 4 5	Marks
OPPORTUNITY	COMPLIANCE WITH SPECIFICATION	Requires major development work	A reasonable fit		Fully compliant	
OPPORTUNITY	TEAM-MATES/ SUB-CONTRACTORS	Diluting	Neutral		Enhancing	
OPPORTUNITY	COMPETITION	Fixed for them	Open		Fixed for us	
CUSTOMER	REPRESENTATIVE/ CUSTOMER RAPPORT	None	Limited contacts		Excellent contacts at all levels	
CUSTOMER	COMMERCIAL TERMS	Penal	Average		Standard	
CUSTOMER	LIKELIHOOD OF PURCHASE	Uncertain	Should occur		Certain	
CUSTOMER	POLITICAL SITUATION	Unstable/ Communist	Neutral		Stable Anglophile	
INTERNAL	BID TEAM	The minimum	Average		The best	
INTERNAL	IMPLEMENTATION	Overloaded	Average		Short of work	
INTERNAL	DELIVERY TIMESCALE	Longer than anyone else	Average		Suits the customer, shorter than others	
INTERNAL	PRICE STRATEGY	Low margin	Average return		Super profit	
		Bid No-Bid	Signature:			
					Total Marks	

Figure 7. The aim of the bid/no-bid form is to help in arriving at a decision based upon a sensible evaluation. The same person should always complete the form, if possible, to ensure consistency in scoring.

In a number of cases, it becomes clear that a decision not to bid is the only sensible one. Examples include the response to the receipt of an unexpected bid request, the situation where an excessive future workload already exists or where the requirement is for the wrong sort of business from the Company's point of view. Other instances supporting a no bid occur when a submission would put a supplier into competition with a customer or the request is effectively only to provide a check price. In all cases of no bidding, take great care not to upset the customer when communicating the decision. This requires both tact and honesty from whoever ends up with this awkward job; usually the sales executive! Consistent no bidding to a customer, however, will eventually lead to the Company's removal from the bidders' list.

Initial win strategies

Any review of competitors will inevitably lead back to the question "Why should the customer choose us?" If, after such reflection, the chance of winning still looks good, decide what key message or messages to transmit to the customer. In addition, some internal examination of the Company's resources is essential at this stage, particularly the availability of any crucial technologies and key skills as well as other resources to carry out the work.

The Company will have to analyse the investment it will need to make before a PPP is deliverable to a customer. As well as bid and proposal costs, this may include Company funded development and capital investment. Finally, the sales executive must look at the probability of the contract being placed at all and the chances of the Company winning the contract if placed. Each of these will require further substantiation, requiring a paragraph response in each area at this stage to eliminate non-starters.

Discriminators are basically strengths and weaknesses, viewed from the standpoint of a potential customer. Their use is a vital element of arriving at a win strategy. They may be real or just perceived. The factors determining the relevant discriminators are the customer's requirements and evaluation criteria, the contract terms and the competition. Discriminators break down into four categories.

FEATURES	**NEUTRALISERS**
The Company's strengths	The Company's weaknesses as perceived by the customer
The competitor's weaknesses	May be real or imaginary
The basic win strategy	May be competitor inspired
NEGATORS	**EXPLOITERS**
Competitors' claimed strengths (often discovered from Strawman)	Customer's fears
Be careful in using negators which knock the competition	Customer's biases
Discover the customer's view	Customer's hopes

Figure 8. If the Company's weaknesses cannot be neutralised, DON'T BID

A number of key factors need addressing to arrive at a winning strategy, of which by far the most important are to start early and ensure that everyone involved within the Company embraces the strategy. In addition, it is necessary to take early action in a number of areas in order to:

- Influence the contents of the specification
- Probe how people in the customer's organisation perceive value
- Select the right partners when required
- Access winning technology from a company with similar culture for customer acceptability
- Get the measure of the competition
- Construct Strawmen of how competitors are likely to bid and ensure such arguments are undermined in the Company's bid
- Submit a compliant bid and generate the winning alternative to convince the decider(s)

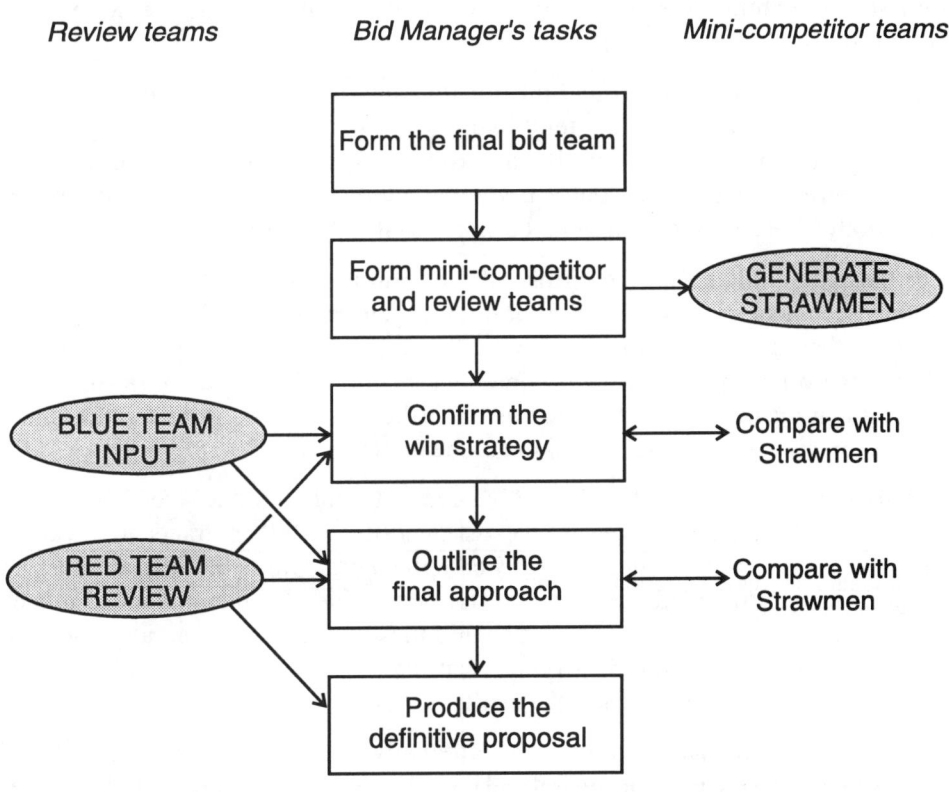

Figure 9. The way in which a company bids requires understanding.

- Stay close to the customer community during the bid and its evaluation
- Answer questions by probing what is behind them whilst respecting their sensitivities
- Influence any weighted evaluation scale
- As appropriate, "help" the customer with the difficult matter of evaluation

Finally, it is most important to learn from success and failure alike, avoid witch hunts and the allocation of blame but, at the same time, benefit from the experience. There is more information on bid win/loss analysis on page 107.

Generating attractive alternatives

The inconsistent use of the words alternatives and options can lead to confusion. The word alternative is used throughout this book to describe a distinct and different solution to a customer's requirement. In contrast, an option means an additional aspect that a customer may or may not elect to purchase. The very complexity of PPPs means that just to offer a compliant solution risks losing the contract on price. The ability to recognise and present attractive alternatives is a powerful selling tool.

Finding alternatives requires real imagination and, in many industries, still needs driving by sales, as engineers tend habitually to concentrate on the compliant solution, regardless of cost. It sometimes requires oblique thinking and "imagineering" to arrive at contract winning alternatives and analysis and inputs from both Blue and Red teams can be significant in this difficult task.

For those unfamiliar with the terms, a Blue team is a group that concentrates on finding technical solutions for a proposal, independently of the bid team's efforts, to see if there is a better way of meeting the requirement. It can also to help find alternative offerings to the main compliant solution. A Red team, on the other hand, is a group of people which acts as if it is the purchaser carrying out the tender evaluation and giving a critique to the bid team. (See page 80.)

A fully compliant base bid will usually need to be submitted to avoid the risk of being rejected outright. However, the vast majority of PPP contracts are awarded to an alternative, rather than to the fully compliant bid. This is because alternatives are invariably attractive because they offer better value for the amount of money the customer can justify spending. It should thus be clear that generating alternatives centrally depends on identifying what the customer considers valuable, the required value to price ratio and the available budget.

Determining what makes an attractive alternative solution is one of the critical factors facing the bid team in general and the sales executive in particular. It requires stepping into the customer's shoes and thinking as they do. The alternative must meet the fundamental need outlined in the specification, though non-compliances in less critical areas are often acceptable, particularly if they save significant sums of money. Clearly the alternative must be within the budget. The use of options can also be important in helping to define a minimum bid, with other items such as a comprehensive support package, being offered as well. Finally, the customer's tender evaluation team must feel able to give an adequate justification to the selection committee and the selection authority for a recommendation to purchase an alternative solution.

Customer sources of value

There is undoubtedly a difference in concept between the words worth and value. Worth is generally a qualitative word and used in the sense of "this benefit is worth a lot." Value is a much more quantitative word, best used in the sense of "We need to measure the value of these features to the customer."

Benefits, such as those which differentiate one PPP from another, are critical and well recognised by sales professionals as valuable. They are, however, one step removed from the four fundamental sources of value:

1. Cost/capital reduction.
2. Risk reduction.
3. Revenue increase.
4. Individual gain.

For maximum impact, benefits need translation into value terms.

The only reason that an institutional customer will purchase a PPP is because of the value derived through its ownership. The sources of value for an institutional purchase, in contrast to an individual one, come from two key areas; the internally generated ones and those which come from external influences. The internal sources distil down to just four key elements, each of which may be split.

CUSTOMER INTERNAL SOURCES OF VALUE	
COST REDUCTION	**RISK REDUCTION**
Direct Costs	Provision of alternatives for contingency purposes
Indirect Costs	Availability of better information
CAPITAL REDUCTION	**INDIVIDUAL CONSIDERATIONS**
Working Capital	Power, control, information, empire-building
Fixed Capital	Status, perk, personal interest, corruption

Purchasers within an institution may influence the outcome of the decision in order to gain individual value for themselves. Their prejudices may result in decisions offering reduced value to the institution itself. This personal influence may arise from considerations such as personality, culture, nationality, or previous bad experience with a particular supplier.

The external sources of value are only two in number, although within each, there are a number of different possible sources of value.

CUSTOMER EXTERNAL SOURCES OF VALUE	
REVENUE INCREASE	**EXTERNAL RISK REDUCTION**
Increased market share	Avoiding reliance on a single customer segment
Access to new markets	Reducing competitor ability to reverse-engineer the PPP
Ability to expand total market	Reducing risk of cannibalisation in marginal cost situations
Increased throughput	Ability to comply with new legislation

Producing and using value cases

Vendors should always compile comprehensive value cases to support the proposed purchase of a PPP. Constructing such a case will help to formulate a winning strategy and the case itself will be a powerful selling tool. The overall case is likely to include elements that reflect the perspectives of each of the customer's dominant influencers. This requires a clear understanding of the customer's business and the dynamics of the purchase process, including who will own the final decision. It should be obvious that the onus of generating such value cases lies with the selling organisation.

These cases represent an essentially positive outlook. "No" votes, which were mentioned in Chapter 1, are essentially negative value and often arise from switching costs, a subject covered in detail on page 199. Redressing the customer's reservations, or overcoming the "no" votes, is one factor, but the disposition and scope of any concerns require consideration.

In looking at Figure 10, it is important to note that in a value case, investment considerations may override profit ones, and likewise profit is usually more important than cost. Take care when using such overriding tactics as they are likely to create antagonists. However, they are justifiable in cases where the competitive offering is more attractive to those concerned, say with cost, yet the Company's

DISPOSITION IN THE ORGANISATION	COST CENTRE	PROFIT CENTRE	INVESTMENT CENTRE
SCOPE OF CONCERN	Direct and indirect costs	Revenue, cost & break-even	ROI & risk considerations

Figure 10. The location of concerns often depends on the financial responsibilities of the different parts of the purchasing organisation.

offering has significant value to those considering profit. In these situations, there is a danger from any uncontacted purchase influencers who are a major source of failure in attempting to steer a decision in the Company's favour.

Although the term investment centre is used, more usually the term profit centre is misused by those also having accountability for capital employed, the strict definition of which includes working capital. Revenue centres may exist in isolation, but they are usually incorporated into profit centres.

There are four ways of demonstrating factual support to a value case and these are shown in descending order of effectiveness.

- Showing results from the same PPP used in a similar customer facility
- Obtaining results from a pilot run through the facilities in question
- Demonstrating results from PPPs owned by comparable customers
- Extrapolation and modelling based on the customer's situation

The translation of value aspects into monetary terms is not trivial, particularly when involving revenue generation and risk reduction. One approach is to pick an arbitrary value to price ratio, say 5:1 and see whether values at five times the price level are reasonable, rather than tackling the problem the other way round!

In each case, the incremental impact of the PPP is the best that can be calculated. Customers are, understandably, reluctant to reveal their total operating situation and this can make the presentation of an effective case more difficult. In most circumstances, it is important to remember to address the impact of source loyalty as well as switching costs, both of which can detract from available value.

There is also a need to distinguish between hard, or quantifiable benefits and subsequent value, together with soft benefits. Failure to do so can make the whole case vulnerable to probing by sceptical customers of the contribution of a soft element, such as handbooks. Worse, once any one area of quantifiable value has been discredited, the credibility of the complete value case tends to collapse in the eyes of the customer.

It is important to remember value considerations when assisting customers to draw up PPP specifications. A comprehensive approach should help to negate the possibility of a competitor coming up with a better solution that has further appeal to those in profit or investment centres.

Cost, value and competition

Cost and value factors need reviewing in the context of a competitive environment since there is a close relationship between all three factors that requires serious consideration to achieve success in the market place.

Excessive costs

- Release from which constraint can lead to attractive alternative bids
- Can an internal case be made for contribution costing?
- Are costs certain? Overhead allocation, learning curve effects?

Inadequate value

- Have value cases been developed and presented to the decision makers?

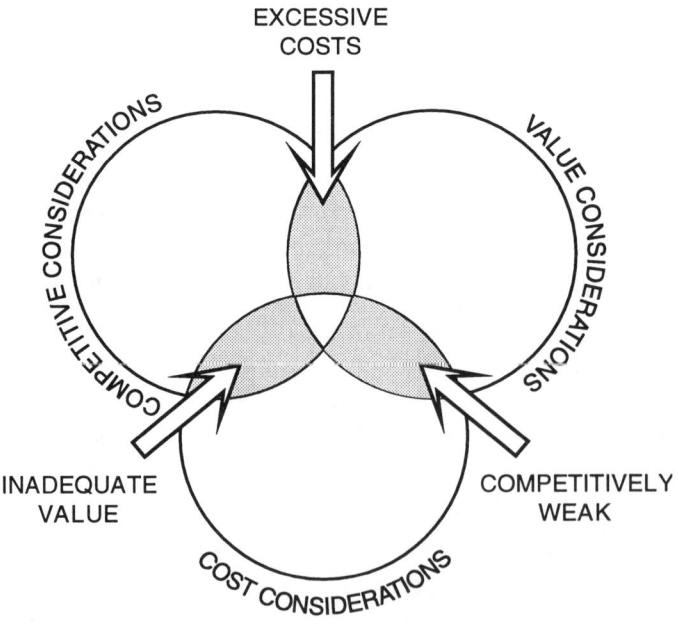

Figure 11. Value, cost and competitive factors all need consideration to achieve a winning position.

- Can the decision be escalated to others who value the Company's offering more?
- Is the value being eroded by switching costs or barriers to entry?

Competitively weak

- Can an attractive bid be made at a lower price?
- Could a beneficial life cycle costing case be made?
- If the current supplier, can a switching cost penalty be demonstrated or another barrier to entry erected?
- Is it possible to leapfrog the competitors' influence?
- Can a competitor's profit sanctuary be attacked?

Learning curves and customer expectations

There is a wide acceptance that the more identical PPPs a company produces in a continuous process at a given rate, the lower the cost of producing each becomes. This is over and above the mechanism of sharing fixed costs over a greater number of units. The causes are the adeptness and familiarity gained by the employees in

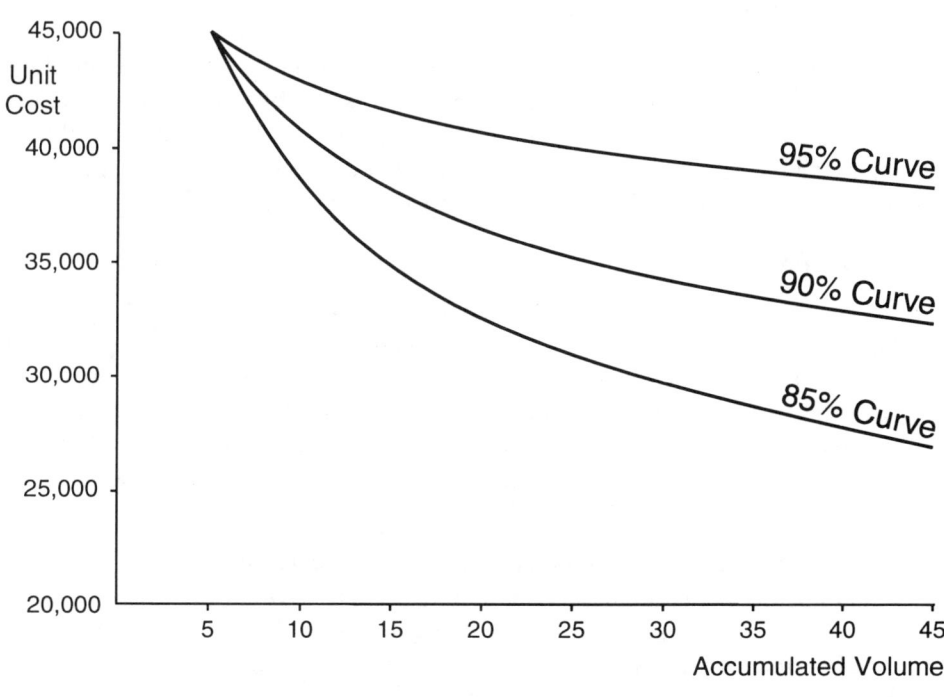

Figure 12. The concept of learning curves is now widely used by purchasers in arriving at "should cost" figures for PPPs produced in volume.

the process of producing the PPPs and reductions in the unit cost of materials as quantities increase. The learning curve, as it is called, plots cost against cumulative volume. This reducing trend of unit cost as volume increases, might, for a typical major product, follow a 95% learning curve. That means that each time the volume doubles, the unit costs reduce by five per cent.

However, enjoying the benefits of a learning curve doesn't come easily. A company has to drive itself down the curve. Perhaps a better way of expressing it is that learning curves give the opportunity to reduce costs accordingly. These may arise from changing manufacturing layouts, bulk purchasing discounts and, perhaps most significantly, the gains through streamlining the tasks carried out by the work force. These tasks are done with increasing speed and efficiency with a resulting reduction in wasted work.

However, learning curve benefits rely on continuous manufacture. Chopping and changing between models erodes learning curve benefits and often results in an overall increasing cost trend. Customers have come to expect learning curve benefits and understand how much the benefit should be. They are one of the main barriers to entry for new suppliers, who will have to work their way down the learning curve to become competitive.

The electronics industry has made extensive use of learning curves when bidding for large quantities of new semiconductors. Companies like Toshiba and Texas Instruments know where they are on the learning curve, even with new products, and where they expect to be when they have completed a new order. This manufacturing cost reduction provides a justification for bidding a really keen price.

Pricing strategies

Pricing targets, how to price major sub-contract quotations and likely negotiating milestones, are all part of a pricing strategy. Large negotiating margins may need to be conceded successively, depending on the country and customer involved. The likely position of the competitors is important as are the Company's investment needs and the recovery policy for that investment. A sensitivity analysis of prices is always useful, as is a profitability analysis, which will take into account further sales of a new PPP.

Customers will usually demand a break down of prices into their individual piece parts and they often have an ulterior motive for this action. Care is needed to avoid the customer "cherry picking." In this, only the low priced items are selected and, conceivably, the remaining items obtained from another supplier, with adverse effect on the margin being achieved by the Company. Alternatively, the customer may use parts of the price breakdown to justify price reductions in other parts. In either case, the pricing strategy needs thinking through to its logical conclusion.

Payback analysis

First, establish the investment required by the Company. This will include bid and proposal funding, any private venture investment in development of the PPP or part of it, any capital plant, buildings or equipment needed and any staff recruitment and training. Finally quantify the risks of implementing the contract.

Balanced against the investment is the return to the Company. Occasionally, the development of a PPP may be funded by the customer, but this is increasingly rare these days. Where it does happen, there is a struggle for who has the rights to the intellectual property, whether royalty fees are payable for sales of similar PPPs to other customers and if so how much.

More usually, customer's only pay suppliers for their specific PPP implementation, to which the subsequent revenue from logistic support throughout the life of the PPP must be added. Finally, earnings from further sales, particularly in export markets, need consideration. The Company's financial function will advise on the required return on investment. Some companies use discounted cash flow to arrive at a figure, which will then be judged against the company's criteria. As a guide, total sales of a PPP should equate to around twenty times the investment for it to be worthwhile. Of all the figures within such a justification, the price customers will pay is usually the most difficult to substantiate. Only a value analysis can make a sound argument and that still with provisos. There is more information on this topic on page 202.

Sales plans

The sales plan will include the chronological evolution of the PPP purchasing programme, which may be a multi-year plan and sometimes run into tens of years. It will allocate bid and proposal funding and be aimed at getting Company resources allocated to do the work in a timely fashion. A lot of the work will involve internal selling and this includes getting a positive bid decision and finding the winning solution and price. In addition, the customer family tree will need updating at regular intervals and contact plans making to deal with all the decision makers and influencers in the customer community.

Capture plans

Having mentioned the need for capture plans at the beginning of this chapter, it is worth considering the final form of the document. Basically, a view graph format is ideal either when making briefings, using an overhead projector, to management and others involved in the PPP, or for handing out as hard copy briefs.

The plan needs to name the key executives and managers responsible for winning the opportunity and should start with a brief overview of the opportunity,

CAPTURE PLAN	Commercial in Confidence

Names of designated:
    Sales executive
    Bid manager
    PM designate
    Technical manager
    Commercial executive
    Red/blue team members	

Time scale of milestones in bidding and implementation	
Customer needs and requirement overview	
History of company involvement to date.	
Sources of technologies or resources not currently available internally	

Win strategy:
    The message
    Key points for the proposal
    Short term issues	

Pricing strategy:
    Strategic issues
    Tactical issues	

Competitive analysis	
Customer family tree and contact plan	
Attach copy of latest bid/no bid form	

Figure 13. Complete and circulate a capture plan to those involved in winning the contract.

including the Company's involvement, and the most likely timescales. Resources and technologies not available internally need highlighting with proposed solutions for overcoming these shortcomings. The win strategy and pricing strategy are the heart of the document, which is completed through an assessment of the competition and the customer's staff involved in the tender assessment and award process.

Deciding the appropriate price for a particular bid is likely to require both strategic and tactical consideration. In the first category are the possibility of a reference installation and the follow-on benefits of having won this particular contract. These factors, in turn, will probably reflect on the Company's recovery policy for any investment. The tactical considerations will encompass the pricing targets and short term need for work, as well as the country and customer involved.

Project/programme management plans

One of the key factors in winning most PPP business is to get the right person appointed as project/programme manager (PM) designate to implement the PPP for the customer. By their very nature, the success of PPPs is critically dependant on the performance of the PM and customers recognise this during their evaluation.

The PM designate will normally act as the bid manager and will need a realistic bidding budget, a team to design/specify the PPP and to write the proposal. A resources plan should be prepared, both for the bidding and the implementation phases. The PM will need to consider, amongst other things, the reporting schedule and the customer's milestones. It is also important to have a contingency plan to deal with the unexpected. The PM will always have to bear in mind the Company's win requirements during the preparation of the bid and will need a personal commitment to the implementation of the PPP. An understanding of who in the organisation really has authority and power is essential to help to get the PPP rolling once the contract has been won.

Exploitation plans

The first sale of a new PPP, or the first sale of an existing PPP into a new market is an important landmark. The potential for follow-on sales may well justify an investment to win the first order, particularly if the cost for a customer to change to a different design for later orders is likely to be high; the sprat to catch a mackerel approach. However, the PM must always remember that the next order is only as good as the last delivery.

Following success in winning a contract for a new PPP, it is important to initiate an exploitation plan without delay. This should encompass production follow-on, logistic support and PPP upgrades. Consideration also needs to be given to direct export, local manufacture by an overseas company or subsidiary and ancillary markets. All of these factors need considering and a financial summary preparing, to allow authorisation and implementation of the exploitation plan. Furthermore, many leading companies consider that work should start on developing a PPP mid-life update as soon as the first order arrives, otherwise the update will be too late in reaching the market. Chapter 9 covers this subject in greater depth.

In fact, winning the first contract, although viewed as a landmark by all involved, is only the start for the sales department. The really hard work of getting the PPP to the rest of the market involves conversion of the exploitation plan into a sales plan. This will involve the sales executive in so called missionary selling to expand the market and find customers who are opinion leaders. Influencing such leaders may well require significant support from other functions within the Company. A well-planned approach might make use of technical papers, seminars and industry association meetings to help in a soft sell the PPP. It may well be that a region by region tactic is better than an attempt to tackle the total market at the outset.

Decisions need making on which of the many of the tools of the public relations manager to use and which will be the most cost-effective ones. This is covered in Chapter 11. Fortunately, the exploitation plan is a logical follow-on to the PPP plan and needs preparation at an early stage, when the PPP is first conceived. Chapter 10 provides more information about PPP planning and development.

Chapter 3:

The Tender Process

Final win & pricing strategies · Life cycle cost (LCC) appraisals · Pricing · The price customers will pay · Cartels · Why customers want PPPs · Estimates · Other cost elements · Subsidising capital sales by spares · Software pricing · Pricing approaches · Price, cost & profit relationships · Marketing decisions & cost accounting systems · New PPP pricing · Final pricing review · Presenting prices · Progress payments · Submitting bids · Unusual bid situations · Tender evaluation · Selection committees · Selection authorities · Bribery & corruption · Negotiating strategies · Negotiating factors · Planning & preparation · Stages of negotiation · Breaking deadlocks · Negotiating contracts · Dutch auctions · Cognitive dissonance · Keeping it sold

Final win and pricing strategies

The invitation to companies to submit offers is variously known as the RFT, RFQ or RFP (Request for Tender, Quotation or Proposal). The term RFQ or request for quotation will be used to cover all such solicitations. Once the RFQ arrives, a number of activities need triggering. The definitive proposal document will have to be written, a price prepared and a set of terms and conditions put forward. It is also the time to review the initial win strategy and come up with a final proposition. A historical review and analysis of what has happened in the intervening period will be necessary, noting any key changes that have taken place. A reassessment of the competitive situation is required, as the competitors will not remain stationary and neither will the customer's thinking (see page 173). Of course the inevitable question "Why should the customer choose us?" must be asked once again.

It may be that the result of this analysis will show that a new message needs putting across to the customer and a reassessment made of the overall benefits to the Company of winning the contract. Finally, a review is necessary of the probability of any contract being placed and of the Company winning the business.

As with the win strategy, the pricing strategy will also need revisiting. This should start with the total investment to date and the investment still to come in the future. These figures will then allow revision of the payback analysis. The competitive situation, in financial terms, will require updating with the latest information. A sensitivity analysis on the various components of the price needs carrying out once again. This type of analysis will identify the key factors that will impact on profit, should they change during the progress of the contract. Finally, requirements for executive approval of the final price require thought, particularly the time taken to get such approval and, therefore, the required dates.

Life cycle cost (LCC) appraisals

Large numbers of PPP purchasers now include the requirement for life cycle cost information in their requests for tender. They ask for the total cost to them, that is the prime purchase cost together with any operating, maintenance and other expenditure likely to occur during the life of the PPP. These calculations involve significant work and must be included in the submission. This does not mean, however, that such information will have much, if any, effect on the purchase decision. Most purchasers still pay lip service to the subject, not the least because they are operating on annual budgets, with five year plans and possibly ten year outlooks. The financial drivers are short term, whilst LCC benefits are long term. The Swedish government is, perhaps, a shining exception in this respect.

With PPP operating lives of twenty to thirty years or more in some cases, life cycle costs are rarely seen as a justification for buying an initially more expensive proposition. Having said that, a better LCC appraisal can tip the balance when all other things are equal. It is thus important to discover who in the bid evaluation process will be looking into this very specialist area and involving the Company expert. It is imperative to get hold of the economic model being used by the customer, if at all possible. In this way, it is possible to massage and present the LCC figures so that they give the most favourable impression in the life cycle costing analysis. A note of caution is again needed as it is rare to let contracts for fully compliant solutions. Much more prevalent is the purchase of attractive alternatives (see page 28).

Pricing

The most powerful single communication that can be made about a PPP is its price. Pricing is thus probably the most important single factor in the whole selling process. Better not to win at all, than to win unwittingly at a money-losing price, unless there is justification. This truism is compounded in the PPP business, where single contracts can be of very large value, and incorrect pricing can lead to mortal losses for the company involved. Loss leaders are generally alien to the PPP business, apart from reference installations. These may be offered at discounts, but only after serious consideration to ensure that there is some way to lock in the downstream benefits.

Pricing in the PPP environment has its own characteristic foibles and challenges compared with the classic product context. For example, it is rare to find a price list and even where there is one, it is common to ignore it. Since the degree of customisation in PPPs is likely to be high, both in scope of choices and in number of variables, as well as in the key role of negotiating, this is not unexpected. In the interests of obtaining some stability in markets and in attempting to manage, or rather contain, the cost of generating prices from scratch for every offering, companies try to formalise their pricing models.

Given these characteristic levels of uncertainty, it is inappropriate to discuss a classical pricing strategy. Instead, pricing guidelines will be considered. First, these are likely to change over time. The objectives at each stage of the PPP life cycle merit different approaches. For example, at the outset, winning reference installations to prove new concepts, gather data and establish de facto standards are likely to be the most important factors. Here, it is traditional for opinion leading customers to be provided with loan equipment, probably with full-time engineering back up as a means of reducing the not inconsiderable risks faced by such customers. Later, premium pricing is often appropriate to recoup the development investment as quickly as possible or finance the next generation of improved PPP.

Second, from a corporate standpoint, it is likely that pricing analysis will be subject to personal influence by the individuals involved. Downward pressure may arise through desire to prove historic arguments or the need to be associated with a successful bid on the grounds of job security. Upward pressure may result from a desire for some slack in the pricing if the head of the bid team is to take the lead in executing any resulting contract and wishes to turn in a good performance.

It is essential to think pricing early in the PPP planning process. It is also important to remember that individuals cannot ever be any good at pricing until they are prepared to walk away from a piece of business. There is more information on this subject in the section on negotiating later in this chapter. The aim of good pricing is to ensure that a company sells its PPPs at the most profitable prices, taking into account the prevailing market conditions. There are, however, other business objectives, which may have a major impact on pricing, and these are shown below.

- Maximise return on sales
- Maximise return on capital employed
- Maximise net cash inflow

- Increase market share
- Establish a new market position
- Utilise available resources
- Develop new technologies

Inevitably, these demands lead to the question "How is price determined?" The price is, in fact, the sum of the costs plus the profit. From this summation, it is tempting to estimate costs and add the desired profit. This is a traditional approach in the PPP environment, but by no means the only one. The theory appears easy but the practice less so. There are, for example, fixed costs and variable costs. Fixed costs include time related costs such as rent and the depreciation of machinery and other equipment like computers. These costs do not alter with changes in the number of PPPs produced over a given time period.

Variable costs, which alter directly with volume changes, include raw materials, direct labour and any shipping costs. It is difficult to decide whether salaries are fixed or variable costs. The laws governing redundancy and associated payments in the UK tend to mitigate against mobility of labour and, at least within a single financial year, the salary bill is likely to be a fixed cost. The fact that so many costs are fixed suggests that it is possible to gain benefit from selling at the marginal cost; an approach examined later on page 50.

Accountants traditionally use the terms direct and indirect costs. Direct costs are those attributable directly to a particular PPP, such as project/programme management, sub-contracts and direct manufacture. Indirect costs, or overheads, include a notional part of the chief executive's salary, the cost of the finance and marketing functions as well as anything else not easily apportioned directly to a particular PPP contract. Convention has it that overhead allocation is pro-rata to contract value. The term G & A (General and Administrative overhead) is one widely used in industry. It is a charge added to the factory cost to cover the expense of running the business and is applied as a percentage mark-up.

The price customers will pay

PPP customers are still inclined to pay too little, almost invariably to their own detriment. NASA, for example, bought the Space Shuttle at a very low price, but ended up paying a far higher figure because of variation orders. Often, a PM who is given a very tight budget will have to charge the customer for even the slightest variation or addition; items that are, with a reasonable price, given away at no additional cost. Thus customers do need reminding of the dangers of contracting at too low a price. It was the nineteenth century philosopher, John Ruskin, who said *"It's unwise to pay too much, but also unwise to pay too little. When you pay too much you lose a little money, that is all. When you pay too little, you sometimes lose everything, because the thing you bought was incapable of doing the thing you bought it to do."* This is still true one hundred years later.

In the PPP arena, because of the very nature of bureaucratic purchasing procedures, customers will often demand a justification for the price. This is particularly so for large, one-off PPPs. Clearly, a contractor cannot charge a market price for building say the Channel Tunnel. No such price level exists and even the price of other tunnels provides little assistance, since the specifics of each job are likely to be very different. Instead, PPP buyers probe into the costs, having made their own estimates. Price negotiations will usually concentrate on these issues. However, the truism is that the price is what the customer will pay, though in practice, the competitive tendering process holds prices down; cartels being severely dealt with.

Cartels

Cartels are perhaps most commonly associated with commodities, such as OPEC in the crude oil market. Cartels are, however, sometimes found in PPP industries but both governments and customers dislike their formation. In many cases, laws prohibit the operation of cartels and PPP companies should avoid the apparent advantages of controlling prices in the market place, as it only needs one player to break ranks for the whole cartel edifice to collapse.

The steel manufacturers in Europe were reported to have paid the penalty for operating a cartel through the eighties, following a probe by the European Commission. It is interesting to surmise, in a recession, whether it isn't the biggest player in the cartel which drives prices down, since it has the largest capacity and will hurt the soonest through failure to fill it. This contrasts with the classically supposed market leader behaviour of leading up and following down.

Why customers want PPPs

Another price determining factor is why the customer is purchasing the PPP. There are many factors that have an influence.

- Will it save the buyer money?
- Is it new and will it provide an insight into new approaches?
- What are the buyer's competitors doing?
- What are the seller's competitors doing?
- What is the cost of the buyer getting it another way?
- Is legislation forcing purchase of a new PPP?
- How much is the buyer willing to pay or can afford?
- Will the PPP replace something else?

It is important to remember that purchase decisions are made on the basis of perceived value compared with the price involved, not necessarily solely on the basis of the lowest priced offering. Thus, the price quoted must be consistent with the buyer's perceptions of the value. This means that a PPP may be able to warrant a premium price if it offers a superior value to price ratio. There is, however, a danger here of offering features that, although nice to have, are not needed by the customer, yet add to the cost and usually increase the price. There is more information on this subject page 66.

Several other factors need assessment in arriving at a price for any particular offering.

- How large is the customer's budget?
- What is the expected winning price?
- What is the competitive PPP situation?
- What are the competitors' workload and cash flow situations?
- What inflation is forecast and which indices will be used?
- Will some or all of the bid be in foreign currency?
- What are the predicted costs and risks involved?
- Will there be any customer cost/price investigation?

Estimates

In the PPP business, estimates, as well as covering the cost of labour and materials, will often include major sub-contract figures. This dependency precipitates the danger of working out the costs of the Company's scope of work to a high degree of accuracy and then making rough estimates of the sub-contract costs, which are often the more significant items in terms of impact on the total cost. The causes of such poor estimating include unfamiliarity with or ignorance of the sensitivities of the particular application, which will have a strong impact on the sub-contract price. As an example, a division of a structural steel fabrication company, operating in the design and construction environment, might be tempted to calculate in detail the cost of washers in the steel fabrication aspect of a cement plant, since steel is their industrial expertise and technology. They might then add an approximate figure for the electrical drives and control equipment, which might be an order of magnitude more in value than the washers.

Contingencies or management reserves are essential to cover risks, which may or may not occur. Such things as a particularly demanding requirement, a tight programme schedule, reliance on key or even single source suppliers and overall systems responsibility all bring risks that are difficult to quantify. There is a danger, however, that at each level of integration of an estimate, contingencies will be included, resulting in contingencies on contingencies on contingencies and an excessively high cost estimate.

In a profit dominated environment, this source of error is particularly difficult to overcome. There is, however, a practical approach which can work. Each department producing an estimate splits out the contingency amount visibly, so that these are subsequently handled by addition. The same approach can be used with interdivisional trading. Such an approach provides the benefit that at the bid review, each of the various contributions to contingency is visible to the bid review management team.

Labour			509,488
Material			737,877
WORKS COST			1,247,365
Escalation provision:			
Labour	8%	40,759	
Material	5%	36,894	
Factory Overhead	10%	124,737	
TOTAL WORKS COST			1,449,755
Major sub-contract items		241,500	
Warranty	2%	28,995	
G & A	15%	217,463	
G & A on major sub-contracts	5%	12,075	
Contingency		76,877	
Liquidated Damages *	2%	50,041	
Representative's commission *	3%	75,062	
ECGD premium *	2%	50,041	
Bank Charges *	2%	50,041	
Profit*	10%	250,205	
RECOMMENDED SELLING PRICE			2,502,055
* Figures expressed as a % of Selling Price			

Figure 14. A typical price estimate summary showing those items that make up the works cost as well as the additional factors to arrive at a recommended selling price.

This contrasts with situation where the price information is handled by adding mark-ups even to contingencies, to cover such things as administration, handling costs and applications engineering. Taking a corporate view can indicate whether there is sufficient contingency in the whole job, or indeed, whether some reduction can produce a more competitive price.

It is, in many industries, becoming quite common to use computer models for parametric cost estimating and customers are likewise taking to these models to arrive at "should cost" figures. Not only can they provide effective Strawman prices for comparison for conventionally calculated costs, but they really come into their own when considering different "what if?" solutions to particular requirements.

A note of caution is necessary here. Gathering cost data is a precarious business and an estimate may come back too high to meet the target price. Going around the loop again can often result in costs being reduced by as much as fifty per cent, using genuine lateral thinking to overcome the challenges. On the other hand, bitter experience has shown that such an exercise will, as often as not, result in a higher estimate than the original one.

Other cost elements

Some costs do not fall directly into the labour, materials or overhead category, yet need to be included in any total cost. The list below covers the majority of these.

- Liquidated damages (Payments for late delivery)
- Interest or cost of money and currency exchange
- Bank and insurance charges
- Royalty payments
- Representative's commission
- Counter-trade, offset and local taxes levied
- Shipping costs
- Negotiating margins, while not really a cost, should not be forgotten when preparing the final price

Subsidising capital sales by spares

In the same way that it is important to know which PPP lines are making profit and which are not, so it is important to understand the relative profitability between the prime equipment as opposed to spares and other support items. The same is also true of consumables. It can be very attractive to win new business by subsidising the initial purchase and recouping the money from the follow on business, particularly where switching costs are high.

Radiosondes, flown two or four times a day beneath hydrogen filled balloons by meteorologists to profile the atmosphere, represent good revenue for the supplier. The price of the long lasting associated ground equipment is almost invariably well subsidised and, on occasions, will be given away free of charge. The corollary to this is where escalated spare parts prices are encouraging customers to explore alternative sources. In this case, modern technology, such as computer aided design, prototyping and manufacturing, is threatening the whole price structure.

Software pricing

A particular and poignant example of the difficulty of pricing lies in the case of software. What is delivered to the customer is likely to include only a number of floppy discs, or programs pre-loaded on a hard disk or in semiconductor memory, probably with an instruction manual. What are the cost elements and how does their size compare with conventional hardware costs?

The tender process

ELEMENT	COST
Raw materials	Tiny, maybe nil
Manufacturing	Small
Documentation	Medium
Production equipment	Small
Development	Very large
Shipping	Negligable

Figure 15. Software pricing can be very difficult to justify to PPP customers.

As a result of the very large one time cost and the tiny repeat costs, also perceived by customers as tiny, together with the ever present danger of pirate copying of software, licensing is a common practice. A software licence is the fee paid to a supplier by a user for the right to specified use of the software. The software's ownership and title remain with the seller.

The various types of licence fee paid divide into four possible options:
1. One-off licence
2. Initial fee plus periodic licence fee
3. Usage linked licence fee
4. A combination of the above

Software licensing can be a minefield and specialist advice is desirable when dealing in this difficult field. Note that bundling software together with its associated hardware is a common practice and the relative benefits of bundling as opposed to unbundling need to be thought through. There is more information on this subject on page 184.

Pricing approaches

Three main approaches to pricing are possible; customer based, those based on a cost build up and market based. Each has different manifestations and its own particular advantages and disadvantages.

Customer based pricing

Customer based pricing is value-based and will depend on the customers' budget, approval limits and tender options, as well as the PPP availability. The dangers of value-based pricing include the difficult situation arising when a new competitor arrives on the scene with much lower prices. This leaves the Company in a nasty predicament. Savage cutting of prices will probably make existing customers angry, since they will feel that they have been over-charged up to that time. Alternatively, leaving prices where they are will result in erosion of market share.

One viable alternative might be to criticise the quality and reliability of the competitive offering in a promotional campaign, unfortunately giving free exposure and possibly appearing a bullying tactic. Another is rushing a cost reduced offering to market as soon as possible to save the lower end of the market. Given these scenarios, it is perhaps worth considering developing such a cost reduced model before competitive entrants arrive at lower prices, in order to be ready to respond without time lag in such an event.

Advantages

- Encourages deeper understanding of the customer's business
- Allows profit maximisation
- Enables predictable market share changes
- Sensitive to market changes
- Usage based licence fees smooth cash flow

Disadvantages

- Increased cost of sales and marketing
- Generally restricted to significant contract sizes, due to effort involved

Cost-based pricing

The system of basing the price on cost is one that has found much support in the PPP arena. The reasons for this include both the simplicity of the method and the appeal it has to the intellect; the more it costs to produce, the more the customer will have to pay for it. The cost build up method of pricing will reflect learning curve benefits, marginal costing and quantity discounts.

Advantages

- Simple mechanistic method
- Fixed profit margins when demand is known
- Enables long term pricing publication
- Ready made case to increase prices when costs rise

Disadvantages

- Susceptible to accounting system foibles, such as historical overhead allocation disguising true profit generating PPPs
- Fails to encourage probing customer needs and sources of value

- Fails to encourage awareness of competitor activity
- Fails to encourage concern over costs

Market based pricing

Market based pricing involves looking across the total market place and using similar pricing strategies to others in the market. It often involves the use of total life cycle cost analysis, demanding consideration of production capacity and will usually involve pricing a complete package, rather than a stand alone PPP. It is not applicable when the PPP is customised to the purchaser's requirements, but may be relevant to some major products. It does require checking against cost-based pricing to ensure that contracts are not unwittingly taken at a loss.

Advantages

- Imitative pricing can establish world wide levels avoiding negotiating ploys by global customers
- Imitative pricing frees company management for other issues

Disadvantages

- Price cutting and retaliation can reduce market viability for all
- Imitative pricing eliminates the opportunity to use an important implementation tool
- Imitative pricing makes cash flow and profitability unpredictable

Price, cost and profit relationships

There are three possible ways of relating price, cost and profit.

1. Price = cost + profit

This is the traditional way of bottom up pricing, which takes the cost, adds the profit and calls the result the price.

2. Profit = price - cost

The correct way to price is to establish the projected costs and compare them with the winning price. The difference is the profit (or loss)

3. Cost = price - profit

This technique can be particularly beneficial when trying to make an early bid/no-bid decision, where the market price, less a reasonable profit margin, leads to a cost target that needs meeting or bettering. It also encourages lateral thinking in design to come up with innovative approaches to provide the required functionality at the target cost level.

There is also the case of marginal costing, where the price does not carry the full share of the overheads. This is most easily understood by considering the case of an airliner where two thirds of the passengers have paid the full price for their tickets. The remaining seats are then discounted significantly, for the airliner flies to its destination anyway and the increased cost of carrying additional passengers is insignificant; any further fares contributing towards profit. The obvious danger is that the full fare paying passengers will become disgruntled with the comparatively high price of their tickets. In the PPP arena, marginal costing applies, for example, to the cost of spares built at the same time as the PPP, or to peripherals packaged with the main equipment.

Marketing decisions and cost accounting systems

Traditionally, cost accounting systems have looked at material and direct labour costs. At the beginning of the twentieth century, when the labour content of all PPPs was high, the division between the three categories was very different from those of today.

YEAR	MATERIALS	LABOUR	OVERHEADS	OVERHEAD RECOVERY RATE
1900	30%	60%	10%	17%
1990	35%	20%	45%	225%

Figure 16. Overhead recovery rates have changed dramatically during the twentieth century.

The traditional dominance of total cost by direct labour in the early part of the century justified levying overheads as a proportion of labour. The search for consistency, one of the tenets of accounting practice, encourages persistence with the same overhead levy today. The result is the significant magnification of any errors in the direct labour figure. Since labour costs are the ones most liable to vary and also the most difficult to measure, resulting total costs can become very unreliable. The act of subtracting total costs from the selling price subjects the result to a further magnification in the impact of the error. Thus even a £10,000 error in the labour costs, out of total costs of £500,000, may end up with a 35% reduction in profitability, as shown in figure 17.

Many PPP companies now levy separate material and labour overheads, but such systems are not without their own pitfalls. While levying material overhead is usually satisfactorily on raw materials and components, the same overhead rate levied

COST	ACTUAL	ACCOUNTED
LABOUR	110,000	100,000
OVERHEAD RECOVERY @ 250%	275,000	250,000
MATERIAL	150,000	150,000
TOTAL UNIT COST	535,000	500,000
UNIT SELLING PRICE	600,000	600,000
CONTRIBUTION PER UNIT	65,000	100,000

Figure 17. The effects of errors in labour costs are magnified, resulting in a severely reduced profitability.

on identifiable sub-systems, results in prices that, after the other normal mark-ups, are clearly unacceptable to customers. The $800 clock and the $500 lavatory seat, identified by the US government in the nineteen eighties during investigations into contractor mark-ups of purchased items, are clear examples of these dangers. A good compromise is to use a lower mark-up on major bought-in items, particularly where these items pass through the Company without being given direct added value.

The difficulty of all overhead systems is that, when combined with the traditional line by line profitability analysis, they often result in the erroneous closure of apparently unprofitable lines. This phenomenon, known as margin retreat, offers no resistance to erosion of market share by a newcomer, as a leading European manufacturer apparently experienced when attacked by the Japanese ball bearing industry. As the European company retreated line by line, fixed overheads increased in rate, so further reducing the profitability of remaining lines.

Fortunately, the accounting profession is recognising this vulnerability within the cost accounting system and is looking at initiatives such as Activity Based Costing (ABC). ABC aims at establishing cheap mechanisms to push the total expense of traditional overhead items back into the direct cost where they belong.

For example some computer aided design terminals can only be used by entering a cost code to activate them, thus allowing the real cost of the use of the machine and its software to be allocated, together with a charge for the time the designer spends working at the terminal. The challenge is to automate the process cheaply, otherwise the costs incurred in gathering the information exacerbates the situation by making the overhead amount even larger.

New PPP pricing

Assuming that a PPP is completely new and there is no competition...yet, it is useful to start by asking four questions.

- What need does it meet?
- What benefits will it provide?
- What alternatives are there?
- How many will be sold?

It is very common for companies in the business to start with bottom up pricing for new PPPs. This is far too simplistic an approach and a number of influential factors need taking into account before arriving at a final price.

1. The risk of cannibalising orders for existing PPPs.
2. The need to get a reference installation.
3. If a genuinely new solution to a problem, the justification for using value-based pricing.
4. If a "me too" PPP, the likely use of cost-based pricing.
5. The effectiveness of any barriers to entry, which will determine:
   - The sustainability of value-based pricing.
   - The licensing policy with the novel parts of the PPP.
6. The paramount dangers of trying to recoup all the development costs with the first order.
7. Any royalty payable if a customer has funded the PPP development.
8. Whether the PPP is being produced in collaboration with other companies.
9. The attitude of the final end user, if not the direct customer.

Note that the price is likely to be different from the one used to justify the development of the PPP. Finally, it is important to consider the total sales volume through the life of the new PPP. If this number is more than, say twenty-five, there is a usually a justifiable case for discounting early sales. The purpose of this will be to win opinion leading and trial sites as reference installations and to establish the standards any later competitive offerings will have to meet. If the total number of sales is expected to stay in single figures, then such an approach is unlikely to be worthwhile.

With the rapid increase in competition for almost all PPPs and the frequent shortage of cash to pay for them, the idea of leasing is finding increasing favour. For some countries, this attraction may result from an inability or reluctance to increase their national debt. Particularly with revenue generating PPPs, it is reasonable for the supplier to receive a proportion of the earned revenues in payment.

This is particularly attractive for suppliers to Third World countries where the new PPP will actually generate the necessary hard currency. Alternatively, some companies actively pursue a leasing policy, finding the necessary finance either from their own resources or by obtaining the cash from a finance house. The competitive advantage gained by such companies is that their sales executives can win business from customers with insufficient capital budgets.

Final pricing review

Inevitably, when the price of something as complex as a PPP is first derived, it is almost inevitably much higher than the competitive market figure. A number of questions need answering to ensure that the right approach has been taken in arriving at the final price.

- Is the design value engineered?
- Is the batch size cost effective?
- Is there contingency on contingency?
- Has the non-recurring engineering been amortised over a reasonable batch size?
- Are the mark-ups realistic?

Presenting prices

There are a number of ways of presenting prices in the PPP marketplace, and the differences will depend both on the customer's needs and the type of industry concerned.

- Including inflation
- At a base price/date, with a price variation inflation formula
- Man hour/day/week/month/year rates
- Budgetary
- ROM or rough order of magnitude
- NTE or not to exceed

In addition to the normal cost information, many PPP purchasers, particularly where the supplier is a sole source, may require or even demand a significant amount of additional data to support the submission of a price. This may need to include a wide range of items.

- Major supplier/sub-contractor quotations
- Cash flow predictions
- Interest cost calculations
- Inflation/variation of price calculations
- Foreign currency calculations

Progress payments

With the long timescales normally found between contract signature and the final handover of the completed PPP to the customer, it is inevitable that companies will look for ways of funding the work during its implementation. The real benefit of progress payments comes from their effect on cash flow and the sales executive may need to fight hard to obtain them. A second advantage, from the company's point of view, is that in a default situation, the onus lies with the customer to retrieve the money. However, failure to satisfy the customer during contract implementation will lead, first, to the holding back of progress payments and the subsequent calling of performance bonds.

Cardinal points specifications usually make it seductively easier to judge as compliant any PPP being offered. However, at hand over, the PM may face great difficulty in actually proving compliance with the contract. To attain agreed progress payment triggers, it is necessary to take even greater care with the wording of the documented contract specification to ensure that fulfilment of the stipulated criteria is provable to the satisfaction of the purchaser.

Submitting bids

There are a number of rules involved in submitting tenders, some unwritten, most specified in the tender documents. The first golden rule is to submit the tender on time. No allowance will normally be made for postal delays or the delivery vehicle being caught in an unexpected traffic jam. Fortunately, the rush job calendar allows additional time for such emergencies!

NEG	FRI	FRI	FRI	THU	WED	TUE
8	7	6	5	4	3	2
15	14	13	12	11	10	9
22	21	20	19	18	17	16
29	28	27	26	25	24	23
36	35	34	33	32	31	30

1. This is a special calendar for handling rush jobs. All rush jobs are wanted yesterday. With this calendar, a job can be ordered on the 7th and delivered on the 3rd.
2. Most jobs are required by Friday, so there are three Fridays in every week.
3. Five new days are added to each month to allow for end-of-the-month panic jobs.
4. There is no 1st of the month, thus avoiding late delivery of the previous month's last-minute panic jobs.
5. Monday morning hangovers are abolished, together with non- productive weekends.
6. A new day - Negotiation Day has been introduced, keeping the other days free for uninterrupted panic.

Figure 18. The rush job calendar highlights the difficulties in completing tenders on time.

The tender documents, however, should not be submitted too early. Doing so not only reduces the time available for their preparation, but also allows an unscrupulous member of the customer community to open the documents and possibly pass vital information to a competitor. Where a tender has a public opening, it is vital to attend and spend as much time as possible copying down competitor data for use during subsequent negotiations, as well as in future competitive analysis.

Any rules that the purchaser may have set, such as the number of copies of the technical proposal and the page count, completion of a pricing proforma or any other forms, require obedience to the letter to avoid being declared non-compliant. It takes careful scrutiny of the requirement to ensure that nothing vital is missed. Quite often, the invitation to tender will prohibit vendors from contacting the customer until the purchase decision has been made. This needs interpreting sensibly but liberally, making the most of the almost inevitable question and answer sessions.

Unusual bidding situations

There are a number of situations where a normal approach to bidding is, for one reason or another, clearly not the right way to proceed. Two occasions when normal timescales are quite inappropriate are bids put together in response to a natural disaster and similarly, in response to the nation going onto a war footing. In these cases, speed is of the essence and following the 1994 Los Angeles earthquake, a contractor succeeded in replacing a concrete flyover on the key Santa Monica freeway within three months, a timescale hitherto considered reasonable for bidding but impossible for implementation, thus earning a handsome bonus worth seventy percent of the total contract value! The rapid completion involved a completely new approach to the job, working two twelve hour shift a day for seven days a week. Such an undertaking in normal times would have taken eighteen months to two years. Similar stories abound.

Other special situations include:
- Bidding for work for the Olympic games, where the deadline is a real date which cannot be changed.
- Bidding to take over work from a failed contractor.
- Trying to win a contract for a reference installation.
- Tendering for "black" programmes; those so secret that they are often carried out in a "skunk" works.
- Trying to meet impossible specifications.
- Bidding with unique offerings; a replacement space shuttle for Challenger.
- Tendering for variation orders.

Tender evaluation

The methods used by customers to evaluate bids need serious consideration. Weighted points scale evaluation finds much favour with PPP purchasers and is used, in conjunction with the price, to decide the winner. In this type of evaluation, the selection team will decide on a number of key technical and commercial items to be scored, together with a weighting factor that relates to the relative importance of each item. The total scores for each bidder are then compared with the price submitted for the required package and a final purchase recommendation made.

However, do not think that this Utopian solution is all that there is to tender evaluation. Recognise the involvement of human beings and thus the possibility of an overridden or back worked weighted points scale evaluations. It is therefore incumbent on all sales executives to try to influence the evaluation, recognising that their competitors will attempt the same thing.

Spec. Clause Number	TECHNICAL			COMMERCIAL			OPERATIONS			TOTAL
	Points Score	Weight	Final Score	Points Score	Weight	Final Score	Points Score	Weight	Final Score	Clause Score
TOTAL:										

VENDOR:

Figure 19. A typical weighted points scale evaluation form can end up a lengthy document

Selection committees

Industries differ in the way their organisations go about buying PPPs. An institutional process is common, as with an electricity utility buying a generating station. Alternatively, an ad hoc committee, set up as a task force for the purchase, is often the case when companies acquire information technology systems.

It is useful, in the PPP arena, to think of the customer's team that makes the purchase decision as the selection committee. It is essential for sales staff to discover the names of the members of the selection committee, their backgrounds and where they fit into the customer's organisation. Those involved directly in the purchase process itself need identification. The power and authority distribution across the committee also need establishing.

The Company's access to the members of the committee should be examined, as well as that of the competitors. Finally, attempts should be made to understand the evaluation process and schedule. Analysis of information gained about the views of the committee members will need matching with an effective plan to influence them towards selecting the Company's offering. A negotiating strategy requires compilation and its interaction with the win strategy considered. There is more information about this subject on the next page.

Selection authorities

The person or individuals most likely to be responsible for the final purchase decision require identification and their background established. Whether anyone in the Company knows them personally can be of critical importance to winning and the corollary as far as the competition is concerned can similarly be bad news. A plan to influence the selection authority is as important as a blocking plan for activation if it seems that a competitor is going to win the contract. Finally, the likely reaction of the selection authority to the win strategy will need careful assessment.

Bribery and corruption

There is little doubt that winning much PPP business results from payments in cash or in kind to people in the selection committee; the more so in the Third World. In many countries, such payments are normal practice despite being illegal and are effectively a different channel of income distribution.

The key rule is that the selling Company should never directly make such payments. Whilst morally unacceptable in the industrialised nations, bribery still occurs and company executives frequently end up in jail for making either offers or payments. It is up to the individual companies and sales staff to set their own moral standards in this difficult area.

Negotiating strategies

Even before bid submission, it is important to have a negotiating strategy worked out and a team of negotiators selected to match that of the customer. The team must decide what concessions will be made, at what stage and in exchange for what from the customer. The posture taken will very much depend on the latest competitive assessment, but will also depend on the customer and whether there is likely to be one or more "Best And Final Offers" (BAFOs). This is where, after the bid opening, the purchaser goes back to the top two or three bidders and requests their best or lowest price.

Other factors for consideration are the size of the customer's budget, the Company's price, alternatives and options, as well as the absolute minimum price below which the Company will walk away from the potential contract. The negotiating plan should include recovery action, if it appear that the bid has been lost. As a last resort, attempts can be made to have the procurement re-tendered, which can result in living to fight another day, albeit at the risk of antagonising the customer.

Negotiating factors

It is common for inexperienced staff, when faced with the idea of negotiating a contract, to think immediately of the need to reduce the price. This is, in fact, the last thing to do. In the complexity of most PPP offerings, there are many other things to negotiate before ever reaching the stage of reducing the actual price. The following list may act as a useful check.

- Delivery
- Quantity
- The package
- Performance
- Concessions to specification items
- Logistic support
- Acceptance
- Warranty
- Contract terms and conditions
- Negotiating margin
- **When all else has failed, price**

Planning and preparation

For any negotiation to reach a successful outcome, a significant amount of preparatory work is essential. In the context of winning a PPP contract, the negotiations are likely to be carried out between teams from the purchaser and the vendor. It is essential that the Company's team agrees the approach during this vital planning and preparation period, and also nominates a spokesperson. The following is a list of questions to address before negotiations begin.

- What do we want from the other team?
  - Must have?
  - Would like to have?
- Starting demand?
  - What we are prepared to concede to get what we want?
  - How quickly will we concede?
- What do we think the other team wants from us?
  - Must have?
  - Would like to have?
- What are the other team likely to concede?
- What are the probable areas of agreement?
- What are the probable areas of conflict?
- What longer term issues are relevant?
- What is the likely sequence of discussion?
- How will "history" affect our negotiations?
- What is our timetable and deadline?

The team needs to be clear whether the chosen approach is based on a one off deal with the customer or whether a long term relationship is the aim. There are many unfortunate examples of the long term aim being clouded by the temptation of a quick hit, particularly where ambitious individuals wish to make their mark in the Company. The consequences in the PPP environment are particularly dire, since most businesses operate on long term horizons and people have good memories. With relatively small customer communities, when the word circulates about cavalier attitudes, a severe backlash may quickly surface. Even worse is the likelihood that the Company will have to deal with the customer again at some time in the future, when any such debts will be repaid with interest.

Briefing the team should include such tactics as whether to take a "nice/nasty" approach, where the "nice," person appears to be on the customers' side. This individual should be able to win their confidence and perhaps gain better favour from them in considering any suggestions personally made. The person may even be elevated to the status of an "intermediary," though not an unbiased one.

The team also need to know how to signal to their leader that they wish to call for a recess. Successful negotiators, in calling for a break, give a summary of the negotiating stage reached and express enthusiasm that a mutually beneficial agreement is attainable. On return, they resume at the point the negotiations had reached, either taking them in a new direction as a result of the recess, or re-opening the issue to hand.

Finally, there is nothing worse than a team member who mentions that a requested change can be implemented at minimum cost. This is particularly so when that change has been previously identified by the commercial executive as a high value aspect for the customer and has worked hard to substantiate a price premium for the capability. At least as important is to prevent a senior executive or director from coming and taking the credit as agreement approaches. Many customers use the ploy of welcoming the newcomer, gaining confirmation that they have the authority over price (many take pride in agreeing) and then asking for the concession that the negotiating team has been struggling to avoid.

Stages of negotiation

There are fundamentally four discrete stages in any negotiation. These are the introduction, the stage where differences are examined, followed by movement of the parties and finally agreement. Each has its useful set of rules.

1. Introduction

Settling in remarks and small-talk.
Developing the climate by the attitudes shown by the teams.
Opening remarks putting the negotiation into a broad context.
As appropriate, specifying time available, agenda and objectives.

2. Examining the differences

Speeches to convince the other team that the current offer is the best available.
Teams circle round, weighing each other up, manoeuvring.
Feelings are expressed and the differences between the teams are displayed.
Each team makes clear what are their issues and their positions on each one.

3. Movement

Movement by both teams is necessary.
Proposals are made in attempts to bridge the negotiating gap.
Teams generate tactics in attempts to get what they want.
Proposals must be hooked onto conditions or are concessions.

4. Agreement

Complete trading of concessions. "We'll do this if you'll do that."
Final trades such as: "If...then we have a deal."
Summarising and writing up the agreement.
Implementation and monitoring of the agreement.

Breaking deadlocks

When two way movement stops, the situation will almost inevitably degenerate into deadlock. There are only three ways to break deadlocks. These are by altering something existing, introducing something new or changing a perspective on something. Some ways to help a negotiator return to the table with minimum loss of face are more obvious than others.

- Change the shape or form of the money even if the total value is unchanged
- Change a team member or leader
- Postpone a difficult part of the discussion until more information is available
- Offer to share some of the risks
- Offer options. These give the appearance of flexibility even if unlikely to be taken up
- Change the stance from competitive to collaborative if appropriate
- If you can trust your sense of humour, tell a funny story

Each of these options re-involves the other party in discussions. They provide the opportunity to change the atmosphere and lead to new alternatives. Often such new alternatives serve to make the existing propositions look better.

Negotiating contracts

Experienced negotiators have two separate mindsets. The first concerns the task and deals with the various issues, making sure they are handled in the most beneficial way. The other mindset focuses on the process, concentrating on the interaction between the two sides and the thinking of the opposing team. It can be useful to nominate one member of the team, who will not participate actively in the discussions, but rather observe the process interactions for insights. These may help to steer the negotiations in a particular and beneficial direction.

Additionally, experienced negotiators occasionally make emotional statements. These are verbalised expressions of how they want the opposition to think they are viewing the proceedings and they can be effective in shaping the approach being used by the opposition. Commentaries about the feelings of the negotiator, the team or the process also frequently occur. They are usually of a supportive nature and can be of significant help in bringing the whole process to a satisfactory conclusion.

The early stages of a negotiation are vital. Remember that the overall objective is to determine as soon as possible what is valuable to the customer and to swap it for something of little cost to the Company. It is probing questions and effective deductions that can reveal how to play the cards for best effect. This may mean being somewhat economical with background information; a stance commonly encountered with experienced opponents.

Negotiating teams face the danger of feeling rushed, accompanied by the inevitable and unhelpful thought that the in-tray in the office is rapidly filling with other vital work. These pressures must be resisted at all costs, particularly since the customer's tactics are likely to appear deliberately slowing; indeed sometimes they are.

During negotiations, it is essential to keep the whole deal in mind or the customer will be able to nibble away around the edges for concessions. Individually, these may look eminently reasonable, but in aggregate, are successively eroding the attractiveness of the deal to the vendor. Avoid one sided concessions; swaps are preferable by far. After trying these and hopefully achieving success, concessions may finally be necessary to get within the customer's limits. Do this grudgingly for two good reasons. First, there can be no foreknowledge of how far the process will continue, regardless of what the customer says. Second, if large chunks of

WHEN NEGOTIATING CONTRACTS IT IS HARD TO DECIDE WHICH OF THE THREE IS THE TOUGHEST.

what is available are given away, the customer will think that in the last resort, there will be yet more to come. If it is not forthcoming, they are likely to end up feeling that they have not done very well.

Thus, negotiating margins need to be conceded gradually, since it is not uncommon for the customer's negotiating team to refer their recommendation to higher authority, who will justify their existence by demanding a further discount; a process that can lead to several iterations.

There are several well-known texts on negotiating which provide comprehensive information about the subject and the bibliography lists them.

Dutch auctions

One of the dangers in the final stages of a tender process is that it will degenerate into a Dutch auction. The so-called best and final offer is rarely actually the final one and keen competition ensures that the prices quoted to the customer by the various companies keep tumbling. There are a number of ways of dealing with this problem. The first is to sit down with the customer and quietly explain that it is not in the interest of either side for the contractor to face insufficient funding to implement the contract. A company making a loss on a PPP is unlikely to do the best job for the customer. It is almost certain to scrimp and save money during implementation and to bicker over changes to the contract specification; both to the detriment of the job.

The second approach involves knowing when to walk away from the contract and telling the customer unequivocally when that point arrives. Some years ago, the US Air Force needed a large quantity of new altimeters for its aircraft. The two incumbents in the business bid very similar prices, whilst a new entrant bid at two thirds of the others' price. The incumbents both refused to reduce their prices to match the lowest bid and, as a result, the newcomer won the business, but never succeeded in delivering a working altimeter, to the detriment of both the newcomer and the purchaser.

Cognitive dissonance

This consumer marketing concept is just as relevant in the PPP arena. After making a commitment, people involved in making the purchase decision may read press comment or advertisements to confirm the correctness of their choice. Cognitive dissonance arises when reading about competitive PPPs, or seeing others using them and thinking that they would have been a better purchase. These doubts may include some or all of the following factors.
- Could the price have been lower?
- Could an extended warranty have been obtained?

- Was the PPP specification the optimum one?
- Will the training be effective?
- Will the delivery be on time?
- How good will the support be?

In the PPP arena, clearly such doubts can arise from any one of a number of causes and it is the responsibility of the sales executive to think carefully to see if any of them are likely to occur.

1. A changing business situation negates the need for the purchase, as happened with the procurement of oil tankers when the long term traffic growth prospects evaporated.
2. Competitive offerings arrive featuring, for example, new technology, better value/price ratios or imminent new standards rather than the current ones.
3. Other aspects of the total contract change, where the customer is the prime contractor, such that a different offering would have suited the recent change better.
4. Relationships do not look so straightforward when finalising design details or tying up contractual details.

Keeping it sold

Once the contract has been signed, never let it be thought that the sales team can relax; far from it! After the celebrations are over, there is more hard work. The customer may get withdrawal symptoms and competitor attacks aggravate these. Inevitably, there will be a communications hangover as projects, programmes, engineering, operations and logistics staff take over dealing with the PPP customer interface. It is also common, on large PPPs, for companies to have some difficulties in increasing the numbers of staff to the level required in the desired timeframe.

When the implementation period of a PPP is long, the customer's budget may well come under attack and the Company should provide assistance in keeping the PPP in the budget. It is also important to maintain an independent source for assessing customer contentment, as well as a "999" procedure, should the customer feel that the PPP is heading for real trouble. The first contract review with the customer often proves to be a watershed in terms of establishing the way things will continue for the life of the PPP.

The PM is the key player in ensuring that the PPP is kept sold and also in winning additional work, through changes to specification, increased scope or logistics support. In both roles, it is essential that the PM and the sales executive maintain a close working relationship, both to obtain the best possible level of further business for the Company, but also to keep customer relations on an even keel. The relationship is particularly taxing if changes to the specification are required and variation orders arise. Such a situation may be innocent, or part of a deliberate vendor strategy at the onset.

One area, which needs particular attention in high-tech PPPs, is the need to keep the design usable, particularly if spare parts cease to be available and minor design changes are necessary to accommodate alternative parts. Sometimes, customers will fund post design services contracts, but generally, such work can only be funded by the Company.

Chapter 4:

Bid Management

Effective solutions · Bid teams · Collaborative bids · Sub-contractors · Competitive assessments · Competitor Strawman proposals · Proposals · Proposals that win · Proposal formats · Executive summaries · A structured modular approach · Boiler plating · Storyboarding · Facilities & procedures · Proposal reviews · Blue Teams · Red teams · Bid reviews · Executive approval

Effective solutions

Having examined how to get to the point of contract award, this chapter examines the role of bid management in getting a company into a winning position. It was Sir Henry Royce (joint founder of Rolls Royce) who, unfortunately, preached engineering excellence for its own sake. It has become a valued tradition, not only in British academia, but also by many individuals in our islands. This has proved to be most unfortunate in today's competitive world. The tendency is still widespread to gold plate and over engineer solutions offered to the customer, rather than design to cost.

It was John Glenn, the first American astronaut to orbit the earth who said that as he sat in the Mercury capsule awaiting lift off, he was thinking: "This complete spacecraft has been purchased on a government contract, awarded to the lowest bidder!" How would the reader have felt? Technical compliance, or even an acceptable declared level of non-compliance is still much more likely to win and commensurate costs may need revisiting several times by the bid team, before they reach a winning level. It is indeed the classic value to price ratio problem.

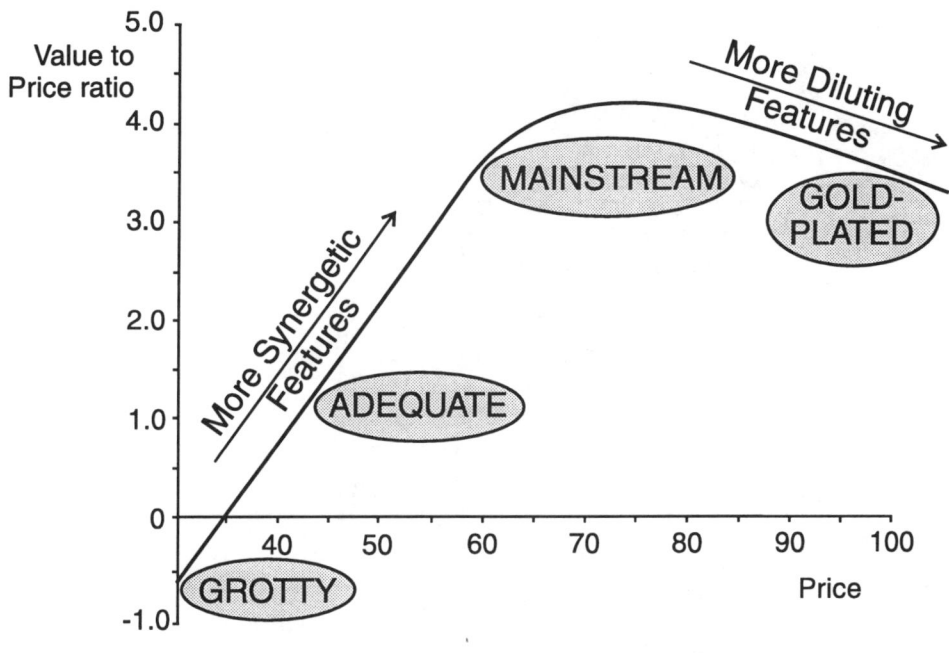

Figure 20. It is the value to price ratio, when compared to the price, which defines whether a PPP is gold plated or not.

Bid teams

Assembling a bid team and choosing the right time to bring the team together are not easy decisions. Planned timescales for the issue of requests for tender frequently slip and judgements have to be made since, by the time the RFQ arrives, the first draft of the proposal should already be complete. However, starting too early can be an expensive mistake and prove to be almost as bad as starting too late. The quality of the bid team is also important and the "A" team needs to be available for "must win" PPPs.

The team should be a balanced one, containing typically a sales executive, a PM and a number of PPP specialists, together with estimating, pricing and proposal skills. In addition, input will be required on the "-ilities"; reliability, maintainability, quality and the other support functions, as well as a commercial input on the terms and conditions. The bid team will need a leader, normally but not necessarily the PM. This choice will be very dependant on the state of development of the opportunity. Its scope, complexity and size will also all impinge upon the selection. To have a reasonable chance of submitting a winning bid, it is essential to employ a strong and balanced team. A second XI just won't do and usually reflects a lack of management commitment to the bid.

The team's first task will be to assess the requirement and then select a baseline bid, alternatives and options, including non-compliant offerings. They will then have to establish technical solutions and start to allocate tasks. Most time is lost at the onset of a bid so it is crucial to get mobilised as soon as possible. Many PPP organisations have a dedicated proposal manager which has advantages in terms of expediting layout, presentation and editing to a common style.

An early priority is to establish any weaknesses, which may demand a teaming arrangement with another company. (See also page 264.) At the same time, any major sub-contractors will need identification. These two items are invariably critical in timescale terms. Thus, investment of effort in these areas in the early stages, preferably well before the RFQ arrives, generally brings rewards later. Key teaming issues require resolution.

- How will these relationships be managed?
- Who will manage them?
- How will the work packages be defined?
- How to resolve interfaces, responsibilities and back to back issues ?
- How will the sub-contract bidders list be established?
- What commitment will be made about sub-contracting if the Company wins the prime bid?
- How will buying in versus internal sourcing be resolved?

Within a short period of the establishment of the team, direct bidding costs will have to be established, figures between 1% and 2.5% not being uncommon; £10,000-£25,000 per million of contract. The cost of any re-bids and BAFO's must be included, as well as travel costs and the time and expenses of the negotiating team.

Supporting bid teams overseas

There is nothing lonelier than being a member of a bid team, working overseas, which experiences poor support from the parent company in the UK. Rapid response to faxes and telephone calls is absolutely vital to keep the morale of the bid team high and to maintain their credibility with the customer. Simple forgetfulness of timezone shifts or consideration that other things are more important differentiate the amateur approach from the professional. The golden rule is that a response to a team overseas always must have everyone's top priority, particularly in view of the expense of keeping a team in an overseas hotel and the team members' desire to get home to their families as quickly as possible.

Collaborative bids

Bidding in conjunction with one or more companies produces a whole host of new problems, particularly if working with overseas companies. There will have to be a lead company and a single site nominated for the integration of the bid. This will mean considerable extra work for the company's bid team either spending time away from base, or picking up the co-ordination and integration role. Where more than one language is involved, it is essential that the lead company is putting the bid together in its mother tongue. Allow additional time for sequential executive approval and the problems of mark-ups, which require discussion at the highest management levels. An agreement of joint and several liability can often be helpful in this respect, leading to all parties having a vested interest that the others take the most appropriate actions.

Some customers welcome bids by joint ventures, while others demand a prime contractor. There are advantages and snags to both. Joint liability clearly forces each partner to ensure the protection of all parties from poor performance of any resulting contract. It can, however, lead to fuzzy leadership, both in the bidding and the implementation stages. Furthermore, mediocre teams often result from the reluctance of companies to see their best staff transferred to a joint venture. Much clearer leadership is available from a prime contractor, but the role of sub-contracting partner can be less than ideal, particularly in terms of workshare and ownership of intellectual property rights.

Sub-contractors

The problems of keeping sub-contractors (subs) and major suppliers in line are many and varied. For a start, no PPP prime contractor wants subs going directly to the customer. Thus, it is incumbent on the prime-contractor's sales and marketing organisation to feed the subs with just sufficient information about any potential contract to fulfil their needs.

Then there is the question of ensuring that their prices remain valid if, as is usual, contract negotiations with the customer become prolonged. It is the task of the PM, in conjunction with the Company's purchasing department, to obtain leeway over and above any back to back agreement, to allow time for eventual contract negotiations with the subcontractor. The danger is that once subs knows that a prime contractor has signed a contact with their offering included, this severely erodes the prime's negotiating position.

The above considerations have led to the setting up of key supplier/purchaser relationships to mitigate these difficulties and also to reduce costs on both sides. Such relationships can be beneficial, particularly when a sub-contractor has put a lot of work into a bid, which the prime bidder has subsequently lost. It can also help to keep key subs bidding on an exclusive basis. The down side is that if, after the prime contract award, a better offering appears from another sub-contractor, the prime contractor will be unable to take advantage of the benefits of the new offering. Such a situation can, however, provide something of a lever for the prime.

Sometimes, the customer will stipulate the use by all bidders of a certain sub-contractor for a particular item of equipment or work. This will always erode differentiation between bidders and can lead to difficulties if that sub fails to perform satisfactorily during the contract implementation. These instances require appropriate handling on the contract side to protect the prime contractor both from poor performance by the sub but even more from any consequential delays, profit erosion and blame by the customer.

Competitive assessments

Bid preparation necessarily involves an assessment of the position of the other leading contenders for the job. The following questions demand a response, despite the difficulties in obtaining all the answers.

- Why should another's solution be chosen in preference to the Company's PPP?
- What are the strengths of their PPP, delivery time and expected price?
- Do they have any technological advantages?
- Have they got an existing relationship with the customer?
- What view does the customer hold of them?

It is also essential to review the competitors as corporations, rather than in terms of their offerings, and to consider their position both in the market place as well as in financial terms.

- What is their financial position?
- How much do they need this contract?
- What are their future business plans?
- What is their reputation in the market?

Competitor Strawman proposals

Once a list has been established of competitors likely to bid, if the bidders list is long, it should be filtered down to the few most likely to win. Then mini competitor teams should be set up internally and tasked with putting together bids as if they were competitive bid teams. Each team must have full access not only to the customer's specification, but also to the Company's bid, competitor's files and data-bases, in order to establish the fullest possible background.

These Strawman teams require quarantining whilst they fulfil their task and full management freedom to act as they choose. On completion, they present the Strawman proposals, in particular the techniques used, type of solution proposed and alternatives, to the Company's bid team for comparison with the proposed offering. The bid team can then improve their own proposal to counter competitor's strengths and highlight weaknesses. Such an approach can effectively negate a competitor's offering, whilst avoiding the pitfalls of denigrating the competitor.

Proposals

A number of reasons highlight the need for effective proposal management in the PPP arena. A good proposal is a critical success factor in winning new business. It

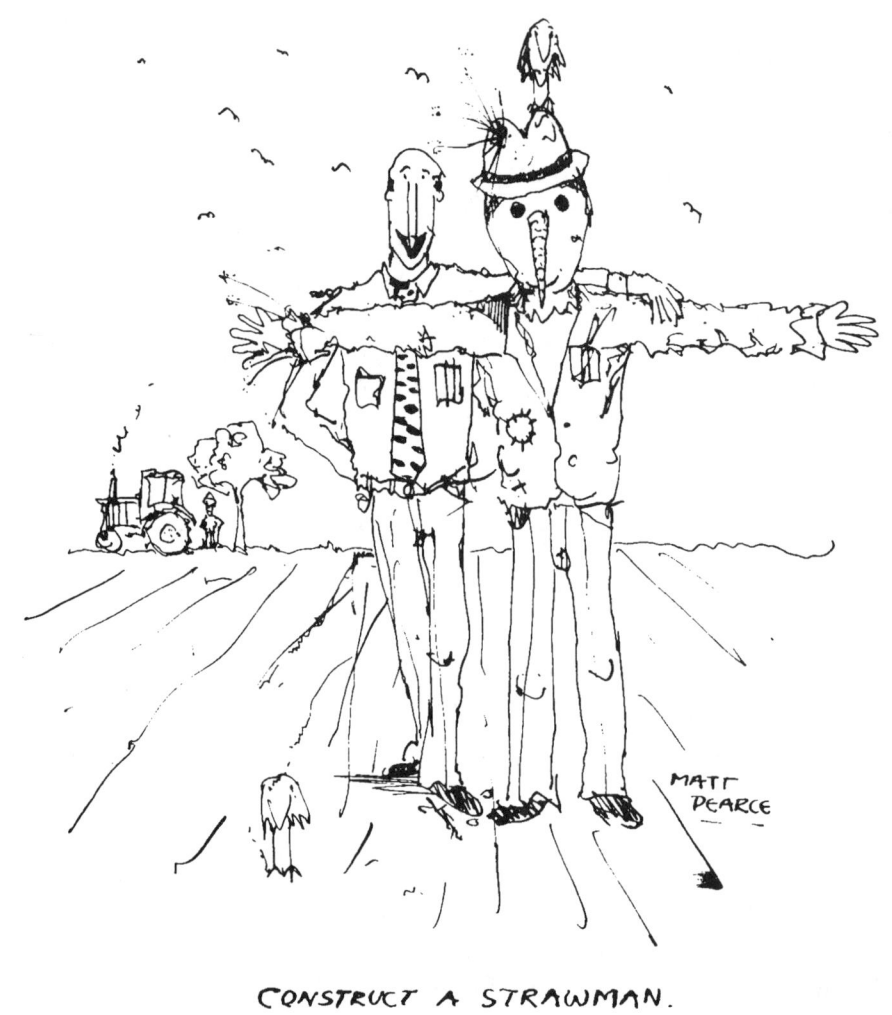

CONSTRUCT A STRAWMAN.

is an expensive and complex activity. It involves multi-disciplinary teams working to demanding timescales and concurrently undertaking such activities as designing, writing and estimating.

A good proposal will maximise the evaluation rating by the customer in terms of the technical solution, while proving its compliance. It will also emphasise the track record and credibility of the Company as well as highlighting any risks and uncertainties involved in implementing the PPP. It must encapsulate the win strategy, which should contain a unique overall theme addressing the customer's needs. It should contain key discriminators that highlight the Company's advantages and resolve any weakness perceived by the customer, while at the same time revealing the competitors' deficiencies. It must also address the customer's key concerns.

Compliance statements should never be long lists of customer's requirements, followed by the word "compliant." Compliance must be proved to the customer and a short supporting statement is essential, often with a reference to the appropriate descriptive section of the proposal.

The aim of every proposal is to be clear, comprehensible and complete. It must answer the question "Why should the customer choose us?" and match the customer's bid evaluation process. Finally, from the Company's perspective, the cost of preparation must be controlled and affordable. This is usually quite a balancing act for those in charge of the overall process.

Proposals that win

A number of key factors need checking if a winning proposal is to result from all the bidding effort. Such a document must contain the following features, which are necessary to avoid it being cast aside unread.

- Sized correctly for the bid value
- Not boring or repetitive
- Show the benefits of the solution
- Easy to read and skim read
- Easy to reference
- Well illustrated and presented

Furthermore, for larger offerings, it ought to include an executive summary volume as well as a PPP overview. It should also divide out well for the customer's specialists to handle effectively. The executive summary is written to persuade the decision makers to choose the Company's offering, whilst the PPP overview is given to each specialist, together with their particular section, so that they can understand the total offering before assessing their particular part.

Any proposal must prove that the Company can do the job and do it better than the competition. It has to take the place of the bid team at the critical time of decision making, when company representatives are normally forbidden contact with the customer. Thus, it must guide the evaluators through the document, explaining reasons and showing benefits. The completed document must prove that:

1. The offering is the best for the job
2. The Company is a credible supplier

The dependence on customer information, which can only be gleaned from sustained customer contact, indicates why it is very rare for a newcomer to be able to assemble a winning bid. Conventional wisdom suggests that newcomers will not become competitive until they have completed at least three bids in a new area.

Proposal formats

The proposal is the key document that tells the customer what is being offered. It comprises an offer in the legal sense and is subject to acceptance, so forming a contract between the parties. However, things are never quite so straightforward.

In the PPP business, both the methods of writing proposals and their appearance have improved significantly in recent years. Before even starting to write the proposal, it is essential to see whether anything in the customer's RFQ will directly constrain the way in which the proposal is produced and whether there is anything in the construction of the RFQ itself that indicates the desired form of proposal. Remember, a competitor may have written the tender specification! It is not uncommon for customers to impose a limit to the number of pages and on occasions prohibit the use of colour. They may well define the contents and even the order of the subject matter, unfortunately often resulting in an unsatisfactory document.

Whilst there are several ways to structure and write a proposal, one approach that leads to a consistent proposal format is the use of the "storyboarding" technique,

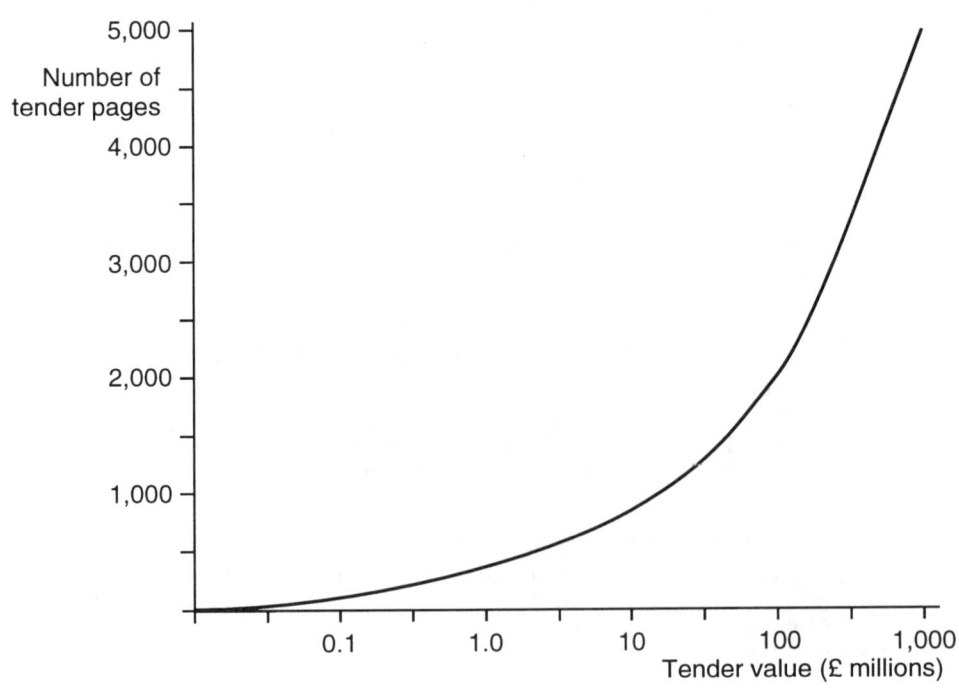

Figure 21. The number of pages in a typical proposal will, to a great extent, be dependant on the total value of the bid.

which will be explored shortly. The other major consideration is the appearance of the proposal. Some customers receive tens of proposals and evaluation teams discard a number unread, making their appearance critical. This requires decision making in a number of areas.

The end result must invite the customer community to read and enjoy reading the Company's proposal. It is the sales executive's responsibility to ensure that the look of the proposal matches the customer's culture and needs.

ISSUE	OPTIONS
Page size	A4 for Europe, AQ (American Quarto) for North America
Language	English or translated
Print face	Must be easy to read and not too varied
Single or multi-column	Two column allows more words per page and easier reading
Pictures in text or separate	In text pictures give impact, easing reading and referencing
Colour or monochrome	Some customers prohibit colour
Attractive, eye-catching cover	To get the customer to look at the proposal
Cover colour	Eye catching
Binding method	Loose leaf or permanent
Number of volumes	May assist dispersed customer evaluators

Figure 22. A number of areas require careful though when deciding the form of a proposal.

Executive summaries

Executive summaries can be particularly useful when making major PPP bids. An executive summary is not a précis of the proposal. It is a short document (twenty pages maximum) explaining to the members of the selection committee why they should purchase the Company's offering. It is essential that the sales executive ensures that every member of the committee, and the selection authority, receives a copy. It should concentrate on value to the customer, benefits, advantages and features. It should give a brief overview of the PPP and must encapsulate the win strategy. It should substantiate key factors, such as logistic support, and possibly cover company capability and track record.

A structured modular approach

Modular proposals give a number of benefits. First, the structure of the proposal is easier to map into large customer evaluation teams, which may be multi-department, multi-disciplined, based at more than one location and on occasions, multi-national. Customers nearly always sub-divide comprehensive tenders and send the resulting parts to different departments. It is important to take this into consideration when deciding the format of the complete proposal. Modular proposals are easier to read since they integrate text and graphics, spotlight key points and have an understandable structure. Such proposals are also a great help to skimming readers.

The modular approach gives visibility of the key elements and the proposal shape to the Company at an early stage, clarifies what is happening during the proposal writing period and improves control of the process. The proposal manager specifies the module objectives and these are used to direct the authors. Such an approach better accommodates the different writing styles, which will inevitably be involved. It significantly reduces the impact of individuals and team members. It focuses the efforts of the writers on the content, rather than the structure, style and procedures. It provides a common framework that eases the rapid run up of the proposal writing team and finally it makes it possible easily to re-use material and tailor standard paragraphs.

Some of the additional advantages of a modular approach include the fact that the writing order is not critical and modules can readily be added, rearranged or deleted. A discipline is imposed on authors in terms both of the length of the text and the level of detail. This can be particularly beneficial when dealing with the verbose and rambling author and can also help the "What am I going to put on this blank page?" writer.

The technique allows an early assessment of artwork requirements, so often the critical path for a good proposal, and eases the management of page budgets. Finally, from a management point of view, it provides an excellent basis for estimating the level of effort needed, the forecasting of cost and schedule, as well as control of the whole process. Modularity also simplifies the check for compliance before submission of a proposal.

Each module has a writing plan and intermediate check point. The module is generally two pages long, though four and eight page modules are not uncommon. It integrates text and illustrations and covers a single theme.

Boiler plating

This valuable technique is the name given to the process that allows the incorporation of standard sections of text into any technical proposal. It is naturally particularly useful when describing the various "-ilities", and of course for company capability statements. However, with complex PPPs, it can be equally effective in describing standardised parts of the offering. The term is common in the commercial section of the proposal, where the term boilerplate clause is used to describe those standard paragraphs that find their way into virtually every contract.

There are, however, dangers involved in the use of boiler plating. There is a risk of making junior staff responsible for preparation of the bid when more experienced eyes are required. Also, it may reduce the tendency to read the contents of the boilerplate sections, so possibly building in inconsistencies, contradictions and omissions.

Storyboarding

The storyboarding technique was developed by Hollywood in the nineteen thirties for the film industry. Each separate scene or shot was illustrated on a single sheet of paper that showed the visual effect and summarised the verbal contents.

This allowed scenes to be shot out of sequence, yet the actors and actresses could see where the scene fitted in the whole film and understand the physical and emotional settings in relationship to the preceding and subsequent scenes. The technique was adapted for proposal preparation by a number of large Californian industrial companies in the period following the Second World War. Every proposal is divided down into a number of modules, for each of which a storyboard is prepared. The storyboard contains the aim of the module, up to six paragraph outlines, a theme or summary sentence, an illustration or diagram, together with a caption.

Once all the storyboards are complete, they should be pinned to soft board panelling on the walls of a large proposals room. The structure and contents of the proposal can then be checked to discover redundancies, omissions, inconsistencies and outstanding problems. This technique also provides an excellent vehicle for dialogue between the writers and management, giving the various authors a fine framework for their writing as well as an insight into the position of their part in the whole proposal.

Other benefits include the ease with which the win strategy can be applied at module level. Changes to the storyboards can be annotated and authorised in a single session and the early identification of problems gives adequate time for their resolution. The benefits of pinning a proposal up on the walls, as opposed to reading the pages clipped into a folder, is even greater than the advantage gained from reading printed copy rather than text on a computer screen. It is highly recommended.

PROPOSAL STORYBOARD	
VOLUME Engine for Earth Moving Machine **SUB-SECTION** Introduction **AUTHOR** J. Smith	**SECTION** System description **PROPOSAL REF** TM 1234 B **TOPIC TITLE** Benefits **DATE REQUIRED** 25th May
MODULE OBJECTIVE To indicate the benefits of our design to both the end user and the vehicle designer.	
SUMMARY SENTENCE The smooth running of the compact lightweight V6 is combined with low fuel consumption and pollution levels in a highly reliable and flexible power unit.	
PARAGRAPH OUTLINES 1. A V6 configuration gives minimum engine length with super smooth running 2. Maximum use of aluminium and magnesium alloys minimise overall engine weight. 3. Direct injection gives best fuel consumption and low exhaust pollution levels. 4. Peak power at low revs gives maximum flexibility and simplifies gearbox design. 5. 3000 hour MTBF and 500 hour service interval ensure maximum availability.	
SKETCH OF ILLUSTRATION 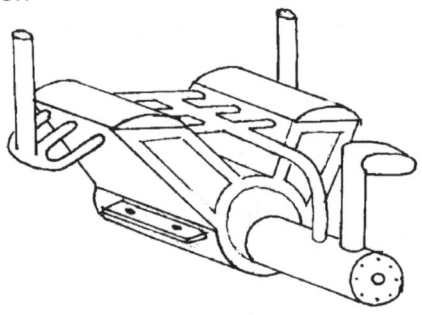	
FIGURE/TABLE NUMBER 3.4	
CAPTION The V6 engine combines minimum size and weight with excellent performance and economy.	
AUTHORISED	**DATE**

Figure 23. A typical storyboard, showing a module including objective, text and illustration, which will occupy two pages in the final proposal document.

Bid management

Facilities and procedures

To carry out storyboarding effectively in a company requires both facilities and training. The facilities include the establishment of a proposals room, with soft board on the walls and a perimeter of some sixty metres. This room will need to include a number of desks, so that authors can come and work in the room. Standard stationary layouts will be required and standardised word processing facilities, together with dedicated photocopying and desk top publishing facilities.

Training in the technique is essential for technical staff, sales and marketing staff, support staff and management. Procedures will need formalising, including the processes of overview preparation, proposal formats, reviews and authorisation. There will need to be agreement on the word processing package used by authors and the desktop publishing system will require selection. Finally, management commitment to the system is absolutely essential.

Proposal reviews

Any proposal must be the subject of regular reviews of its contents. In a well-organised bid, there should, typically, be five proposal reviews.

TYPE	PURPOSE	WHAT IS REVIEWED
LAUNCH	Check win strategy	Customer requirement, outline solution, win strategy, bid/no-bid
BLUE TEAM	Check technical solution	Design schedule, preliminary costing
STORYBOARD	Review proposal contents, organisation and emphasis	Proposal outline, storyboards
RED TEAM	Evaluate draft proposal and Red team report	Draft proposal, Strawmen
BID REVIEW	Establish proposed price and commercial terms & conditions	Cost estimates, pricing, proposal overview

Figure 24. It is important to ensure that the review team members have the time and commitment to undertake the necessary tasks.

Blue Teams

A Blue team concentrates solely on the technical solution being offered. It consists of creative engineers with complementary skills. They should know the customer well and understand the PPP requirement. Given good team spirit and commitment to involvement in the Blue team, the members can help the Company's team reach the right technical solution. This may involve developing independent solutions to the requirement and then comparing them with the bid team's proposal to see if there is a better way of meeting the requirement. It can require lateral thinking; re-interpreting the specification in terms of similar facilities used elsewhere or something called by a different name.

A good example came when bids for telephone exchanges included a requirement to provide short form dialling. By recognising that the already incorporated UK 999 facility was, in fact, a type of short form dialling, the winning supplier was able to avoid expensive changes to the system, whilst using the existing facility to provide other short form dialling capabilities. In addition, a Blue team can be of particular assistance in finding alternative offerings to the main compliant solution.

Red teams

The presence of Red teams needs planning into the bid process at an early stage, though the majority of their work occurs fairly late in the process. Their task is to evaluate the Company's bid prior to its completion. The members need briefing well before the team assembles to allow them time to get up to speed and they should attend the launch review. They should aim to adopt a bird's eye view. They must act as if they were purchasers carrying out their evaluation and must have a destructive intent, though with constructive suggestions for the bid team at the subsequent Red team review.

Red teams need to employ the best people in the Company, who must have a high reputation, preferably both internally and with the customer. They must be doers and hard workers as there is never enough time in the bidding schedule for an adequate Red team review. They will need to understand the customer and their operations, as well as knowing about the PPP being offered. The employment of former members of the customer's selection committee as consultants for this task can be immensely beneficial. Finally, they will have to be willing to commit significant time to the Red team work.

Bid reviews

A comprehensive, though not necessarily long, document should be prepared for the group that is responsible for authorising the submission of bids to customers. The following checklist is useful in ensuring that the text covers all the necessary topics. It divides into four main sections. The first gives the background to the proposal, then follow the costs and pricing factors, ending with a number of other issues not be forgotten. The review team should consider four items; the bid review document, the technical proposal, the commercial proposal and the price together with its supporting estimates.

BID REVIEW CHECKLIST	Commercial in Confidence
OVERVIEW:	**PRICING:**
Description of customer requirements	Inflation/price variation
Description of Company offering	Warranty
Risk assessment	G & A: General & Administrative charge
Importance to Company and competition	Liquidated damages allowance
COSTS:	Royalties and IPR
PVR&D	Bonds and bank charges
Factory cost estimates	Interest adjustment
Major suppliers and sub-contractor quotes	Counter trade/offset requirements
Spare parts, tools and test gear	Customer finance
Installation and training	Currency risk
OTHER ISSUES:	Freight and insurance
Capital expenditure	Representative's commission
Transfer of title	Profit
Resource availability	Gross selling price
Technical feasibility	Recommended selling price
External approvals required	Negotiating margin

Figure 25. The bid review document needs careful checking to ensure that nothing has been missed.

Executive approval

The level of authority needed to sign off a bid will principally depend on its financial value and this figure will usually define the signatories and the order of obtaining the signatures. Other key factors include the minimum profit level proposed and the possible imposition of onerous terms and conditions. It is important to remember that senior management diaries get filled very quickly and plenty of warning of an impending bid approval meeting is essential. It is not unusual for these to have to tie in to the day of a company board meeting, which could mean a month's delay if the authorisation process is badly scheduled or delayed through an inadequate submission.

Almost invariably, for the larger PPPs, the signatories will require pre-briefing before giving the final approval. The bid manager will need to assign tasks to the bid team to ensure that this part of the proceedings runs smoothly. Alternate plans may be needed, especially due to the penchant of busy senior executives to reschedule meetings at the last minute. It will also be sensible to have a rapid response plan ready, should the final bid be rejected for any reason (usually price!) and need reworking in a short time to meet a rapidly approaching tender closing date. Here, a personal computer with an effective operator can really earn its keep.

It is usual to hold a series of meetings to approve a bid. The technical and production issues, including the cost estimates are the domain of the bid manager/PM designate and PPP design engineer in conjunction with the project/programme management director, engineering and operations directors as appropriate. A review of the terms and conditions, probably chaired by the commercial director, will involve the sales executive, the bid manager/PM designate and the commercial executive.

The final bid meeting should be attended by the sales executive and the bid manager/PM designate on the one hand and the managing director/general manager, sales and marketing director, commercial director and finance director on the other. With the significant involvement of many departments in any bid, every effort should be made to avoid duplication or unnecessary attendance at any of these meetings.

Chapter 5:

The Sales Function & Sales Management

The selling function · Split sales & marketing functions · Customers' views of sales executives · The role of sales executives · The tools of the sales executive · Account management · Buying influences · Danger signals · Selling stances · Managing sales departments · Commercial confidentiality · Sales funnel instability · The dangers of rat holing · Sales control meetings · Monthly reports · Bid/no-bid decision factors · Bid launch · Increasing order intake · Stock orders · Using private venture funding to support bids · Bid win/loss analysis · Collecting & sharing market information · Visit reports · Prospect management systems & order intake forecasting · Order intake & phasing of deliveries meetings · Competitor data-bases · Sales staff · Recruiting sales staff · Incentives · Relations with engineers · Training sales staff · Resignations · Sales & marketing training for other staff · Caring for customers · Organisational structures · Budgeting

The selling function

In companies involved in the PPP arena, the head of the selling function is variously given such titles as the sales director, the marketing director, the sales and marketing director or the business development director. For companies with American leanings or parents, the term director is normally replaced by the title vice-president. Throughout this book, the single term sales director is generally used to describe any of these titles.

The role of the sales director and for that matter the sales manager, is never an easy one. The prime pre-occupation must be with winning orders and gathering prospects, whether from existing or new customers. This will involve the management of a team of sales executives and supporting sales engineers, as well as proposal and sales office administration staff.

In larger organisations, sales managers will usually have a number of sales executives and sales engineers reporting to them. Additionally, the sales director is likely to be responsible for the business and PPP planning processes. A good information system is an essential tool, recording market opportunities and forecasting workload for the business as well as providing a data-base of customers and competitors.

The sales director will be the sales and marketing function's representative on the board of management and may have to lead any change within the Company to a market driven culture. Any number of examples highlight the dangers of remaining with an engineering led culture. A classic one is the hovercraft, an engineering invention still to find its full potential some thirty years later.

Split sales and marketing functions

Whilst companies in the consumer market, as a matter of course, have separate sales and marketing departments, this is much less common in PPP companies. The classic distinction between sales and marketing hinges on who has responsibility for bringing in the orders.

In the PPP context, this division is much more difficult and there are a number of good reasons for a joint approach. The PPP's themselves are difficult to understand technically and this mitigates against a marketing department carrying out market research in isolation; the task being better carried out by sales and support staff under supervision. Furthermore, in many cases, the volume of PPPs sold through their market lifetime is so low as to make any statistical analysis meaningless. Indeed, in markets where the total number of potential customers is small and the market itself, as a result, international, the cost of sending separate selling and marketing staff to visit potential customers proves an unacceptable financial burden.

What is found in many large corporations is a central marketing function, which is associated with international operations. It is responsible for discovering new sales leads and providing the political, economic and cultural background to the prospects before handing them over to an operating division to bid and close the sale. However, this split does not mean that the operating divisions only carry out a selling role, since, as defined previously, the marketing task will also be carried out by them. In fact, the role of the central marketing function is addressing the customers and carrying out the early stages of the business development process.

The divisiveness which usually exists between headquarters staff and the operating divisions is well summarised by the hackneyed joke "We're from headquarters and we're here to help you." Corporate marketing can at times appear to be a bottomless sink for information demanded with alarming regularity, but by building relationships, much useful work can be obtained from the function. It is the age old problem of communication and understanding each other's needs.

Customers' views of sales executives

In many PPP markets, the word "sales" is a dirty one and in extreme cases, customers will refuse to see anyone whose business card includes the word "sales." This can be very limiting for sales executives, sales managers and sales directors. It has spawned the use of alternative titles, such as "business development" and the use of "marketing" in place of "sales."

The reasons for this are quite straightforward. The majority of PPP customers don't want to be subject to sales pressure; the feeling being that their tender system will enable them to select the best solution to meet their needs. This is understandable, bearing in mind the type of high pressure salesmanship found in consumer goods markets. The result is that sales executives and their superiors need to be sympathetic to the attitude of their customers and choose titles which will not cause offence. Alternatively, many sales staff carry legitimate cards with a range of suitable titles, not the least because some customers refuse to see any company representative below vice-president level.

A regional sales manager of a large international company, trying to win business in Nigeria, recognised the importance of having the right title to impress his customers. The title he chose for printing on his cards was "Chairman." The problem arose when the real company chairman visited the country and attended an official reception. There, several members of the embassy staff were confounded when introduced to him, since they thought that they already knew the company chairman!

On occasions, a sales executive and a key individual in a customer organisation may be mutually incompatible. This problem needs early identification and, wherever possible, a change to another sales executive made. It is not a reflection of the capabilities of the sales executive, but rather of the world as it is. Sales directors need to watch for this difficulty and sales executives must recognise that it is not necessarily a slur on their professional skills.

The role of sales executives

The tasks of sales executives are never easy ones. A good analogy is that they should act like the conductor of an orchestra. They should see the whole picture, co-ordinate the Company's efforts, ensure good balance, give feedback, but not play an instrument themselves. Sales executives should always resist the temptation of returning to play their instrument.

In dealings with the customer community, they need to be able to analyse and present benefits, overcome objections, negotiate the sale and, where necessary, interpret and translate. They should ensure that the Company has the right proposal, solution, price, delivery, contract terms and negotiating posture. These are the requirements for winning new business. Clearly, sales executives need to have a comprehensive understanding of the customer's purchase process. They must know how, where and when to exert influence on the purchase decision.

The sales executive must establish the following factors about the customer.

- The budget and the winning price
- The key PPP parameters
- The bid evaluation scoring system
- The customer's view of the bidders
- The customer mood

When the time comes for bid submission, the sales executive is responsible for ensuring that it has been prepared in such a way that it meets the key criteria below. Success will depend, to a large extent, on the ability to read the customer's signals. From a company point of view, winning is about closing the deal at the right time and at the right price. Both are critical.

The bid must

- Be what the customer wants
- Meet the operational requirement
- Avoid including anything not needed
- Have the right approach to baseline, alternatives and options
- Be a winning one

Sales executives may sometimes judiciously have to go out on a limb, especially when a number of potential customers are all waiting for one of their number to contract, exaggerating the degree of commitment, after which the others will all follow suit. However, such overstatement in describing the details of the PPP to potential customers is likely to be lethal. Here, absolute honesty is the only way.

There are two other dangers worth mentioning. The first is that any letter written on company headed writing paper and signed has the potential to commit the Company. Sales executives, in particular, need to be wary not to make unauthorised commitments to customers in writing, or verbally. The second danger lies in the provision of budgetary or rough order of magnitude prices, where it is essential that customers understand the exact basis of any price quoted. It is also important that the sales executive understands the straight jacket which will then encompass any future quotations by the Company.

In addition to selling to customers, a second task needs recognition and acceptance by any sales executive. This is internal selling; persuading Company colleagues to undertake the work necessary to bid for opportunities, as well as gaining access to the necessary bidding resources. Thus, sales executives need to know their way around the Company's "real" internal processes, as this is critical to their success in winning new business. Internal and external selling provide roughly equal workloads in the PPP arena.

It is, however, important to recognise that the sales executive also has to undertake a number of secondary functions. Keeping abreast of developments taking place in the customer industry and a good understanding of the competition are necessary roles, as is carrying out market research and helping to position new PPPs. Other important tasks include the selection and motivation of overseas representatives, acting as the customer care point of contact and deciding which selling stance to take (see page 90).

Not recognised as work by other members of the Company, attendance on the cocktail circuit can be important in some PPP markets, both for meeting customers and for picking up useful information. Over indulgence in alcohol, with its consequent loosening of the tongue, is a danger to be avoided at all costs. It is also essential to remember the ever present ears of both the competition and customers.

The tools of the sales executive

For the new sales executive, it can be quite daunting knowing where to start in terms of establishing the tools of the trade. Considering the basic needs, some form of customer address book is essential and for many, a small portable computer is proving invaluable for this and other tasks such as visit reports and prospect records. Secondly, the sales executive should never be without a reasonable number of business cards to give to new contacts. It is amazing how quickly these get used. Finally, a telescopic pointer is always a useful standby when making presentations.

Moving onto PPP specific tools, there is the need for a range of literature, starting with a simple data sheet and moving through a technical description of the PPP to a copy of a recent proposal. This literature can be supported by copies of the relevant portions of the full set of technical handbooks for the PPP, as well as reprints of published articles about the PPP and possibly a list of existing customers.

On the audio-visual side, a series of view graphs is essential, showing all the aspects of the PPP, including its benefits, features and advantages, together with a well-rehearsed presentation. Hard copies of the view graphs, as well as a selection of glossy photographs of the various aspects of the PPP, make an excellent back up. A short video may also be appropriate. For some PPPs, parts of it or even the whole item may be portable. In such a case, it is vital that the sales executive has access to suitable hardware when meeting potential customers.

88   How to win business

Because of the importance of Company credibility, capabilities and financial stability, the new sales executive must be ready to deal with these areas. Literature, presentation material and even a video outlining the Company's capability are necessary, supported by copies of the Company's capability brochure and latest annual report. Similarly, any sales executive needs to be "five minutes survivable" on any of the Company's other PPPs, since enquiries about these during meetings with customers are not uncommon.

ACCOUNT MANAGEMENT FORM							
Customer	PPP						Sales executive
	Current Position					Authority holder Person responsible	Call objective Agreed next action
	NO				YES		
	-4	-2	0	+2	+4		
NEED Defined & agreed?							
FIT With customer needs? With Company needs?							
EXCLUSIVITY Of Company offering?							
TIMETABLE Established or not?							
MONEY Approved for expected outlay?							
SIZE Can you/they handle the deal?							
INFLUENCERS Are they identified/committed?							
ENEMIES Is the competitive/political process stable?							
ANSWER Have you an agreed solution to their needs?							

Figure 26. A typical account management form used by sales executives involved in selling major products.

Account management

In selling major products, but not usually in dealing with programmes or projects, account management is a useful tool. It is a customer based system which, in effect, provides a checklist for the sales executive of customer actions and the status of each opportunity. From a sales management point of view, it is a useful tool for reviewing progress with the sales executives, as well as providing an excellent receptacle for information should the sales executive ever be unavailable.

Buying influences

The people within the customer community who influence the purchase of PPPs can be divided into four groups, depending on their motivations.

These are those who's influence is economic (usually accountants), those who are users, those who are technical specialists and those who's involvement is purely as a coach or adviser to the decision makers and other influencers. The coach provides help to colleagues in the purchaser's organisation in deciding which PPP to select. It is useful to list the individual names under the four headings, so that the right person from the Company can deal with the concerns of each of them.

ECONOMIC	USER
Release funds	Judge operational useability
TECHNICAL	**COACH**
Screen out non-compliant	Advise decision makers

Figure 27. The area of customer influence is dependant on the role of each individual.

Danger signals

There are a number of factors, which any experienced sales executive will recognise as danger signals that the Company is going to lose the business. These key signals are usually fairly obvious, but are frequently missed in the rush to try to win a new contract, resulting in just the opposite effect. It is an essential part of the sales management role to find the time to review the possible existence of such signals with the sales executive and agree on a corrective course of action.

- Critical information missing
- Uncertainty about information
- Any uncontacted buying influencer
- Buying influencer(s) new to the job
- Customer re-organisation

Selling stances

There are typically five different stances which can be taken by sales staff in the PPP business and in general, they are mutually exclusive.

ROLE	TASKS
Missionary sales executive	Educating sales prospects, helping PPP specification
Creative sales executive	Selling the PPP to the purchaser
Applications/Technical sales executive	Professional adviser/consultant
Sales office manager	Inside order-taker
Logistic support sales executive	Selling through operators & maintainers

Managing sales departments

While there are several ways of managing the selling function, there are some tools and skills which are universally applicable and need to be understood. These include a number of meetings, reviews and techniques.

- Monthly control meetings and reports
- Bid/no-bid reviews
- Bid launch meetings
- Recruiting and managing sales staff
- Dealing with overseas markets

Sales directors will need to stamp their personality on their function but must avoid, at all costs, the temptation to revert to being sales executives themselves. Such reversion can only result in them spending too much time out in the field and not enough time directing their staff. Furthermore, it will undermine both the authority and the confidence of their sales executives and managers. Certainly, they will need to support their team, particularly when the going gets sticky with a potential purchaser, but they must recognise the need to draw back from the situation once the difficulty is overcome.

The opposite approach, of never going out into the field, will cause sales directors to lose contact with reality, both in the way customers behave and in terms of what is a reasonable level of travel, subsistence and entertainment expenses. They will also quickly lose credibility with their team.

It is essential to recognise that there are a number of sensitive issues that need careful handling and which escalate into the sphere of the sales director. Entertainment of customers can, at times, be lavish, as can gifts given to them. In overseas markets, representatives' commission can amount to considerable sums of money. A sensible level of confidentiality is needed to avoid embarrassing the customers involved, and also to prevent "moles" within the Company building and leaking sensational stories.

Commercial confidentiality

It must be self-evident that the information gathered and used by any sales and marketing function could be of great benefit to any competitor and in some cases to customers and potential purchasers. Thus, sensitive information should always carry a "commercial in confidence" label so that people are reminded of its sensitivity. The circulation of some documentation, such as pricing data, should be severely restricted. Even greater care is needed with data stored in computers to prevent unauthorised access. Page 117 discusses the problems in this area when a sales executive resigns.

Sales funnel instability

One way at looking at the cycle of the selling process from a management point of view is to liken it to a funnel, with a wide top tapering down to a narrow bottom. The analogy is to start with a large number of potential opportunities, sift them down to prospects, forecast the best prospects and bid for them, sign contracts and achieve deliveries. In the PPP business, where both gestation periods and delivery periods can be very long, the needs of a business at any particular time tend to concentrate maximum effort on one particular area in the funnel.

A shortage of potential opportunities may lead to a major drive on opportunities and prospects. A lack of contracts can result in concentration on forecasts and bids, whilst an excess of unfulfilled contracts can lead to a dramatic cutback in all the selling activities to concentrate on achieving deliveries. The changing of priorities leads to instability running down the sales funnel and when this gets to the bottom, inevitably, it starts at the top again. The difficulty for any company in the PPP

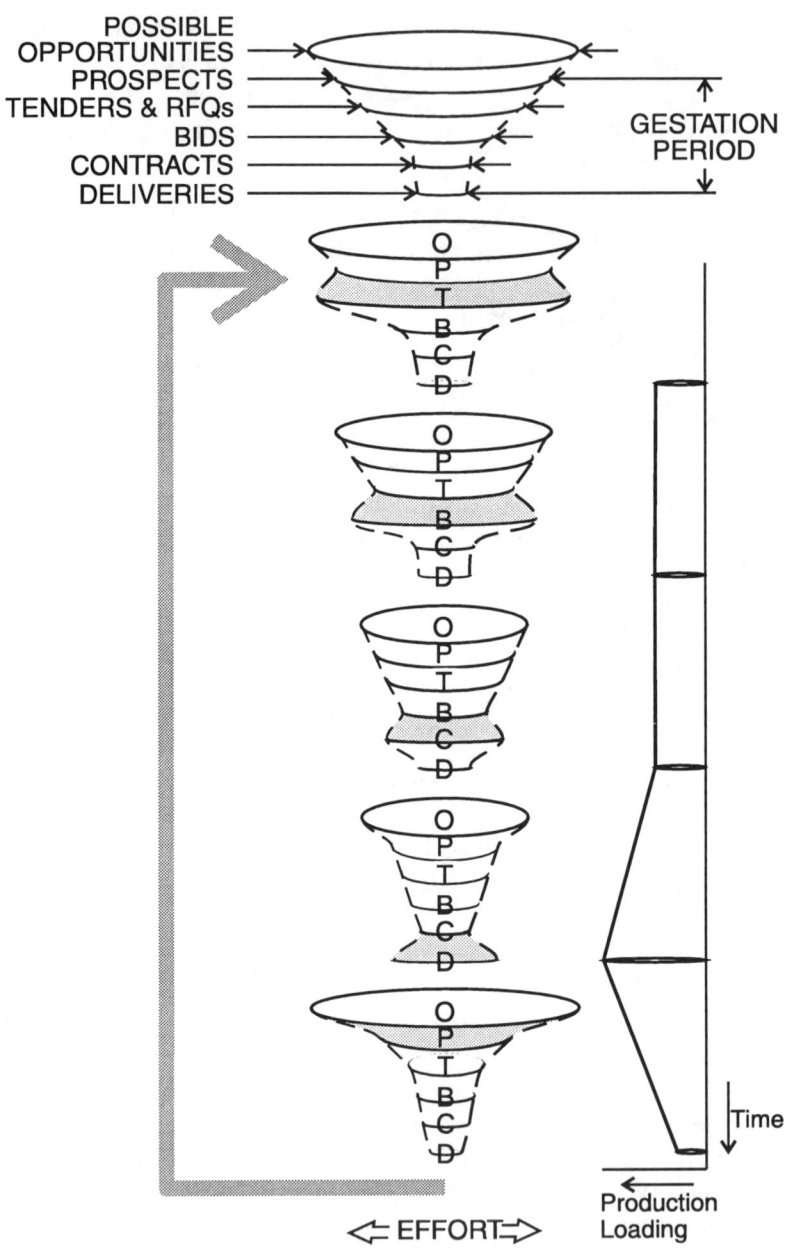

Figure 28. Instability flows down the sales funnel as the business outlook for a company changes with time.

business is that moving effort is fundamentally inefficient and can lead to loss of morale among staff involved in any of the processes.

Whilst recognising this widely experienced phenomenon is easy, overcoming it is a major challenge with few if any proven remedies. The following points should, however, be born in mind:

1. The further an opportunity progresses down the funnel, the greater its resource demands both in terms of duration and continuity. The disruption to continuity arises mainly because of the presence of deadlines.

2. Instability arises from lack of resources to progress the contents through the funnel. Thus, some opportunities will have to be abandoned, requiring a new start back at the top of the funnel. The commitment of all the required resources at the bid/no-bid stage can curtail this return to the top.

3. If resources are committed to bidding immediately they become available, no attention is given to progressing the contents in other parts of the funnel. Bid decisions based solely on resource availability are thus highly undesirable.

4. Having a mix of sizes of bids has much to commend it. Small bids are usually quicker to mature, helping cash flow and contributing to the cost of larger bid teams. The percentage of capacity involved in each size of bid may be a useful measure. In addition small bids can utilise less able staff and help to train new people.

5. There are obvious advantages in winning some ongoing business in order to sustain the company and reduce the degree of oscillation at the output end of the funnel.

A case occurred where a company was coming to the end of implementing two very large projects, and was short of opportunities to turn into new contracts. The managing director called his fifty most senior staff, together with the whole of his sales department, into a conference room. After making a presentation on how to win new business, he allocated a senior member of his management team as "godfather" to each significant major prospect. These "godfathers" worked with the relevant sales executives and proved singularly successful in circumventing a tortuous hierarchy and providing lateral thinking. After a year, the system was disbanded, as by then the problem was once again moving down the funnel.

The dangers of rat holing

Continuing the analogy of the sales funnel, physical funnels suffer from a phenomenon known as rat holing. When a real funnel clogs, a condition can occur where material only flows through a narrow tunnel. The parallel business situation

94   How to win business

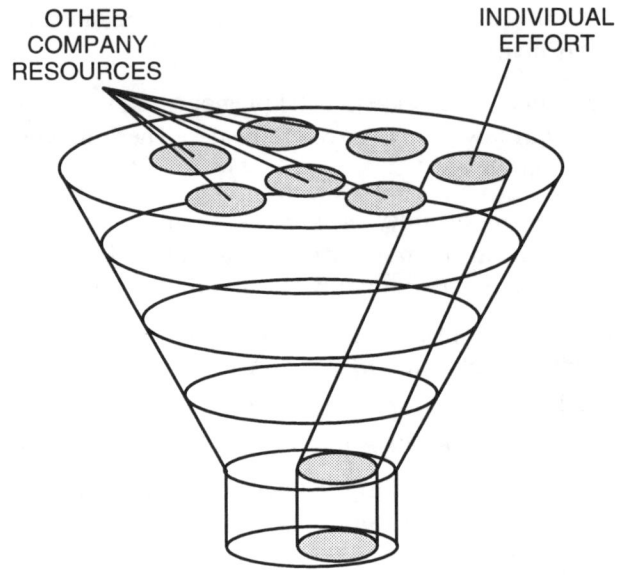

Figure 29. Ratholing is extremely wasteful of company resources.

is where an individual takes possession of a piece of potential business and takes it all the way through the funnel.

Ratholing may be a symptom of under-resourcing and usually accompanies a person's lack of trust in the rest of the organisation and their perceived need to become indispensable. A particular variant may occur where a senior member of the Company has visited a customer with an opportunity or prospect. Feeling ownership, that individual drives the process through the Company, being too close to see the wood for the trees or too senior to be countermanded. Ratholing may also arise if someone is assigned to develop an opportunity, when others in the organisation are unwilling to get involved with the work.

The unfortunate consequences of such action include self-delusion and the erosion and eventual breakdown of communication channels. The self-delusion arises from the sense of desperation that comes from being so closely identified with the success of a particular piece of business. It usually results in continuing to spend resources on chasing the business, where the chances of success have become minimal. At the same time, failing to identify and progress other worthwhile business increases the negative impact of this phenomenon.

A final drawback is that should a contract actually be signed, the individual clings to the business, rather than moving back to the initial stages of business development. This stickiness is likely to worsen the instability of the sales funnel.

To overcome the problems of ratholing, a number of factors need remembering and acting upon.

1. Someone must be available who is likely to know what will prove to be a waste of time.
2. Customer visits need to be made, with the sales executive, to get a first hand feel of the opportunity.
3. Errant staff should be re-allocated to worthwhile opportunities with short-term bid workloads.

Sales control meetings

A monthly control meeting is a crucial tool in the sales director's armoury. The attendees should include all the segment sales managers, the public relations manager, the administration or support manager and whoever is responsible for marketing or business planning. Attendance must be compulsory and, with dates set up a year in advance, the sales director should only accept customer demands or illness as reasons for absence.

The agenda shown overleaf should start with an analysis of orders won and bids lost. Page 106 covers this subject in more detail. A review of the orders forecast over the next eighteen months to two years should follow; this time frame varying with the type of PPP. The level of enquiries is an excellent indicator of the state of the market and some analysis of new opportunities may be appropriate, together with a review of the status of bids submitted and under preparation.

Performance against the budget for order intake is the key measure of the performance of a sales department. Feeding back the state of the Company's forward work load to staff allows them to understand the true urgency of winning new business. This also has an impact on resourcing of current and future bids. A discussion of customer relations can highlight not only dissatisfaction within the customer community, but also possible areas within the Company that are creating or accentuating such problems.

The discussion on public relations should include consideration of exhibitions being attended and future possibilities, literature under preparation and impending needs, as well as any advertising campaign planned or underway, including media schedules. Press releases and press briefings need airing, as does the need for internally written articles suitable for publication. A discussion of audio-visual requirements is important and, from time to time, a review of company facilities covering everything from conference rooms to reception areas and company signs.

Overseas representatives and their performance are a critical item for companies in the export business and plans for their motivation must not be ignored. Rather than discussing every country on every occasion, it may be beneficial to cover one

SALES CONTROL MEETING AGENDA

1. Actions from minutes of previous meeting
2. Orders received during the month compared with budget for month and cumulatively for year
3. Orders forecast during next month and to year end
4. Changes to order intake forecast, forward load & delivery problems
5. Bids lost
6. Level of enquiries & significant new prospects
7. Bids in progress & under adjudication
8. Overseas representatives (if exporting)
9. Customer relations
10. VIP visits planned
    Inwards
    Outwards
11. Trials and demonstrations
12. Competitors
13. Public relations
    Exhibitions
    Literature
    Audio-visual
    Press relations
    Advertising
    Company facilities
14. Company funded PPP developments and mid-life updates
15. Staffing levels and personnel issues
16. Sales department budget
    Expenditure to date
    Forecast expenditure to year end

Figure 30. The agenda for sales control meetings needs issuing in plenty of time and should be informative about the topics to be discussed.

region of the world each month. VIP visits require scheduling and organising, both into the Company by senior customers and outward by the sales director and other directors of the Company.

The department's internal budget expenditure needs reviewing with a comparison of the latest figures to the budget. A forecast should be provided of likely expenditure to the end of the financial year and warning given of the imposition of any possible expenditure cut backs.

New PPP developments and mid-life updates need airing, but not in great detail. More important is to get agreement on the priorities for spending the Company's valuable private venture investment money. News about the competition is always important, but avoid the tendency for the department to look over its shoulder continuously. It is, however, a good opportunity to set specific tasks in terms of monitoring competitor activity.

An informative agenda needs issuing to all attendees at least one week before the meeting and minutes producing within two working days of the meeting. Actions require highlighting and review by the chairman at the next meeting.

SALES EXECUTIVES ARE ETERNAL OPTIMISTS

Monthly reports

Preparing written reports are the bane of most people's life, yet their provision on a regular basis is the lifeblood of the management of any PPP company. The sales and marketing report to the managing director should always start with the order intake compared both with the budget and the figure forecast in the previous report, including details of key orders won and bids lost. It should follow with an update on the key opportunities that are in the order intake forecast. New opportunities of significant value or importance to the Company need detailing, together with an indication of the level of enquiries. No-bid decisions need highlighting together with progress reports on current bids. Information is required on key public relations items, such as major exhibitions, new literature and videos, as well as new press releases and briefings together with details of VIP inward visits.

The next part of the report is likely to be inward looking and consider such factors as performance and forecast against internal budgets, particularly on bids and proposals. Other details include staff shortages and recruiting, together with progress on marketing issues such as the five year plan, PPP plans, PV progress and expenditure. Clearly the contents of the report will necessarily reflect the reporting structure of the sales and marketing organisation. The relevant sales executives should produce the part dealing with new opportunities and those already being pursued.

Bid/no-bid decision factors

Avoiding the trap of bidding for every single opportunity requires a method of rating the relevant attractiveness to the Company of each opportunity. A bid/no-bid form is just such a tool. A number of questions need answering when filling in the form, so that an objective bid/no-bid decision can be made.

The importance of this is illustrated by a company which decided to bid for the construction of an electronics factory in Iraq during the nineteen eighties. With the bid complete, the final price was submitted to the company's main board for approval, at which point the board decided that they were not prepared to provide a 10% bid bond, valued at £40 million! The total expenditure on the bid was thus wasted because the impact of the requirement for so large a bid bond was overlooked at the beginning of the bid process.

It is important to fill in the form as part of an inquisitorial process and the sales director should do this in discussion with the appropriate sales executive. Regardless, it should always be the same person who completes the form, at least for each market segment, to provide consistent ratings for the various opportunities that arise over a period of time. This does mean finding someone who will be available to carry out the task; not always easy in a busy sales and marketing function. A number of important questions need answering while the form is being completed.

1. Is the project real and will an RFQ be issued?
   - Customer needs, wants and justification?
   - PPP champion in the customer community?
   - Project funding by customer or foreign aid?
   - Project authorisation?
   - No other problems: moratorium on orders, political?

2. Does the Company have a real capability in the area?
   - PPP developed?
   - Private venture or recoverable development?
   - If second or subsequent phase, who is incumbent?
   - System aspects, integration capability & logistic support?
   - Past reputation?

3. Is there ongoing customer contact and has it influenced the specification?
   - Purchaser's specification writers provided with a baseline?
   - Has PPP been, or should it be, demonstrated?
   - Has customer visited the Company to:
     Prove hardware exists.
     Demonstrate understanding of the problems.
     Give confidence that requirements can be met.
     Demonstrate availability of facilities and resources.

4. Does the customer consider the Company a front runner?
   - Customer known at all levels?
   - Competition known, including all companies on bidders list?
   - Budget known?
   - The specification reflects Company inputs and is known to make competitors' solutions expensive?

5. Will it make money or provide other downstream benefits?
   - Profit or margin?
   - New PPP (recoverable development?) or PPP launch?
   - Reference installation (and deprive competitor of one)?
   - Market dominance or extension?

6. Are the commercial terms acceptable?
   - Size and terms of bid bond?
   - Export licence?
   - Can IPR be protected?
   - Payment terms and currency?
   - Offset, credit, counter-trade or barter?
   - Funding source?
   - Acceptance terms?
   - Retentions?
   - Law and arbitration?
   - Liquidated damages?

100　How to win business

7. Are there adequate funds and staff available to prepare a winning bid
   - % of contract value for bid.
   - Sales lead?
   - Bid lead?
   - Engineering lead?
   - Estimating lead?
   - Commercial lead?
   - Proposal manager?
   - Supporting staff?

8. Are there the facilities and management commitment to complete the PPP successfully?
   - Commitment, including a champion within the Company?
       Managing director?
       Directors: Marketing/sales, engineering, operations, projects/programmes?
       Implementation team: PM designate, technical lead, sufficient team members?
   - Facilities: Engineering? Operations? Logistics?

Country:		PPP:	Customer:		Date:	
	Bid Factor	Negative 1　2	Neutral 3	Positive 4　5		Marks
OPPORTUNITY	COMPLIANCE WITH SPECIFICATION	Requires major development work	A reasonable fit	Fully compliant		
	TEAM-MATES/ SUB-CONTRACTORS	Diluting	Neutral	Enhancing		
	COMPETITION	Fixed for them	Open	Fixed for us		
CUSTOMER	REPRESENTATIVE/ CUSTOMER RAPPORT	None	Limited contacts	Excellent contacts at all levels		
	COMMERCIAL TERMS	Penal	Average	Standard		
	LIKELIHOOD OF PURCHASE	Uncertain	Should occur	Certain		
	POLITICAL SITUATION	Unstable/ Communist	Neutral	Stable Anglophile		
INTERNAL	BID TEAM	The minimum	Average	The best		
	IMPLEMENTATION	Overloaded	Average	Short of work		
	DELIVERY TIMESCALE	Longer than anyone else	Average	Suits the customer, shorter than others		
	PRICE STRATEGY	Low margin	Average return	Super profit		
		Bid	No-Bid	Signature:		
				Total Marks		

Figure 31. A bid/no-bid form is an essential tool to help avoid wasting bidding effort; this one being designed for export opportunities.

If the Company is not the favourite, are there genuine ways of unseating the favourite? These reasons fall into two categories; those concerned with the Company's offering and those involving the lead competitor. Finally, it is worth remembering the following table.

	TECHNICALLY BEST	TECHNICALLY SECOND-BEST
LOWEST PRICE	Almost always wins	Can win
SECOND-LOWEST PRICE	Can win	Invariably loses

Figure 32. In the PPP arena, the lowest priced technically compliant bid almost invariably wins.

A unique selling proposition means that the PPP is the only one to provide certain features and thus may still win the contract even though not the favourite. These features fall into one of three categories. Failing the ability to provide such a unique factor, there must be some other realistic reason why the favourite won't win.

POSSIBLE USP'S FOR OWN PPP	COMPETITOR'S PPP
Price	Price will be too high
Performance/Specification	Will have an unmaskable technical weakness
Delivery	Can be unseated politically, a double-edged weapon

If the answer to virtually all the questions in this section isn't yes, DON'T BID

Bid Launch

A bid initiation form (BIF) is an excellent way to start the internal bidding activity and not only is it a good discipline for the sales executive, but also greatly assists in communication of all the relevant information to everyone involved in the bidding process. Clearly, the BIF needs to be customised to the particular industry and company concerned, but the basic outline shown is a practical starting point. The amount of information contained in a BIF requires careful thought to avoid omissions. In essence a one to two page document, it can also be a useful trigger of a forthcoming approval meeting to those involved in authorising the final bid.

BID INITIATION FORM	**PART A**	**Commercial in Confidence**
Customer	Bid manager	Ext
Address	Bid Team	
	Bidding budget	
Sales executive Ext	Bid review dates	
	Tender closing date	
Summary of situation	Order date	
PPP	**TENDER**	
Schedule of equipment	Budget available	
Logistics package	Validity required	
Training and handbooks	Bid bond requirement and value	
Services to be provided	Customer special requirements	
Major sub-contracts		
Alternative solutions		
Options		
COMPETITIVE POSITION	**PRICE BASIS**	
Importance of business to company	Method and terms of payment	
Company investment	Delivery period to be offered	
Development needs and PV expenditure	Delivery terms	
Capital expenditure	Bonds	
Bidding cost	Handover	
Key competitors	Retention	

Figure 33a. There are a number of different ways of laying out a bid initiation form, of which this example is just one. It continues opposite in figure 33b.

BID INITIATION FORM	PART B	Commercial in Confidence
EXPORT BIDS		**BID ASSESSMENT**
Representative's name and address		Compliance with specification
		Team mates / sub-contractors
		Competition
Commission requirement		Representative / customer rapport
Export licence requirement		Commercial terms
ECGD cover		Likelihood of purchase
Shipping terms		Political situation
Currency / exchange rate		Implementation
Credit / offset requirements		Delivery time scale
Local manufacture		Price strategy
KEY DATES		**OTHER INFORMATION**
Launch Cost review Proposal inputs Blue team review Red team review Pricing complete Internal bid review		

Figure 33b. The back of this bid form includes a section for export opportunities and carries a copy of the information from the bid/no-bid form.

Convene the bid launch meeting as soon as convenient after making the decision to bid and circulating the BIF. It is the time and place where the bid manager briefs everyone involved in the bid and explains who is going to do the work to put together a winning bid in a timely manner. The briefing should cover what the customer wants, the submission date, why the Company has decided to bid and what in essence is going to be offered. It is an exercise in communication and the sales executive has a dual role to play; not only to make an active contribution, but also to listen to ensure that the bid manager is communicating the right message.

Increasing order intake

Improving order intake means submitting better offers and being highly selective in bidding. This, in turn, requires realistic win strategies and effective proposal writing to allow pursuit of opportunities in the most effective manner. The price submitted must be the winning one, which implies a knowledge of the budget, as well as competitor pricing. For companies operating in the home market, exporting can be an excellent method of building the size of a business, though management will have to commit to the necessary investment and timeframe.

To turn any particular opportunity into a contract, there must be a bid champion, both within the customer community and within the Company. The latter must have several important attributes.

- Determination to win
- Knowledge of what it takes to win
- Ability to motivate Company staff at all levels
- A logical approach to the winning process

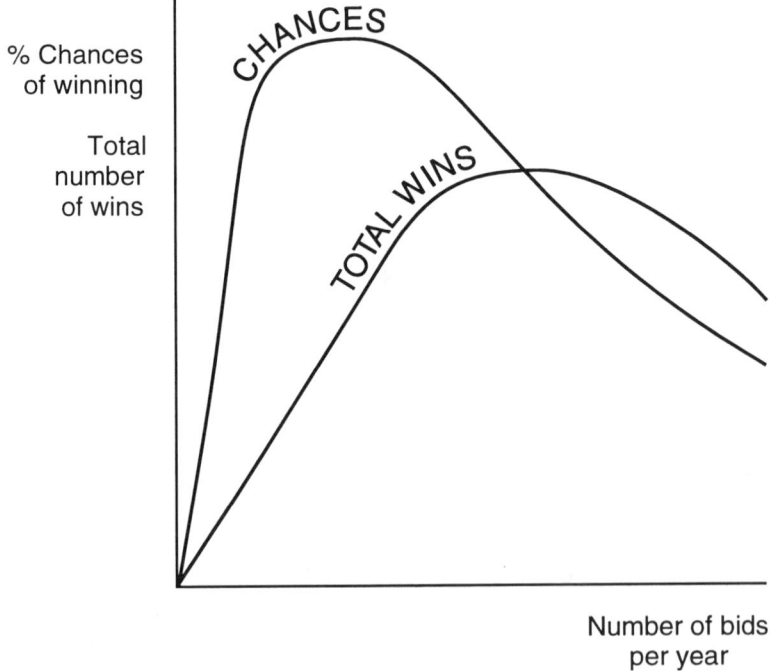

Figure 34. There is an optimum number of bids per year to maximise the number of wins, since attempting too many concurrent bids reduces the quality of submissions.

Stock orders

The use of stock orders can give considerable competitive advantage. Their application will depend on the type of PPP business and factors such as the volume of production, customer delivery expectations, competitor actions and any existing contracts from which equipment can be diverted. All need taking into account and no one is going to suggest the creation of inventories of such PPPs as power stations or infrastructure telecommunications.

The great benefits of stock orders to customers are that they reduce delivery times, enhancing competitiveness. They need not cost money if timely orders are obtained. They also show customers a high level of commitment to the business allied to a clear understanding of what customers require. They are, not unnaturally, anathema to the finance function, as they tie up capital. However, in addition to reducing delivery times, they have a number of other benefits.

- Can be used to smooth production peaks and troughs
- Help to provide a consistent standard of build and avoid component obsolescence
- Allow cost effective production of small runs of PPPs
- Put extra pressure on sales staff to win timely contracts

Building to stock may not literally mean that. It may mean just completing long lead items, to cut delivery time. With a modular PPP, it may be feasible to produce standard items, with just the customised parts being produced to order. Never consider stock orders in isolation, as similar benefits may accrue through a wide range of advanced manufacturing techniques.

There are dangers to be avoided. In the boom years of the oil industry, when new oil rigs were being installed at a furious rate, an American rig supplier laid down stocks of major components based on the latest sales projections. When the orders failed to materialise, following major cutbacks in exploration, the supplier was left in an unenviable position.

Use of private venture funding to support bids

One way of reducing the development cost being charged to potential customers of a PPP is to fund part of the development using the Company's private venture (PV) development funds. It is not always necessary to spend this funding before any bidding commences, although time to market is often a critical driver. When applying PV in such a manner, remember three important rules.

- Not a commitment until the contract is signed
- As a result, can be bid more than once when the same PPP is offered to different potential customers
- Should be subtracted from the direct costs in any price build up calculation

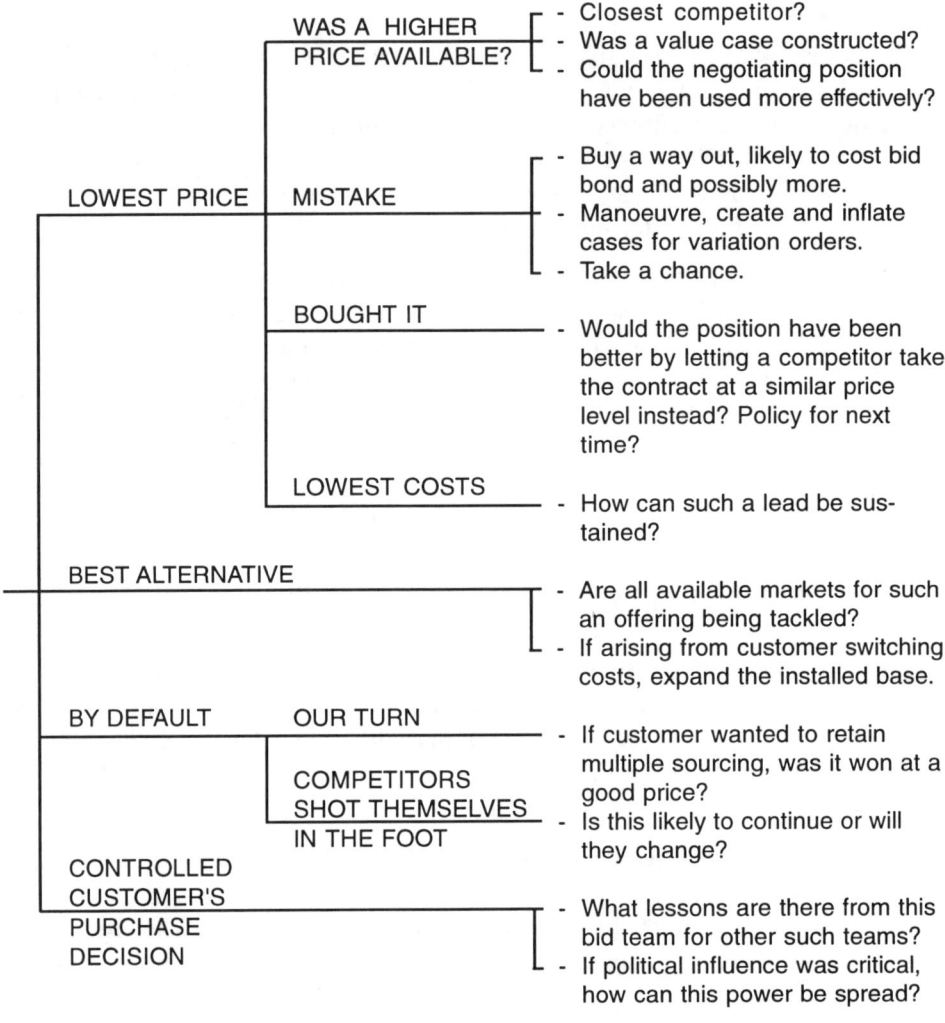

Figure 35. The completion of a bid win analysis can produce useful lessons for improving the Company's win rate in the future.

Bid win/loss analysis

It is important, after a contract award, to have an independent team provide a balanced analysis of why it was won or lost. It is easy to forget the former in the euphoria of a win, but is well worth the small amount of effort and self analysis required. It is the time to review whether a higher price could have been achieved, what mistakes if any have been made which need correcting and, indeed, whether costs can be lowered. Lessons will need learning and honesty used in deciding whether the contract was effectively won by default.

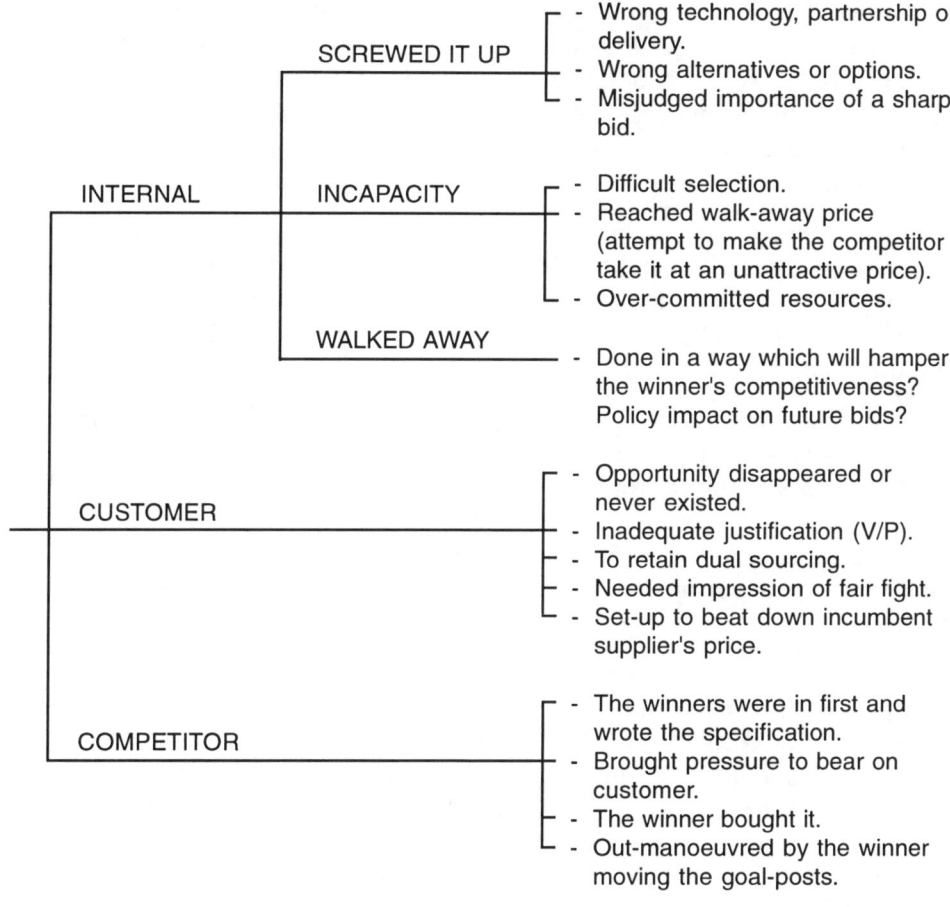

Figure 36. The results of the bid loss analysis need communicating to all those involved in the bidding process.

Bid loss analysis is more common and, in the PPP field, many customers will give a debrief on the reasons for not selecting a company. Was the right offering made and were both the final proposal and bid competitive? Alternatively, was either the customer or the competition inaccurately assessed? Again, it is important to learn any lessons accurately and note that some of the lessons impact on the original pricing. Page 40 covers this aspect of pricing in more detail.

Collecting and sharing market information

Today, the two cornerstones of good marketing information systems are a modern computer network and an efficient method of ensuring effective data capture and up-date. These demand a disciplined approach; something for which sales staff are not renowned to say the least! In a PPP company, it is not just the sales department that gathers facts and figures about the market. Anyone in the Company with customer contact is likely to be able to gather useful material; the other primary sources being PMs, engineering, customer support and commercial. It is important to encourage these staff in this role, but, much more importantly, to ensure that there is a method of inputting the information into the sales and marketing data-base.

The use of computer networks considerably eases this task. However, these other functions must never forget that it is sales and marketing which is the final owner and keeper of the data-base. It is imperative to distinguish between reading access and writing access. The storage of the information can be costly and ultimately fruitless, unless senior management takes ownership of it.

Use of standard data-bases requires categorisation, which will start by being intuitive. Almost invariably, the categories will need changing and this is difficult with most data-bases. Typical problems include how to enter America; as USA, US, United States of America or United States? Free form data-bases have much appeal through being able to search for word associations and chunks of text without the prior need for categorisation. The output is usually a list of file names containing the search data that is subsequently examined for relevance, source and corroboration.

Both prospect and competitor data-bases need an owner if they are to flourish; someone who will cajole the other members of the department, as well as those outside it, to submit the valuable data. In addition, steps need taking to ensure that there is a strict limit to those empowered to change data. One particular use of these data-bases is in market research and Chapter 8 covers this subject.

Visit reports

In gathering information about prospects, customers and competitors, visit reports are an essential tool. They are also the bane of every sales executive's life. However, discipline must be imposed and a format produced to ensure that nothing is missed. The distribution list for the report will also need careful consideration. Because the average sales executive will make several customer visits each month, it is essential to complete visit reports in a timely manner, thus avoiding details of meetings blurring and vital information being lost. Furthermore, a means needs establishing to condense the essential information into the department data-base.

Prospect management systems and order intake forecasting

All sales executives seem reluctant to sit down and prepare a detailed list of prospects for their area of responsibility. They appear to feel that this information is the only thing that keeps them in employment. It is also seen as a safeguard in case the forecasts identified in the order intake budget get delayed or are lost. The advent of computer based prospect systems has done little to improve the attitude of sales

The sales function & sales management   109

VISIT REPORT	Commercial In Confidence
Visit report by sales executive to country/customer	Date(s) of visit
Distribution list	
Name and address of customers visited	
Name and address of others visited (Representatives, embassies, banks)	
Summary of key information including any new opportunities	
Detailed report of each meeting	
List of actions and actionees	
List of any documents obtained & their location	

Figure 37. A visit report needs to completed every time there is contact with a customer.

staff. Yet prospects are the very life blood of a company and detailed information about each one is essential to allow the efficient allocation of resources, not only in the sales department, but also in other key functions within the Company.

Prospect analysis systems are usually needed in two forms. The first gives as much data as possible about each individual prospect and should include the items detailed in figure 38 overleaf.

The second form required is, in effect, a summary produced by computer, which shows each group of PPPs, listing them by customer, value and order time scale. The sales director should review this list monthly and select prospects to form the basis of the order intake forecast.

Order intake and phasing of deliveries meetings

The order intake forecast is the sales department's commitment to operations/production and engineering, detailing the quantity and timing of new orders. This forecast needs a multi-disciplinary review before feeding into the Company's production schedule. If the latter is a computer based system such as MRP 2, it may be possible to automate the data transfer, but this will require a somewhat different meeting format. The sales director and the directors responsible for project/

PROSPECT RECORDING FORM	Commercial in Confidence
Reference number	
Type of PPP	Sales executive
Market segment	
Customer name and address	Names & phone numbers of key contacts
Customer family tree	
End user if different	
If export, overseas representative's name and address	
Expected order content including logistic support	
Quantity of PPPs required	
Budget amount and availability	
Percentage chance of customer placing order	
Percentage chance of Company being awarded the business	
Main competitors	
Order placement date	
Communications record: date of last visit, last letter/fax, last telecon	
Other information	

Figure 38. The prospect recording form is the heart of any marketing information system.

programme management, operations and engineering should all attend the review meeting. The managing director should chair it and divide it into two parts.

In the first part, the sales department has to report progress on winning new business and reveal any delays in obtaining forecast contracts. In the second half, there is a review of the performance of the business in achieving timely deliveries and action agreed to inform the customer of any major slippages. In this way, the sales team can understand any company actions that may affect their relationship with their customers, whilst the other functions can obtain the best possible information to help in resource planning.

Competitor data-bases

All the problems that apply to prospect recording systems also apply to gathering competitor data. A systematic approach is essential, with company reports and sales literature being gathered from a variety of sources. These can include visits to competitors' stands at exhibitions, letters from the Company librarian asking for information and selected requests to overseas representatives to obtain photocopies of competitors' proposals.

Pricing data is essential and must be dated, to avoid becoming misleading at a later date, due to the effects of inflation or exchange rate variations. A friendly customer can also be persuaded to provide an amazing amount of useful information about competitors. A significant quantity of general information is also available, particularly in the United States as a result of its Freedom of Information Act. As an example, CD ROMs now provide details of United States government procurements. It is even possible on occasions to discover actual overhead rates, allowing the development of very accurate Strawman prices.

Sales staff

One particularly significant area of sales management is dealing with subordinates. Whilst many think that managing sales staff is just like dealing with the staff working in any other function, there are some significant differences that need understanding. The natural characteristics that make good sales executives, the training of sales staff and those who support them, as well as dealing with resignations all require special attention.

Recruiting sales staff

Recruiting sales staff in the PPP sector is never easy. It is indeed rare to come across the specialist technical knowledge combined with selling skills. What is important is to find the right attributes, so that the person can be trained to be effective. It is useful to consider any potential recruit in three ways.

- Their interaction with other people
- The way they think
- Their emotions

RECRUITMENT CHECKLIST	Staff in Confidence
HOW THEY INTERACT WITH OTHER PEOPLE	Like setting targets & forecasting trends?
Persuasive?	Able to work to deadlines?
Tenacious?	Can adapt to change & enjoy doing new things?
Independent?	Interested in people & understanding them?
Socially confident, outgoing, extroverted?	**THEIR EMOTIONS**
A team worker, not authoritarian?	Competitive?
Able to identify with customers' perspective?	Optimistic?
Knows customers, purchase procedures & requirements?	Free from anxiety?
Able to survive in overseas environment? (export only)	Cool under pressure?
HOW THEY THINK	Able to keep their emotions under control?
Innovative?	Able to switch off?
Numerate?	Energetic?
Enjoy complex problems?	Decisive?
A forward planner?	Quick thinker on their feet?
Beware of the candidate's selling skill, persuasiveness & ability to mask weaknesses	

Figure 39. *A checklist will help to avoid missing anything during the time available for interview of potential new recruits to the sales function.*

Interaction

The first consideration is how they interact with other people; a critical factor for sales staff. Perhaps persuasiveness is the key attribute in anyone who is going to succeed in selling PPPs, together with a high degree of tenacity. A socially confident, outgoing, extroverted personality, the classic characteristics of a sales executive, should also be apparent, as should the capability to operate with customers at all levels. There is little room for an authoritarian approach in any PPP business, where team work is so essential.

The ability to identify with the customers' perspective (perhaps through having been an ex-employee), sympathising with their problems and desires, and even with some hangover of loyalty towards them, are all desirable attributes. Despite the need for team membership, selling, particularly selling overseas, can at times be very lonely requiring the ability to survive in such an environment. Furthermore a strongly independent personality is necessary, particularly in arguing the market issues and putting the customer's point of view to the Company, no matter how unpopular such a view may be.

Thinking

Looking next at the way the person thinks, PPP selling really does require innovative people who are very numerate and enjoy complex problems. Less commonly found in potential sales executives, but very desirable, are the ability to forward plan, think things out well in advance, set targets and forecast trends. The ability to complete tasks to deadlines is particularly necessary during any tendering process. In today's competitive PPP world, the ability to adapt to change and to enjoy doing new things is almost a sine qua non. This ideally needs matching to an interest in people and a desire to understand them; how they think and how they behave.

Emotions

From an emotional point of view, sales executives need to be free from anxiety and cool under pressure. Being able to switch off can be a great asset. Almost inevitably, they must be of an optimistic nature, energetic and most importantly, incredibly competitive, for winning new business is what it is all about. Finally, decisiveness, the ability to think quickly on their feet and keep their emotions under control are all necessary attributes.

The above qualities are very useful ones to bear in mind when dealing with a first interview. The real problem is that a good seller, and that is what is being sought, may not only be successful in obtaining the job through pure selling skills, but may also mask a number of serious weaknesses that will mitigate against success in PPP markets.

Internal recruits have often moved from development engineering to applications engineering, where they are involved in tender preparation. The alternative source is from people who have occupied a role in the project/programme management field. A useful source can be staff from customer organisations. Their recruitment is usually the result of a number of factors. Their understanding of the complexities of the customer purchase process may be the justification. Alternatively it may be their knowledge of requirements or the individuals involved in procurement. Regardless, the danger of this practice is that the recruit may not have the attributes necessary for a selling role.

Incentives

The provision of incentives to sales executives, be they in the form of commission on orders won or any other form of reward, is a contentious issue. The pros and cons need studying and understanding. Perhaps the most important factor in their favour is that incentives seem to motivate sales executives to put in that final extra effort to win the business and gain the reward. In addition, sales executives live with opportunities from birth to contract award and beyond. Thus, particularly with export opportunities, they are likely to spend more time away from home than anyone else in the Company. It is a sad statistic that sales and marketing staff have a higher divorce rate than any other function. This may, of course, be more related to their natural characteristics than to absence.

The case against the provision of incentives is that PPP selling is a team effort and an incentive given to the sales executive can act as a disincentive to the other members of the team. Furthermore, in many PPP sectors, orders are few and far between, but of extremely high value when they do arrive. This makes benchmarking for reward purposes very difficult. Neither of these reasons is usually sufficient justification for precluding the use of incentives.

There are two possible approaches with incentives. The first is to allocate them annually, preferably at appraisal time when order intake targets should be set. The incentives should be a percentage of additional salary awarded if a contract or contracts are won. A maximum limit of twenty to thirty per cent of salary should suffice. Alternatively, an ex gratia payment of say £5,000 to £10,000 (at 1994 levels) can be made on contract award.

There was a sales executive who was chasing a key contract in South America. He had already spent an excessive amount of time there not the least because, after the usual number of delays, the Minister involved died in an aircraft accident just before making the final decision. Faced with a further six months abroad, the executive's boss agreed to pay for a contractor to cut the grass in his sizeable garden throughout the summer. By way of recompense, the Company also provided a significant incentive payment following contract signature.

The sales function & sales management 115

The difficulty the sales director faces is in deciding what is a reasonable order intake prediction. The past history of the customer community and the Company normally drive this, together with the personal experience of the sales director and the track record of the sales executive both in identifying prospective timescales and in bringing in business. The situation is clearly easier if the number of orders received each year is large, but this is, in itself, uncommon in the PPP arena.

Relations with engineers

The traditional difference between marketeers, sales staff and engineers dates back to the start of the Industrial Revolution, but the joking and teasing which goes on

GETTING ENGINEERING TO WORK WITH SALES AND MARKETING CAN BE TOUGH.

is as old as mankind itself. In the UK, one good way to stop conversation at a party, when asked what one does is to reply "I sell." It always seems to conjure up the image of a door to door salesperson or a commercial traveller and leave the questioner speechless.

Respect between the two functions needs building up and it is incumbent on the sales and marketing function to take the lead in this task. One particularly common problem is the facility that some sales executives have for upsetting engineers. It is probably something to do with the former's extrovert personalities, but it is a danger that needs careful watching and any ruffled feathers quickly smoothing. The problem can be more difficult to resolve when the personalities involved are the sales and engineering directors.

It is a fact that in many PPP companies, engineers think that sales executives are a waste of time and money. They feel that either the PPP will sell itself (fortunately a dying view), or that they can sell the PPP better themselves. They also think that they know exactly what the market needs and that it just happens to be the new idea they are intent on developing into a PPP. In truth, engineers, as part of their training, need to understand how market forces operate and the benefits of developing an effective PPP plan before starting engineering development.

The down side can be that sales and marketing staff fail to recognise the innate selling skills of some engineers and the fact that their understanding of the technicalities of a PPP can be particularly valuable, not only at the PPP planning stage, but also in promoting and selling the PPP. Engineers with such skills need encouragement to use them and even to consider a move into the sales and marketing function.

Training sales staff

It is unlikely that this book would have been written if there had been adequate training available for sales and marketing staff operating in the PPP environment. Unfortunately, almost all training currently is from the consumer goods field and definitely does not suit aspiring sales executives in PPP companies. There are a few enlightened teachers in this specialist field and by far the best solution is to use them to develop a course tailored to specific company needs. Since the majority of companies in the PPP field are large ones, this is not an unaffordable approach, particularly if there is collaboration by a number of operating divisions in this endeavour.

It is important to involve senior management in the planning process in order to gain overt endorsement for any training programme. This should take the form of insistence on delegate attendance on the courses, nomination and release of the staff as required and attendance themselves, either as speakers or as delegates, whichever is appropriate.

Resignations

When sales staff resign, the chances are that they are going to a competitor. They must, therefore, leave the Company the same day that they resign. This should prevent them having any further opportunity to gather sensitive information to take to their new employer. Unfortunately, once such a practice becomes the norm, vigilance is necessary to ensure staff do not collect sensitive information prior to handing in their notice.

In any case, once sales staff have decided to leave, their influence within the company can be destructive and with customers, downright dangerous. Thus, "clear your desk by lunch time" is a realistic rather than a vindictive approach to the problem. The person can always be invited back a few days later to clear up any loose ends with the human resources function and have a farewell party.

Sales and marketing training for other staff

Accepting that non-sales staff are generally well trained in their specialisations, their knowledge of sales and marketing varies from woefully inadequate to nil. Graduate and new entrant training should certainly include a one or two hour briefing on sales and marketing, preferably carried out by the Company's sales director.

For the many non-sales staff who have customer contact, some training in the basic principles operating in the market place is essential. The need is for a two or three day introduction to the subject and this requires customising to the operating conditions of the particular company. It is possible to run such courses using only company staff, but an external tutor does give such training much greater authority.

One of the key issues that needs inclusion in the course is the subject of commercial sensitivities and when it is right and proper to say nothing. Inexperienced staff can behave in very unpredictable and at times expensive ways in the presence of customers. This is never more so than when a contract is in the offing. Sales staff quickly learn who needs a judicious kick on the shins to silence them during meetings with customers and will position themselves strategically at the table to be within range of known offenders.

Far better is some professional training so that potential offenders understand the problem, including what not to talk about and how to signal for a recess. Given an insight into the problem, they are much more likely to adapt to the needs of the hurly burly of customer contact. Furthermore, some will recognise early that this is not for them and they can then move to roles that do not involve direct dealings with clients. It is clearly sensible to integrate the training of sales and non-sales staff, both from an efficiency point of view, but also to build mutual respect and team spirit between the functions.

One area that frequently gets forgotten is that a customer's first contact with a company is usually with the telephone operator and their first face to face contact with a security guard. Training of both groups in the basic business of the Company and its customers, together with an explanation of their own importance in the selling process, can reap rewards. Similarly, learning a good telephone manner is particularly important for all those who deal with customers; not forgetting the secretaries.

Caring for customers

The sales executive's interest in customer care should come primarily from the fact that, as the person in the Company best known to the customer, the sales executive is, not unnaturally, the first person whom the customer contacts when something goes wrong. Furthermore, motivation to improve customer care should automatically come from the fact that a company's next order is so dependant on its performance of the last one. This is particularly true in some export markets, where it is the personal credibility and track record of the sales executive that is a key factor in determining which vendor wins any contract.

It is surprising how many people in a PPP company have contact with customers and thus the opportunity to upset them. Engineers, both at pre- and post-contract stages, logistic support and commissioning staff, invoice issuers chasing for progress payments and, most importantly, PMs. By the very nature of their work, PMs have plenty of opportunities to annoy customers with delays and demands for increased payments. They all need training that it's not what they say, but the way that they say it!

That great Americanism: "Have a nice day" is only a small part of owning problems. A good telephone manner is not an inbred habit, but rather one that needs training and constant vigilance. Keeping promises made to customers is essential, and not making rash promises is part of being in that position.

As an example, two sales executives, one female, one male, arrive at their homes from the office three hours late. One has phoned her partner to say she'll be late and is greeted with a commiseration for a long working day, a stiff drink and supper on the table. The other has given no warning and, when he gets home, his partner, worried that he's had a car accident, shouts and lays into him, saying that supper is ruined. He gets no sympathy at all.

The only difference between the two situations is the expectations of the two partners. It is the same with customer expectations. Keep expectations at such a level that they can be met or bettered. The fundamental issue is to empower the employees and thus get the organisation to respond effectively to customer problems. In this way, customer loyalty will be built through customer satisfaction.

Organisational structures

Normally, sales departments are organised by market segment and Chapter 7 gives more information on segmentation. For export-oriented companies, a geographical split is probably the most popular but in the home market, in particular, a split by industrial sector can be very effective. E.g. government, banking, retail, leisure.

The alternative is to organise by different class of PPP. The advantage of the former system is that it ties the sales staff to the customer organisations. The latter organisation provides the best technical knowledge of PPPs and their application, at the expense of customer understanding. Probably the best solution of all is a mix of the two, with sales executives oriented towards their customers and sales support staff specialising in particular PPPs. It is worth noting that different companies have a range of views on how best to split the world geographically.

Budgeting

Any sales department will require an adequate operating budget and the costs involved can be high. To build up a budget, start with employment costs for each member of staff, not forgetting the company cars still provided to the majority of sales executives. Both secretarial and clerical help must also be included. It is costly to keep a salesman in the field, particularly if working in export markets, where the cost of air travel and hotel accommodation need consideration, as does the figure for entertainment; be it in country or at home.

It is also important to remember that these international items are not governed by UK inflation and change with exchange rate fluctuations. Such prices often rise much more quickly than UK inflation would suggest; several hundred per cent per annum in some countries, matched to a devaluation of only some tens of percentage points.

The cost of public relations, including major items such as new equipment launches, literature, exhibitions and audio-visual materials can be significant and if an advertising campaign is considered appropriate, the cost of this also needs inclusion.

Probably the largest single item in a PPP company's sales and marketing budget will be the bids and proposals figure. This will need to cover the cost of the engineers' time, bid management and proposal publishing, together with any necessary travel and subsistence. A figure of 1- 2% of current sales is the minimum. Demonstration costs need inclusion and can be high if shipping a major product overseas and operating it for any length of time.

The bids and proposals budget is also the one most difficult to keep under control in PPP companies. With large teams working on bid preparation and, on occasions, a shortage of contracts on which to book their time, it is easy for bidding costs to spiral out of control. It is therefore essential that bid managers recognise their role in completing the bidding activities to cost and carefully allocate agreed funding to those working on the bids.

Any potential or actual overspend needs immediate reporting to the person who allocated the initial budget either for authorisation of further funds or to call a halt to the bid. Another need is not to spend too much money in the first part of the financial year, resulting in a famine of funds in the latter part of the year and cut backs that will result in severe demotivation of the sales team.

While it is unusual for the sales and marketing function to hold the Company's private venture (PV) development funds, it is essential that the function provides an input into the PV budget. Having responsibility for PPP plans, the function also needs involvement in decisions relating to the authorisation of any PV expenditure.

Finally, there are the so called internal costs, of which communications by telephone, fax or video-conferencing can be a large item for a company operating internationally. There will also be the cost of office accommodation, photocopying and computer equipment maintenance, including new or upgraded software.

Capital items needed by a sales and marketing department are few and far between. Apart from desktop and laptop PC's, the only likely items of any consequence are a quality conference room and demonstration facility, together with any associated equipment.

Chapter 6:

International Selling

Exporting · Choosing the countries · The regions of the world · Cultural differences · The suitability of PPP's to overseas markets · Sales teams · Communications with staff overseas · Export quotes & contracts · Overseas public relations · Customer visits to the UK · Local representatives · Making the right selection · Appointing representatives · Commission payments · Managing overseas representatives · Representatives' conferences · Sacking representatives · Local offices · Government supported export drives · Export rules & tools · Air travel · Customs & immigration · Road travel · Food · Medical care · Breaking the law · Security of information · Foreign languages · Reporting back · Commercial code

Exporting

This book has, so far, mainly focused on winning business in the home market. Whilst the content is relevant to overseas markets, there is a further layer of complexity that applies to these markets. For a start, some form of geographical segmentation becomes essential and, for the sales manager, a balancing act is necessary in dealing with the various territories, sales executives and overseas representatives.

Many people not involved in it, think that exporting is easy but nothing could be further from the truth. Exporting is not fun, nor is it an inexpensive undertaking. Unless applying significant resources and employing experienced staff, any foray into export markets is likely to end in frustration. Exporting can, however, be very rewarding financially and provide protection for a company against the vagaries of the home market. Increasing the volume of sales of a PPP, through exports, helps recoup the original investment in the development. It also allows improvement of the competitive position of the PPP through the learning curve cost benefits gained with increasing volume throughput.

The Department of Trade and Industry (DTI), together with its associated Board of Trade, is the government department responsible for helping to ensure there is an environment in which UK exports can flourish. It provides a number of services to exporting companies and has regional offices across the country. Particularly for those new to international trading, the DTI can provide valuable assistance in a number of specialist areas. The DTI library is a good starting point, and there is more information about this on page 180.

Choosing the countries

There are some 170 countries world-wide and few companies either wish or can afford to export to them all. Thus, the first question is how thinly can an exporting company afford to spread itself. What is an appropriate process to arrive at a manageable number of countries? A selection by elimination is not a bad way to commence. Start by considering those countries to eliminate.

- Which do not need or want the Company's PPP's
- Which are too small or cannot afford the Company's PPP's
- Where export of the PPPs is embargoed
- Which produce their own PPP's locally
- Which are historically tied to another country's suppliers
- Which are too difficult, risky or unstable

The first group is very PPP specific and as an example, maritime PPP's are hardly likely to find a ready outlet in any landlocked country. The second is the largest grouping and may amount to anything from a few to many tens of nations. The third group may further reduce the number; particularly if the PPP's are of a high-tech or military nature. The fourth category is the "coals to Newcastle" problem, although, as the Japanese have shown, even this difficulty can be overcome. However, for the fledgling exporter, it is probably best to avoid such countries in any initial export campaign.

The fifth group dates back to the era of the large European empires. Typical of the problems are those experienced by UK companies selling to Francophone countries; the historical ties to France and the overwhelming language advantage that French companies enjoy making life difficult for a UK supplier, but not impossible. The last category is something of a catch all. It will include those nations that are politically unstable and those where the risks of failing to achieve a successful implementation of a PPP are high.

Having now probably eliminated a majority of countries, group the remainder by region and by market size, or, if this latter point is yet to be established, by GNP or some similar statistic. This analysis may lead to an obvious means of segmentation, with one or more groups becoming apparent where an initial export drive should prove the most cost effective. All other things being equal, groups nearer geographically, or culturally similar to the UK will provide the easiest starting point.

Do not imagine that, just because a PPP has been developed for the UK market, it will automatically suit the export market. Simple considerations of environmental conditions such as temperature and wind speed may eliminate the feasibility of deploying unmodified solutions overseas, while cultural or national need taking into consideration. Electricity supply or quality assurance standards may also cause problems, with many former colonies using the standards of their erstwhile parents. There is still the occasional company that tries to sell heavy plant without air conditioning in the Middle East!

The regions of the world

There are a number of ways of categorising the countries of the world, but possibly the most convenient is by region and culture.

- The English speakers - North America, Australia and New Zealand
- Western Europe
- Eastern Europe and the countries of the former Soviet Union
- The Middle East
- The Far East - The Northern Pacific Rim and the Southern Nations
- Sub-Saharan Africa
- Latin America

It is easy to define most of the regions, but the border, for selling purposes, between the Middle and Far East is less clear. Often, the divide is taken at the western limit of the Indian sub-continent, but there is advantage in including Muslim Pakistan in the Middle East.

The English speaking nations

The United States is as large and diverse as many of the other regions themselves, stretching from New England to Hawaii and from Alaska to Texas. With its industrial might, the first factor in trying to export there is to consider if the PPP being offered is a unique solution to the customers' problem, followed quickly by the question "Will they buy from an offshore company?" Canada has close though not always amicable ties with the USA, particularly in industrial terms, and there remains a large French aligned community in Quebec.

Australia and New Zealand are the most distant markets from the UK and are increasingly being dominated by suppliers from the Pacific Rim. These two countries are both relatively small markets, but well worthwhile if penetration can be achieved, not the least because of their well developed infrastructure and their use of the mother tongue. They also offer the opportunity to try fighting it out with Japanese competitors, learning about their approach, offerings, strengths and weaknesses.

Western Europe

European countries tend to be intensely nationalistic, often to the detriment of trade. The strugglings of the European Community (EC) have visibly demonstrated many of the problems still not overcome. One of the biggest barriers is that of language, though thanks mainly to the influence of both television and films, English is becoming very widely spoken. Many have a strong national capability in PPP development and manufacture and the southern nations, traditionally the poorest, receive significant EC grant aid. Because of the common roots of the culture in all the nations, many companies rightly consider Europe, even those countries still outside the EC, as part of the home market.

Eastern Europe and the countries of the former Soviet Union

The countries of the former Soviet Union and its Eastern European satellites certainly need a wide range of new PPPs, particularly to improve their infrastructure. As a result, travel and making telephone calls can be surprisingly frustrating, thus making the pursuit of business a time consuming activity. The nations are mostly industrialised, but their output is generally uncompetitive and largely outdated. Language difficulties abound and the communist upbringing of the people is making all forms of change difficult.

The region is the largest of all, stretching from the Danube in Central Europe across Asia to Vladivostock on the Pacific. There is a mixture of religions, from Christianity in the European part to Islam in southern Asia. Similar variations in language and culture, topography and climate exist, whilst communications in many parts of the region are primitive. Regrettably, political instability, local civil wars, difficulties in finding out who really has authority, as well as a severe shortage of both cash and foreign exchange, make this a difficult area in which to do business at the time of writing early in 1994. However, some companies are starting to make serious inroads in the region, often using creative approaches.

The Middle East

The Middle East is basically all the Arab nations plus Israel. It is difficult if dealing with the latter to trade with the former. All the Arab nations speak a common language and range in wealth from the richest in the world like Saudi

Arabia to some of the poorest, such as Yemen. The climate is generally hot and dusty, with any sense of urgency non-existent except on the subject of the delivery of PPPs. Female members of a sales team are generally unacceptable to customers, due to the strong Muslim tradition.

The Arabs are natural traders and drive a hard bargain. Negotiating is their stock in trade and reaching an agreement can be a lengthy and exhausting experience. Business dealings are difficult during the holy month of Ramadan and the other awkward period is Haj, the month of pilgrimage to Mecca in Saudi Arabia, when the air flights in the region become very over subscribed. Due to differences in the Islamic and Julian calendars, the former being based on lunar months, the dates of Ramadan and Haj advance by about three weeks each Julian year.

The Far East

The Far East is not homogeneous as a region and, in general, the Asiatics are extremely hard working. The region is enormous and the southern nations are maritime ones, enjoying a hot and humid climate. Always eager to learn, the people have a wonderful sense of patience and inscrutability that makes contract negotiations long and tough. It is hardly co-incidental that the rate of industrialisation and growth in the last part of the twentieth century exceeds that found in any other part of the world.

The Far East has led the Third World in demanding the technology to produce PPPs themselves. One exception to the rule is China. With over a billion inhabitants and a communist regime, they have lagged badly behind the rest of the region. There are, however, increasing signs that this slumbering giant is starting to awaken to the realities of existence in a competitive world.

India, with the second largest population in the world, shows great contrast between the educated minority and the huge peasant community. It is something of a bureaucratic nightmare. Inevitably, including Australia and New Zealand on a geographically basis does not mean they fit well from the point of view of selling PPPs and they have therefore been included with the other industrialised, English speaking nations.

Sub-Saharan Africa

Sub-Saharan Africa is one of the poorest regions of the world and only South Africa and Nigeria have significant GNP's. There is, however, a voracious demand for PPP's that helps to improve a nation's basic infrastructure and international aid funding is a significant factor in making many PPPs feasible. Tribalism is a key factor in politics and is also critical in choosing the right representative.

Air travel in the continent is generally easier in a north/south direction than an east/west one. Despite its poverty, the degree to which a company may see opportunities is highlighted by the well-known story of a pair of salesmen from two UK shoe companies visiting the continent in the early part of the twentieth century. One cabled back "No-one wears shoes, no market." The other's message read "Unlimited opportunities. No-one wears shoes…yet." It is still a region of huge possibilities.

Latin America

Latin America features some of the poorest states in its Central American region, but further south there are some well-industrialised countries, of which Brazil is the foremost. Stretching from Mexico in the North to Chile in the South, the region is effectively split in two by the Andes mountains. Spanish is the common language used for business, except in Brazil where Portuguese is spoken.

Heavily burdened by international debt, the nations are all struggling in terms of available finance for PPP's. The World Bank and other United Nations organisations do provide funding for some PPPs, but their terms of contract tend to be very restrictive, demanding the selection of the lowest price regardless of the advantages offered by any other bid.

From a selling point of view, there is definite benefit in giving a sales executive one or more particular regions to cover, but segregation is usually necessary when allocating potentially unfriendly nations such as Israel and the Arab nations, not the least because of problems in obtaining visas for one country after a passport has been stamped by another. However, the use of two passports can provide a simple solution to this particular problem.

Cultural differences

Obviously, a grouping into the industrial nations and the Third World, though broad, might suffice for many purposes. Regardless, the important point is to remember that not only the regions, but the individual countries vary significantly and that what is acceptable in the UK can and does easily cause offence overseas. The first two groups listed above include only industrialised nations and, being Christian democracies, similar rules ought to apply. To an extent they do. All have a Sunday based weekend, but the European countries have their own languages and woe betide the sales executive who thinks that American English is the same as the language spoken in the United Kingdom!

The moment a move is made into the Third World, things become a lot more difficult. Not only is everything different, but even simple communication has its pitfalls. The use of non Roman script means that signs appear incomprehensible, though fortunately this is not a universal practice. Many countries provide dual language signs, with English or French the most popular second scripts.

It is essential at the earliest stage to identify the team leader on the customer's side and to continue to make him feel important; it is still rare to find this role filled by a woman. Never contradict him in front of more junior members of his staff. It is also important to recognise the reciprocation of this view by the customers with whoever they consider to be head of the Company's sales delegation.

Many Asian counties, hearing a response of "yes but" will only hear the "yes," missing the qualifying "but" which changes the "yes" to a de facto "no." In negotiation this can be a convenience for them as well. In other countries, 'Yes" means "I hear you." Signals are often used to show a willingness to negotiate. Interpreting their meaning requires careful listening even in the home market. It can be particularly difficult when dealing with foreign cultures and languages.

Many countries take offence to being shown the sole of a foot, as might easily occur when sitting cross legged. In the Middle East, the use of the left hand for eating or drinking is taboo and failure to accept the offer of a drink when arriving at someone's office or house is also very rude. In Brazil, the serving of coffee means that the meeting has come to an end, whilst in the Middle East, guests are expected to leave immediately after the end of the evening meal.

The Department of Trade and Industry, Foreign and Commonwealth Office, Joint Chambers of Commerce, as well as a number of the major banks, all provide booklets on doing business in the various overseas countries. They form a starting point but can, by their very nature, only give limited information. Similarly, organisations such as Reuters provide country reports in the form of on-line computer files, sorted by country, covering both news and useful statistics.

A characteristic found commonly is that of people saying what they think the other person wants to hear. A good example of this from the Middle East was of a visiting salesman asking a secretary whether it was possible to see the boss, who was a potential customer. The response to the question was that the boss was not there and that the salesman should come back in half an hour. Realising what was happening, the salesman then asked the critical question. Where was the boss? Unabashed the answer came back "In New York!" It is always worth cultivating lowlier members of the customer's staff. A small gift such as a pen or diary, given to the boss's secretary, can facilitate making an appointment and avoid the disaster of secretarial shutout. Unthinking rudeness can also provoke this awful syndrome.

The work ethic of many of the industrialised nations is not a universal one. The "Manyana" approach of the southern European nations also exists in Latin America and matches the Middle East's "Bokra" (tomorrow) syndrome. People in these countries simply do not have a sense urgency. They live on the basis that if it can't be done today, then it will be done tomorrow, or the day after that or…"What's the great hurry?" is the question they often ask. The traffic situation in many major cities can compound this, making the M25 look like a speed track in comparison. The lack of urgency can mean immense frustration for the sales executive waiting for business to develop to the point where a contract can be signed. Interestingly, for different reasons, similar delays seemed to have crept into Western acquisitions, all of which take their toll on the time scale.

The main differences in dealing with customers in Third World nations arise from a number of factors, all of which require careful attention.

- Language and resulting communication difficulties
- Bureaucracy
- Lack of delegation
- Fear of taking risks, especially where these may effect the well-being of their organisation
- Their need to justify everything in writing
- Shortage of cash
- Frequent changes of staff and organisation

All of these variances, together with the differences in culture, suggest that for the first visit to a country, anyone representing their company should travel with an experienced colleague. This can not only stop gaffs being committed, but more seriously prevent the unwitting newcomer having their visa withdrawn, or even ending up in jail.

In many countries, it will be an unofficial part of the Company's role to walk important papers from office to office to ensure they get the requisite signatures. This can result in gestation periods just as long as the worst found in the developed world. The big difference is that UK directors and senior managers can understand Western style delays. The impermeability of the Third World culture means that companies are less prepared to accept the inevitable delays in the procurement process of these countries. One senior Sri Lankan government official once said that their bureaucracy worked at the pace of a lame snail and Sri Lanka is not alone in this respect!

The suitability of PPP's to overseas markets

PPP's designed for the UK market are not necessarily immediately suitable for the export market. Obvious environmental difference such as the operating temperature range may involve major modifications to equipment, whilst actual requirement differences can also cause quite a headache. A helicopter designed for European use may be quite unsatisfactory for operations in the Himalayas, as may a microwave communications system. Building designs may need to be proof against earthquakes, as well as hurricanes/cyclones/typhoons, tornadoes, snow and whatever else mother nature may throw at them; fortunately not all at the same time! Careful thought can avoid attempts to sell the proverbial "refrigerators to the Eskimos" or "sand to the Arabs." Problems with the mains electrical power supply in many countries are legendary, varying from non-existent, through very intermittent to insufficient even to warm a soldering iron.

Often, Third World customers will be unable to provide a requirement specification and will state "You make the PPP, you should know what we want." While this is perhaps an exaggeration, it is the opportunity for the sales executive to prepare and submit an "unbiased" outline specification to the customer. Preparation of this document may involve a considerable amount of work by the Company, first in territory and then in the UK, putting together a sensible requirement.

Differences in user behaviour are also a problem. The environment in which major computer systems operate is a good example. Usually located in airlocked, air-conditioned rooms, it is not uncommon in Mediterranean countries to find the double doors wedged open, or smoking taking place in the computer room. Both potentially cause expensive damage to the equipment and sadly, the rule breaking does nothing to negate the reputation of the system supplier for unreliable equipment. Likewise, an electrical trip is often considered an equipment failure, despite a quick reset bringing the PPP back on line within seconds.

Sales teams

Export sales departments are frequently organised on a regional basis, though occasionally by PPP or market sector is preferable. Exporting can be a lonely business for the sales executive, but in the PPP business, after some initial contact, a sales team will normally be required to answer all the customer's questions. During the transition from an opportunity to a contract, the constitution of the sales team will inevitably need to change. At the start, it may consist of the sales executive alone, who will soon need specialist help to develop a solution for the customer. As the situation progresses, a commercial or contracts executive will also be needed and towards the end, a PM designate. This team, at least four strong, is quite a resource drain and the numbers needed can multiply for large contracts.

Usually, but not always, the sales executive will lead the team. He or she will certainly want to and the customer will have a similar expectation. The sales executive will need to advise the other members of the team on local factors. The team members will need to be "inoculated" during the negotiation process to prevent them from inadvertently providing information which may jeopardise the Company's negotiating position. In fact, people who spend long enough overseas tend to "go native" and take up many of the less desirable traits of their host culture.

Communications with staff overseas

Two common problems relate to dealing with sales staff who are abroad in distant timezones. The first is that the communications time slot can be extremely narrow. In California, where the working day starts at 8.00 am, it is already 4.00 pm in the UK office. Thus a communications slot of perhaps two hours is all that is available during the normal working day.

Allied to this problem is the need for a rapid response to questions posed by sales staff overseas. A call placed from the Far East at the end of the day, local time, is received in the UK early in the morning. A delay in responding the same day means the sales executive will have to wait two days for the reply. This is expensive in terms of wasted hotel and subsistence cost, but even more irritating for the sales executive, eager to solve the problem and move on to the next customer or return home.

Export quotes and contracts

Contracting in foreign countries is very different from the UK. The law of the country and the language may both be very different. Many other practical differences will and do occur. Customers prefer to pay in their local currency and will, of course, expect shipment of all equipment to their country. These differences also need reflecting in the terms and conditions included in export quotations.

Bear in mind that some customers require the signing executive to hold a power of attorney and, in some countries, the document will need countersigning by their embassy in London. Export sales staff need a basic understanding of letters of credit and bank guarantees but their detailed workings require specialist contractual staff. Chapter 12 gives further information on this subject.

Whoever has the authority to sign the contract with the customer will need careful watching, owing to the risks of starting to become sympathetic with the customer's view point after prolonged exposure to negotiating. In fact, dealing with Third World customers bring a special set of problems in its trail. These people have been brought up in a negotiating culture where everything purchased, even items for home consumption, is subject to a negotiation between the buyer and the seller. The result is that such people have a wealth of negotiating skills, honed by the practice of a lifetime, which are undreamed of by the average UK executive. Negotiating a PPP contract with such people can be a demanding and time consuming occupation as their key ammunition is that time is almost always on their side.

Overseas public relations

The six main roles of public relations are all affected by the different needs of the export market.

- Advertising
- Audio-visual
- Direct mail
- Exhibitions
- Literature
- Press relations

One of the biggest difficulties faced in thinking about overseas public relations is that even companies that are household names in the UK may be unknown in certain parts of the world. Increasing the level of corporate awareness in targeted countries is important, but can be an expensive process. As with the PPP's themselves, public relations work needs tailoring to the country or region being targeted.

Most customers like to read brochures and look at audio-visual material in their own language and this can be costly. It is generally necessary to make some compromise, either by limiting the number of languages to the more widely spoken ones or, for literature, by inserting translation sheets into existing English brochures. The cost of mailing literature to overseas customers is high so lightweight paper and bindings need consideration. It is also worth noting that the brochures themselves are subject to the export licensing procedure. Press contact, press releases and advertising can target regional or national trade magazines, of which there is an increasing proliferation. Ulrich's and Willing's directories list the names of suitable publications.

Overseas trade fairs and exhibitions are a target for overseas public relations, but three things need watching. The first is that many so called international exhibitions are far from being just that. They are more likely to be national, with a small sprinkling of overseas visitors from adjacent countries. The second point is that many Third World countries will take offence at any company seeking business which fails to support their pet national show. Accept this type of moral blackmail for what it is when deciding which overseas exhibitions to attend. Finally, it is important to recognise that exhibitions arranged for industry are very different from those organised for end users. The British Overseas Trade Board (BOTB) can often give some financial assistance to companies attending, both in terms of exhibiting cost as well as in airfares and hotel charges. There is further information about public relations Chapter 11.

Customer visits to the UK

When overseas dignitaries from the customer community visit the UK, they will expect VIP treatment. It is, therefore, essential to be well prepared. Hopefully the sales executive will know the visitors and their interests. Only use very clear speakers for presentations and promptly follow up any enquiries coming out of meetings.

The sales executive should meet the visitors at the airport and transport them to their hotel, arranged by the Company. Whilst many customers will insist on paying their own hotel bills, others will expect the Company to cover this cost.

Visitors will generally prefer their national cuisine and timescales, so these should be provided if at all possible. The timing of meals has its own pitfalls. Americans are usually starving for their lunch by midday at the latest and will be more than happy to break for a meal at 1130 am, though they will usually ask to pay for their meals if they are government employees, as they cannot be seen to accept "bribes!" Arabs will prefer to work through until 2.00 pm and then break for the rest of the day.

Beware of offering pork to Muslims or beef to Hindus and look out for vegetarians. With visitors from China, two hours work in the morning and the same in the afternoon is good going. With an interpreter essential, actual working progress will be slow. Beware of casual conversations in the presence of the interpreter, who may turn out covertly to be the chief negotiator as well! Entertainment will usually be a part of the visit and requires careful thought, not only to provide enjoyment, but also not to cause offence. Dignitaries from some countries may expect female company and it is as well to recognise who in the sales department is capable of making this type of arrangement!

Local representatives

Because all countries are different, it is almost essential to have a local representative in each country, or group of small territories. These representatives in the PPP arena, variously known as agents, distributors or even consultants, are the guide to the behaviour and attitude of the customer community. The purely legalistic view of an agent being someone who can commit the Company is not the one used here. The roles of local representatives divide into two parts. The first group of needs is really essential.

1. Provision of the entree into the customer community. (Sometimes a legal requirement, though at times illegal.)

2. Effective connection to the current political/presidential power base. (Some are very powerful.)

3. Advice on the local culture and customs, including verbal and written translations.

4. Ability to meet and greet at the airport, arrange hotels and provide local transport. (This is much more important in the Third World.)

5. Dealing with administrative tasks, such as import documents and letters of credit.

6. Acting as the sponsor in obtaining visas, where necessary, and work permits.

The second group of roles are desirable, rather than essential, and future business ambitions need consideration in deciding their relative importance.

1. Understanding the technology of the principal.
2. Helping with technology transfer.
3. Providing a maintenance and support service.
4. Acting as the local partner in any joint venture. (Laws may affect local ownership as well as manufacture)

Making the right selection

Selecting the right local representative, agent or distributor can be as difficult as successfully choosing a marriage partner for life. Divorce is unfortunately commonplace in both. There are various avenues of approach. Depending on the country involved, some desk work prior to a visit to territory may be useful, but on the whole, real progress is only possible once in the country itself. If anyone is known in the local customer community, they should be the first port of call. The second place is the British embassy, where the commercial section will provide a list of individuals and companies with relevant business experience, though these lists can be of very mixed quality. A local chamber of commerce, where one exists, may similarly be helpful.

With a starting list of possibles, the next task is to set up a comprehensive programme of appointments, since talking to local businessmen will help to establish their own capabilities and will often lead to further introductions. Meeting local people and talking to them is the key to success. It should lead to the establishment of a sensible short list. In the Third World, do not be surprised by a lack of punctuality, either by representatives or by customers. It is no reason, however, for a sales executive ever to be late for an appointment.

There are several key rules when appraising local companies and individuals.

Never select a local representative:
- On the sole basis of meetings in the UK
- On the recommendation of a single company employee
- Who already represents a competitor
- Where the key people are not the same ethnic group as the customers (e.g. Chinese in Malaysia)
- Where the office location is not close to the customer community
- If any other local representative is offering another of the Company's PPPs to the same customer community

The importance of getting a second opinion cannot be over stressed and, as it is commonly the sales executive who make the initial contact, their immediate manager is the natural choice for this task. A visit to the representative's office, as well as an introductory meeting with potential customers, should be set up before travelling to territory. Not only can these visits avoid obvious errors, such as choosing the wrong race or creed, but may help to avoid selecting those without the necessary influence with the ruling party or family. It is important to be able to recognise the shut out policy, where a relative or friend of a representative is encouraged to sign up a company and then do nothing, at least slowing down their entry into the territory.

Fundamentally, potential representatives divide into two groups; those who are lean and hungry and those who are fat and happy. It is clearly essential to be able to establish into which category any particular individual or company falls. It is also important to consider the possibility of the key staff, who deal with the market sector of interest, leaving the representative's company to work else where. This can be even more of a problem in the case of an individual, rather than a company. Despite the risk of sickness, injury or death resulting in a loss of representation, some cases justify the use of an individual, rather than a more substantial organisation.

While there is wide acceptance that overseas representatives should not act for two competing companies, it is not unusual to discover that the company owned by a representative's brother-in-law represents a competitor, usually with dire adverse effects. This ruling does not apply to anything like the same extent in terms of prime contractors and sub-contractors using the same representative. The great danger for the sub-contractor is that the prime may not be as impartial as first appears. For the prime contractor, the problem is that the sub-contractor will either try and move up the supply chain, or vertically integrate and end up winning the next major chunk of the prime contractor's business. Once this risk is clearly identified, it is more readily manageable.

In the Third World, be prepared for a very unprepossessing office. They do vary in quality enormously, but the appearance of the office seems to bear little relationship to performance. There is some merit in talking to an opposite number in a competing UK company, who may be a friend or former colleague. Support for "UK Limited" in adverse overseas markets can often lead to the revelation of skeletons in the cupboard for particular potential representatives. These can range from "Not as efficient as they appear to be." to "On the blacklist!" At the end of the selection period, it is essential to have the answers to a number of questions about each potential representative.

1. What is their track record in obtaining business in the required marketplace?

2. Have they got sufficient customer contacts within the target market, at all levels from the working ones to the decision makers and politicians?
3. Are they of the correct creed, family, tribe or nationality and what is the risk of them losing influence following a change of government?
4. What portfolio of existing PPP's do they have from other companies?
5. Are there any competitive companies or PPP's which they already represent?
6. What is the size of the company and the staying power both of the company and its staff?
7. What is the location of their offices in relation to the customer community?
8. What is their administrative capability in relation to the required role?

Appointing representatives

Having reached a decision on the company or individual to appoint, a formal agreement will need drawing up. A trial period is usually the best way to start a relationship with an overseas representative. The length of this period will depend on a number of factors, but should not exceed six to twelve months, otherwise de-motivation may set in.

A baseline agreement for all a company's overseas representatives is highly desirable and should include some sort of annual renewal system. This system can initially require positive action, but after two or three years can move to the more relaxed approach of management by exception, when renewal is automatic unless...! Regardless, an internal annual review of the performance of each representative should take place, with all those involved in dealing with the representative solicited for their views. Well established exporting companies will often run a quarterly review of 25% of their overseas representatives to avoid a log jam at the end of the year.

It is worth remembering that even in a market sector where contract values are substantial, the representatives themselves are usually self-employed or work in small organisations. As a result, they can have difficulties coping with the large company approach of their principals. They much prefer to deal with one person, usually the sales executive who was their first contact with the Company. They will need careful nurturing through the various departments and staff of any large organisation they represent.

Finally, in some large companies, there may be internal difficulties before a representative can be appointed. Other parts of the Company may already be

136   How to win business

represented in territory and even with the same customer community. Such difficulties will require either a central overview and approval procedure, or excellent communications between the sales directors of the various parts of the Company; a sensible approach in any case with a shared customer community. A different approach to distribution between programme/project based parts of the Company and those involved with major products can compound these problems.

Commission payments

The payment of commission can cause more problems than any other factor, not least because representatives will demand commission on all contracts which surface within their territory. Bootlegging is the term given to the problem that occurs when a company sells a PPP to a prime contractor which then exports it to another country. The arrival of the PPP in that country leads to an immediate demand, by the representative of the sub-contractor, for commission on the sale, even though the representative has had no involvement in the placing of the contract. Experienced exporters will anticipate this difficulty and always include a small commission in such cases, or preferably air the problem in advance with their representative and agree that no commission will be payable.

The other major difficulties include the level of commission and the timing of payments. Clearly, the level of commission paid will depend on two main factors;

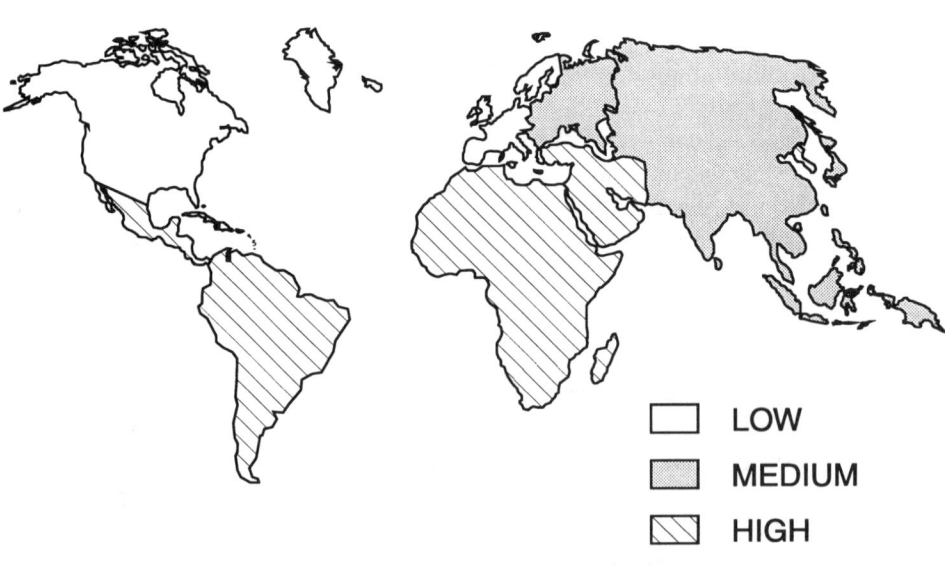

Figure 40. Commission payment levels vary from place to place and care is needed to establish the correct levels.

the value of the contract and the country to which the equipment is sold. Recognition is needed that in some areas of the world, high levels of commission are normal. The world divides into three loose areas with different rates of commission; high, medium and low.

Sales managers and directors need to establish the correct level of remuneration, since local representatives will invariably start by asking for a lot. The inclusion in the representative's agreement of a sliding scale of payments for varying contract values will ensure a reasonable reward on the smaller contracts, while avoiding exorbitant payments on the large ones. Never enter into an auction situation with a customer, where the payer of the largest commission wins the business.

Commission payments should be pro-rata to receipt of payments by the principal. The likely persistent request for up front payment requires steadfast rejection. A number of companies have found themselves blacklisted for failing to pay their representatives the commission level due and reneging on their agreements. Such bad news spreads very rapidly, limiting a company's ability to re-establish effective local representation there in the future.

Managing overseas representatives

By its very nature, the feast or famine situation commonly found in the PPP business makes managing and motivating overseas representatives quite a problem. The staying power of the representative between large orders can be a key factor influencing the initial choice. Motivation is basically a question of communication, even when there are no immediate business opportunities in prospect. Such lean periods can easily last up to five years.

Means of Communication

- Letters
- Brochures and newsletters
- Proposals and quotations
- Telephone
- Facsimile and telex
- Visits by sales staff
- Local equipment demonstrations

Of all the methods of communication, regular visits are the most important, with the telephone and the written word close behind. It is worth remembering, particularly when relationships are not going well, that representatives will often send long faxes filled with difficult questions and demand responses in quite unreasonably short timescales. It should go without saying that rapid response to all communications is critical.

138   How to win business

There are, regrettably, many ways of demotivating representatives, some obvious, some less so. Regardless, a demotivated representative is, at best, unlikely to be of much assistance in winning new business and, at worst, a positive obstacle.

Demotivating factors

- Lack of communication and lack of cover during key staff absence
- Lack of regular visits
- Inaction leading to the representative failing to meet promises made to customers
- Arbitrary or vacillating Company policy

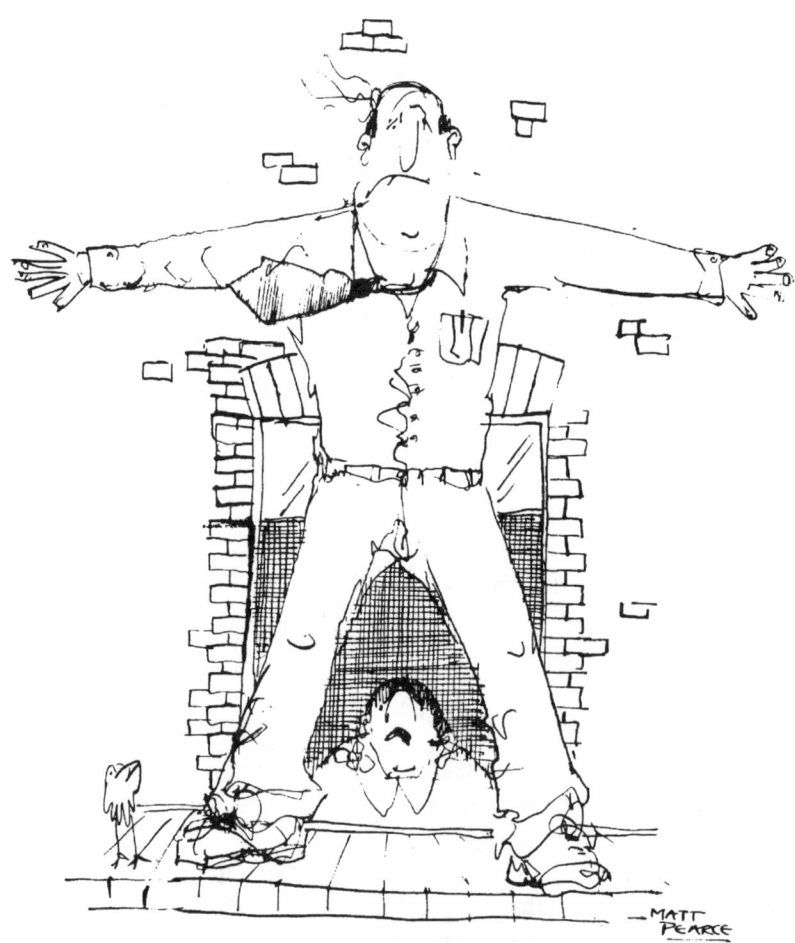

OVERSEAS REPRESENTATIVES WORRY ABOUT WHETHER THEY WILL BE PAID.

- Refusing to bid for suitable opportunities and failing to justify reasonable "No-bids"
- Payment of less than acceptable commission levels
- Slow payment of commission, or failure to pay
- Late delivery of purchased PPPs
- Poor support of equipment already in territory
- Not keeping the representative up to date with what the customer has been told, leading to tremendous loss of face, quickly followed by loss of business

Representatives' conferences

Conferences for overseas representatives, held by the Company in the UK or even overseas by region on an annual or biennial basis, can be wonderful motivators. The future plans and aims of the Company should be presented, together with details of any new developments in the PPPs being offered. The chance for the representatives to express their views is important and workshop sessions or clinics, with the sales director or very senior sales managers, are well worth the time and effort involved.

With a formal programme lasting typically two days, the most useful aspect of these conferences lies in the visible commitment of senior management and the ability of the Company's staff really to get to know the various representatives. An informal evening is excellent value, where everyone talks to everyone else and representatives can also chat with those from other countries. A formal dinner, possibly with a guest speaker from the UK customer community, can add to the sense of occasion.

Sacking representatives

It is a sad reflection that from time to time agreements with overseas representatives will have to be terminated. Usually, there is fault on both sides, but sometimes the cause is loss of influence in the customer community by the representative, as for example, when the government changes and his relatives who were in the cabinet, lose their jobs. As with all divorces, there are two ways of approaching the problem, the acrimonious way and the mature way. The latter is obviously preferable, not the least because the representative may surface again and enemies in export markets should be avoided at all costs.

Terminating a representative's agreement needs preparation to achieve a satisfactory outcome. It will almost certainly, in any case, cause pain to the representative who will:

- Be shocked, even if warnings have been given
- Lose face in the market place
- Blame the Company for the divorce

- Try to stop the Company cancelling the agreement
- Ask to be paid for work done, which has yet to reach fruition

It is thus essential to deal with the termination sympathetically. Whoever is delegated to do the task should accept the need for a face to face meeting, rather than sending the bad news in a letter or fax. The seniority of person who actually faces the representative to pass on the bad news can be critical. It should not be the representative's day to day contact, who will have to continue to operate in the territory. It must be someone senior enough to gain respect and to ensure that the representative does not go back over their head to the managing director.

A director, either the sales director or the export director, should normally undertake this task. An explanation of the reasons for the termination must be given, together with an acceptance that there is blame on both sides. In the PPP business, a reducing rate of commission payable on any orders received over the next two to three years can help to ease the pain considerably; for example two thirds in the first year and one third in the second year. At all costs avoid the dangers of the representative taking umbrage and damaging the Company's image with the customer community or even the local community of representatives. The final critical rule is to avoid sacking a representative until a suitable replacement is found.

Local offices

It can be very difficult is to decide whether it is worth setting up a local sales office. Particularly when travelling to the Far East, the problems of travel time and jet lag make regular travel from the UK both tiring and expensive. A local office can significantly reduce this wear and tear. It can also allow the locally based sales executive to spend more time with customers. Establishing a local office is a costly proposition and the pros and cons shown in the table opposite will need weighing up carefully.

Either the local company office or the local representative can undertake after sales support and this can be a valuable source of new sales leads. Maintenance staff will inevitably be in regular contact with the customer community. Providing they keep their eyes and ears open, they can find out a great deal about new opportunities for business at the earliest sign, as well as the potential for add on sales to existing PPPs.

Government supported export drives

The UK government has, over the years, provided several initiatives to try to increase exports. Led by the Department of Trade and Industry, in conjunction with its British Overseas Trade Board, certain of the schemes target small companies. Some, however, are well worth consideration by PPP companies and two areas spring to mind.

LOCAL OFFICE PROS	LOCAL OFFICE CONS
Reduced travel costs & wear & tear on staff	Cost of setting up and running office
Better and more regular contact with customers	Difficulty of control. The staff can "go native"
Better understanding of customers	Problems of communication
Visibility of national politics and economics	Staff lose touch with the parent and its developments
Visible commitment to the customer	Profit repatriation & local tax commitments
Visible commitment by Company management	Sponsorship needs, visas and work permits
Eases local translation and interpreting	If regional, considerable travel still required
A base for setting up a PPP service and support organization	Some customers unhappy with local office in adjacent adversarial country e.g. China/Taiwan

The first is for the exporter considering entering a new overseas territory or region. Specially organised tours of business people interested in selected industries are arranged to the more distant countries. Subsidised travel and accommodation can make these tours financially attractive. They must, however, be aimed at the particular markets of interest to the Company. A similar scheme subsidises the attendance at overseas exhibitions in new markets. As is the case with re-location incentive packages, the body of evidence suggests that companies will go where they want to, taking any concession as a perk rather than a rationale.

Export rules and tools

Having considered the issues likely to affect any company dealing with overseas markets, the remainder of this chapter considers the various factors likely to be of concern to individuals travelling into those markets. These factors are many and varied, and are a potential stumbling block for all those who are new to exporting.

It is important to consider how much time an export sales executive should expect to spend overseas and the maximum duration of each overseas trip. As a guide, once someone is spending more than one third of their time overseas, they start to get out of touch with their company and problems with their home life start to multiply. Much less than 90 days abroad each year suggests they are not earning their keep. The duration of individual trips will depend on the region to be visited.

Almost the first question asked by any buyer will be "When do you leave?" Typically, for the Far East, three to four weeks at a time seems a sensible length of trip, though this obviously needs tempering with flexibility when actually negotiating a contract. One favourite ploy used by experienced customers is to time the end of negotiations close to Christmas or Easter, thus putting extra pressure on the sales

HOW PEOPLE BACK AT BASE THINK EXPORT SALES EXECUTIVES PASS THEIR TIME.

team to compromise on the final price or terms and conditions in order to get home in time for the holiday.

Air travel

The overseas travel demanded of an export sales executive can be very wearing. First, there are the effects of jet lag to consider. These impact on different people in different ways. Air travel is dehydrating, with passengers losing as much as a litre of fluid every two hours in the air. This liquid loss requires replacing if uncomfortable dehydration is not to occur. Unfortunately, drinking alcohol merely exacerbates the problem, so a regular intake of soft drinks is essential. Long flights, commonly fifteen hours non-stop to the Far East, demand regular movement to keep the blood flowing. A walk around the aircraft from time to time can be very refreshing, as well as being helpful in preventing the blood from pooling in the legs.

Finally the time zone shift needs consideration. It is a good idea to alter watches immediately on boarding the aircraft, to eat light meals and, for day time flights, to keep awake when flying East, but get a snooze when flying West. Research by the United Nations has shown that starting a flight at the time when normal work commences and arriving at the destination at the end of the afternoon has much merit in reducing fatigue. This ideal is frequently impossible.

Adjusting to time zone shifts takes about a day per hour of shift and the obvious effects are difficulty in sleeping, being woken in the night by a full bladder (the kidneys always seem to be the last part of the body to adjust) and general fatigue. Tiredness seems to be worse at some times, better at others; the relationship between the two appearing to be quite random. The best advice, to take time off to recover at the destination, is unrealistic for the sales executive wishing to get things moving, but it is imperative to try to defer making major decisions when jet lagged.

Note that some airlines offer less than satisfactory levels of safety when judged by Western standards. Both the UK Foreign and Commonwealth Office and some air travel organisations can give advice on those airlines to avoid, if at all possible.

Customs and immigration

On arrival at the destination, customs and immigration formalities can be quite daunting. Many countries still require the purchase of visas from their embassy in the UK before travel commences, whilst a few sell them at a counter on arrival; not usually to be recommended. The duration of stay will always be defined on the visa and getting an extension in many countries is effectively impossible because of bureaucracy. Over staying one's legal welcome can result in a missed flight at best and a sojourn in jail at worst. Anyone travelling frequently overseas should obtain two passports; not a difficult procedure. This will enable the holder to travel on one passport whilst the other is at an embassy for a visa.

In many countries, a full search of all baggage is normal and samples or pieces of equipment require perfect documentation, stamped by customs on the way out of the UK. This includes portable PC's, where there may be export restrictions to some countries for the fastest machines. The passage of these items is eased in the Third World by attaching a few national or hotel stickers, acquired during previous travels, to make them look less than brand new. Even then, any item can easily be impounded for a day or two, often only released in return for a suitable payment. Never carry prohibited items, such as drugs, firearms, explosives and, in some countries, centrefold magazines and alcohol. It is not only the sales executive who is at risk, but the reputation of the Company as well.

Road travel

On arrival at the destination, the local representative usually provides road transport. Taxis are very useful, though their cost can quickly mount up and they may not always be available. Reduce costs by negotiating a non-meter rate of payment for longer periods. Car hire is fine in the industrialised nations, but can be rather more problematic in the Third World. A minor accident can result in a night in jail, regardless of who caused the accident. For those who think the traffic is bad at home, just try Jakarta or Rio in the rush hour!

It is worth remembering that in some countries, government servants are grossly underpaid and rely on backhanders to supplement their income. Stopped in Lagos one day by a policeman, two sales executives had the car documentation examined and were told it was faulty. A hefty fine was demanded. Deciding to risk bluffing it out, they told the policeman that they would rather go down to the police station to sort out the matter. The policeman, realising that this would take two to three hours and would mean the loss of valuable backhanders during this time, immediately signalled them to proceed as if nothing untoward had happened.

Food

Eating can be quite a problem for Westerners in the Third World. Some delicacies are less than inviting. Sea cucumber and sheep's eyes are two items that are often offered as delicacies by the host; the first in China, the second in the Middle East. They must be eaten with relish if offence is not to be given. Avoid saying how nice anything is unless wanting a second helping and, for peace of mind, avoid asking what it is! In the Middle East, some banquets still take place sitting on the floor, eating using the right hand without knife and fork. It takes some practice to get used to it! Remember that the meal is always served at the end of the evening there and that it is polite to leave as soon as the meal is over.

Expect continuous refreshments throughout meetings. In the Third World it will be tea or coffee, generously sugared unless asked for without. The Eastern Europeans are also inclined to offer alcohol. Slivovitz (plum brandy) at 9.00 am can certainly dull the senses and be disadvantageous during any serious negotiations. The Americans offer coffee, or decaff, together with a selection of Danish pastries. Wonderful to eat, but not so good for the figure! Even Western Europe can have its problems. In France, it is not uncommon to sit down to lunch at one pm and finish between four and five in the afternoon. To stay the distance, do not be tempted by the excellence of the food to eat large quantities of each course.

Medical care

Taking sensible precautions minimises the chances of getting ill abroad. The relevant inoculations are essential, as well as anti-malaria tablets where necessary. Avoiding drinking local tap water or drinks containing ice cubes and do not eat salad or freshly washed fruit. In the Third World, the local dishes are often a great deal safer than Western cuisine as the latter is often inadequately cooked through ignorance.

The large international hotel chains generally offer a safe standard of food and water, but the advice to clean teeth with bottled water is still wise. If it's flat water, make sure the seal is unbroken precluding the possibility of a bottle refilled with tap water! A useful tip is to drink the local beer as it seems to help in avoiding stomach upsets; an effect usually put down to its disinfectant properties!

Being ill away from home is a most unpleasant experience and in the Third World, if things go really wrong, give serious consideration to flying out immediately to a country with a First World reputation for medical care. There are government forms, obtainable beforehand from any DSS office, which detail reciprocal arrangements between many countries and the UK to cover any medical costs incurred.

A simple first aid kit is well worth carrying. This should include a general antibiotic, anti-histamine cream, salt tablets if visiting the tropics, a syringe and needles to avoid any chance of HIV contamination from locally administered injections. Another real health problem is that of venereal disease. Long absences from home, coupled with the temptations of cities like Bangkok and Hongkong, can prove irresistible to the sexually active sales executive. With low standards of healthcare and the increasing spread of HIV, avoid such attractions at all costs. Do not imagine that this is exclusively a problem of the Third World. Single's nights in First World bars hold just the same risks.

Breaking the law

Ignorance of the law is no defence and never more so than when overseas. Many Muslim nations ban the import of alcohol, so do not try and bring in a bottle of duty-free liquor. However, if offered alcoholic drinks by locals in the privacy of their homes, it is quite acceptable to drink them, but not, under any circumstances, to get drunk. This may be difficult since the drinker may not have had any alcohol for some time and the drinks offered tend to be both large and strong.

In "dry" states, being found drunk is an imprisonable offence and locally made alcohol will often be offered at expatriate parties, so take care. As already mentioned, even a minor car accident can result in the driver spending the night in jail, if he or she is a foreigner.

Photography may seem a harmless occupation, particularly when sight-seeing during some spare time. Do be careful. In the background of some apparently harmless tourist snapshot may be a top secret military installation and the photographer may quickly end up in the local jail on a spying charge. This is a particular risk in the vicinity of airports, some of which are shared with the local air force.

The use of drugs faces a similar prohibition to that found in the UK, but there is frequently a death penalty attached to being found with a significant quantity, or being caught pedalling them. If asked by any individual, or the Company, to carry a package, even of spare parts, always examine the contents and leave the parcel unsealed for customs checks.

The Muslim attitude to women is strict and this also applies to the import of some magazines, or even paperbacks with suggestive illustrations on the front cover. For female staff visiting these countries, appearing in public with bare shoulders or a knee length skirt may be illegal, as may wearing jeans, and some countries do not permit women to drive cars!

Security of information

Whilst espionage, as such, is fairly uncommon in industrial and commercial terms, it is not unknown. Far more common is the unintentional letting slip of information in a hotel bar or on an aeroplane. On the whole, the business community tends to use the same flights and same hotel chains. A competitor may well gain useful information from overhearing a loose conversation and may win the next order as a result.

Discuss sensitive information only in the privacy of a hotel bedroom, or a secluded corner of a public room. In the Third World, in particular, hotel staff may take photocopies of interesting faxes or work being typed in the hotel business centre and sell them to a competitor, or even to the customer.

The use of portable computers, fitted with modems and portable printers can help to minimise this problem, but never completely eliminate it. They also bring an alternative danger of losing the computer especially if there is sensitive material on the hard disc. There was publicity about one RAF officer whose laptop, containing UK plans for the Gulf War, was stolen from his car in outer London.

Foreign languages

Of all the languages of the world, the three most common are English, Spanish, and French. It is worth noting that English and French are spoken in virtually every country, either as a first or a second language and are thus a useful combination. However, usage can vary significantly from place to place.

Classical Arabic, both written and spoken, is understood in every Arab country. However, despite the thought that Chinese and Indian would be widely spoken, because of the size of their populations, both countries suffer from a lack of a single language. For example, Mandarin, or Pitangua as it is called in China, is the official language and its use is being encouraged despite being only one of some six hundred Chinese languages. With the opening up of the former Soviet Union, Russian is rapidly becoming more important. The choice of foreign languages used by a company's staff will depend on the particular markets being tackled.

There is no doubt that sales staff who can speak the local language fluently are a wonderful asset. However, unless they speak the language as their mother tongue, complex letters and contractual documentation should be left to professional translators. With the widespread availability of the fax, it is easy to get written material translated in territory, although there may sometimes be difficulties with commercial security.

One of the problems in getting sales staff to learn a language using tapes, or a language laboratory, is the difficulty of achieving fluency without spending a large amount of time in territory speaking and practising the language. On the other hand, customers much appreciate any knowledge of their language and it helps sales staff to achieve a better understanding of the culture of the country. However, the use of a familiar foreign phrase can lead to a conclusion of fluency, followed by a rapid torrent of the local language and subsequent bewilderment. There is a corollary. The vast majority of foreign customers, even if their English appears fluent, will have some difficulty in comprehension. For this reason it is important to remember a number of factors in talking to them.

1. Speak slowly and clearly. Do not shout.
2. Avoid the use of slang and abbreviations.
3. Try to use the same word for a given meaning, rather than using synonyms to give variety.
4. Check that what has been said has been understood.

The second and third points also apply to the written word. To emphasise the fourth, a speech was being passed through an interpreter at a banquet in Russia. The English speaker said "The spirit is strong but the flesh is weak." The translation was "The vodka is fine but the meat is off!"

When an interpreter is being used, double the time allowed for any presentation or discussion. In many countries, a formal government interpreter will be provided. If at all possible, use a second company interpreter, probably covertly, to check the accuracy of the translations of the first and also to translate any informal conversation as well as to indicate the tone of the discussions. Cultural considerations in a foreign country are critically important. Body language can be very different and it takes quite some time to get use to Indians shaking their heads from side to side as they say "Yes, we definitely will" and mean it!

Reporting back

It is very easy, on a lengthy overseas trip, for sales staff to become slack about reporting information back to the home base. A key rule is never to delay writing the visit report, but to get it done immediately, using a laptop computer, Dictaphone or even handwriting. This is never more true than when a number of customers, or, even worse, a number of countries are being visited in quick succession on a single trip. The meetings soon blur together. A visit report done immediately after each meeting can be a useful reminder of things that otherwise might be forgotten. There is a suitable format in Chapter 5.

The use of fax for less sensitive reports and either a simple commercial code, or even airmail post, for the more sensitive information is recommended. Direct computer links are perhaps the best solution of all. Finally, it is essential for sales executives to ensure that their offices know exactly where they are at all times and how to contact them.

Commercial code

The following example of a commercial code, purporting that the company involved works in the interior design field, rather than its actual line of business, is straightforward to construct. It avoids immediate and obvious decoding, though it is not very secure. It needs some imagination to construct readable sentences, but this quickly comes with practical use, as does rapid coding and decoding.

ITEM	CODE	ITEM	CODE
Country A	*Snowdon*	Embassy	*Shop*
Country B	*Everest*	Head of...	*Cement*
Country C	*Matterhorn*	Head of State	*Mortar*
Country D	*Amazon*	Company A	*Harrods*
Country E	*Thames*	Company B	*Lewis*
Country F	*Seine*	Company C	*Fortnums*
PPP A	*Carpet*	Company D	*Heals*
PPP B	*Chair*	Company E	*Dickens*
PPP C	*Table*	Company F	*B & Q*
PPP D	*Sofa*	Division A	*Gamages*
PPP E	*Cupboard*	Division B	*Selfridges*
PPP F	*Bed*	Division C	*Debenhams*
Customer A	*Apartment*	Division D	*Evans*
Customer B	*Penthouse*	Budget	*Colour*
Customer C	*Villa*	£ K	*Green*
Customer D	*House*	£ M	*Pink*
Customer E	*Premises*	US Dollars	*Yellow*
Customer F	*Skyscraper*	Local currency x K	*Purple*
Customer seniority 1	*Timber*	Local currency x M	*Vermilion*
Customer seniority 2	*Painted*	Commission	*Tint*
Customer seniority 3	*Papered*	5% commission	*Fiesta*
Customer seniority 4	*Sprayed*	10% commission	*Orion*
Customer seniority 5	*Varnished*	15% commission	*Mondeo*
Customer seniority 6	*Lacquered*	20% commission	*Granada*
Local representative	*Store*	25% commission	*Scorpio*

PART 2:

BUSINESS STRATEGY AND MARKETING

Strategic planning & segmentation · Market research · PPP strategy · PPP planning & development · Promotion strategy & public relations

The second part of this book looks at the whole range of marketing issues. It starts with strategic planning including business charters and mission statements, planning for growth and the critical issue of market segmentation with its various associated strategies. The chapter on the principles and practice of market research is followed by two further ones; the first on PPP strategy, including life cycles and barriers to entry, the other dealing with the preparation of PPP plans and the development of new PPPs to meet market needs. Finally, consideration is given to promotion strategy and public relations, covering everything from the preparation of quality literature and attendance at exhibitions to making presentations; important factors in opening markets to PPP offerings.

Chapter 7:

Strategic Planning & Segmentation

The vision of the future · Marketing planning systems · Business charters · Mission statements · Marketing & engineering cultures · Routes to growth · Churn · Market segmentation · Segmentation strategies · Segment strategies · Numbers of segments · Strategies for competitive advantage · Know your competitors · Retaliation

The vision of the future

One of the greatest difficulties facing anyone tasked with developing a strategic plan for a business is to succeed in creating a meaningful vision of the future. The great companies of the present day usually have a chief executive who has dreamed up or created such a vision. Bill Gates of Microsoft is probably the leading example in the USA, with Richard Branson of Virgin and Alan Sugar of Amstrad in the UK. The difficulty is in following such visionaries.

The need is for the ability to create such thoughts and develop them into a meaningful way forward. A chairman often has the role of working out the corporate strategy, and more time for this task than a chief executive. This strategy will define the business, or businesses, into which the Company will channel funds and resources. It should also indicate the markets where the Company will seek sales to achieve its profit and growth objectives. It is quite common to find major consideration being given to financial issues and it is interesting to consider four areas of value achievement. Whether the Company decides that the most important is the achievement of profit, stable growth, cost structure or exposure reduction will depend on risk/return trade offs and where the compromise lies between investment, cost and growth. See figure 41 on page 155.

Marketing planning systems

Probably the biggest single determinant of success in marketing planning systems is good support from the Company's chief executive and top management team. A lack of support can be very demotivating for all those involved in the planning process and is often further excentuated by the lack of a plan for actually undertaking the planning work itself. This is particularly common in "fire fighting," short termist organisational cultures. Lack of management support can result from a number of causes.

A VISION IS ESSENTIAL FOR LONG TERM SUCCESS.

- Inadequate organisational structure
- Lack of skills
- Lack of information
- Lack of resources
- Hostility

Confusion over terms can further worsen these difficulties. Numbers may be used instead of written objectives and strategies. There may be too much detail, inappropriately so when looking far into the future.

In many PPP companies, marketing planning is a once a year ritual, frequently delegated to a planner. Management often fails to use the result as a tool and can make matters worse by separating operational planning from its strategic

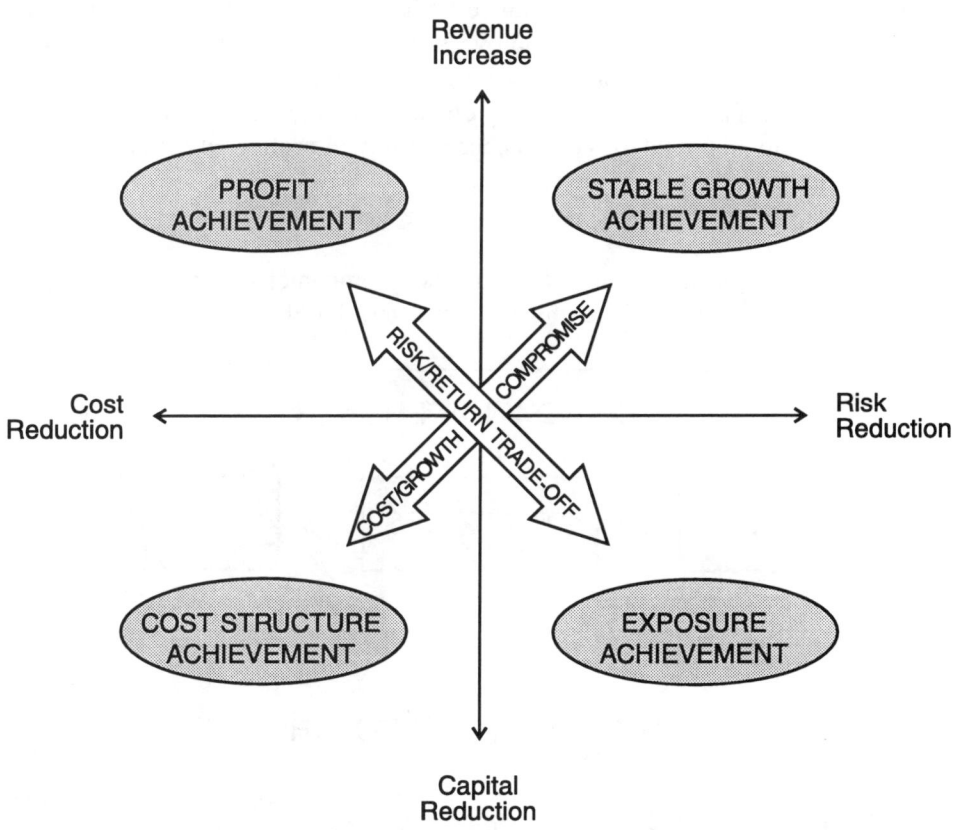

Figure 41. The approach taken by a company will often depend on the relative importance of the key financial issues.

counterpart. This failure to integrate marketing planning into a total corporate system can eventually have catastrophic effects either directly, or indirectly at the hands of competitors with effective and systematically implemented solution.

There are two fundamentally different styles of planning found today.

Top down

Western industrialised nations typically take a top down approach. Goals are defined, then strategies and tactics worked out to meet these goals. The approach works well in a stable environment, but shows its shortcomings in periods of change, such as recession, the collapse of a market, or the introduction of a novel PPP or process by a competitor. In such circumstances, tactics may well end up being based on what have become obsolete strategies.

No facet of the approach is enduring, except financial considerations, reducing commitment. It is difficult for employees at the grass roots to relate their work to its place in the overall achievement of such objectives. The approach also infers a divisionalisation and splitting down of the organisation, with balancing across divisional boundaries only occuring through protracted escalation to the top, rather than directly at the sharp end.

Bottom up

The method typically employed by Japanese companies is quite different. The board of management of a company will determine their strategic intent on a

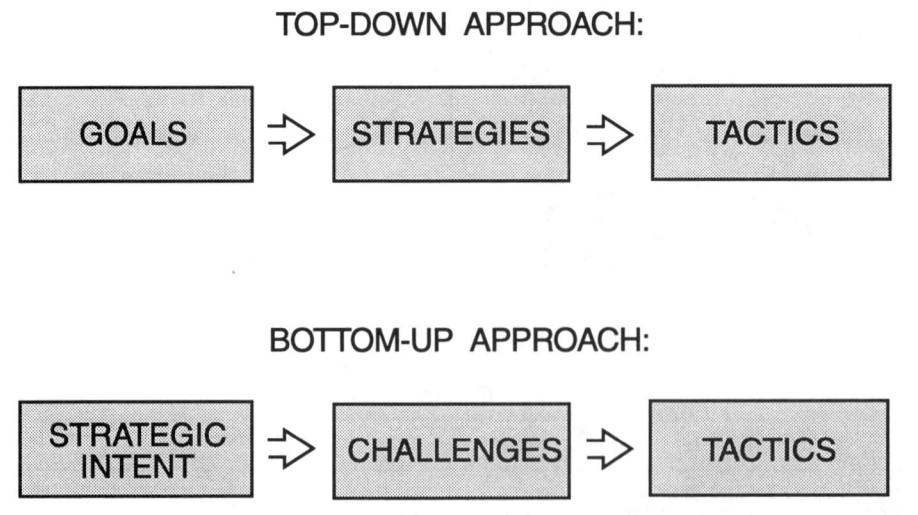

Figure 42. There are fundamental differences in the approaches to planning between the companies of the Western industrial nations and those in the Far East, notably Japan.

long term basis and then get the tactics defined from the bottom up. These top level strategic statements are expected to endure for twenty to twenty-five years, outlasting the current and probably the next generation of top management.

In the absence of such clarity of purpose, the dangers are inconsistent resource allocation and, in all probability, quitting when the going gets tough in the short term, even if the business has good medium and long term prospects.

The outcome from competition between financial short term goal driven businesses and long term strategic intent driven ones repeatedly manifests itself. Regrettably, there is still a lot of loyalty to the view that whatever is best in the short term must also be best in the long term.

The difficulty is in adhering to a long term intent in a rapidly changing world. With continually reducing timescales for each generation of new technology, there is the ever-present probability of a step function breakthrough rendering even complete industries obsolete. The approach does, however, have the great advantage of being more flexible than the Western approach; a significant benefit in today's fast-changing global markets. It also empowers those involved in implementing the tactics and encourages the co-operation of divisions in overcoming shared challenges.

It is possible to learn four interesting lessons from the Japanese

1. Aim and price competitively for a large market share.
2. Changing the rules of competition is more attractive than competing on someone else's playing field.
3. Negate currency fluctuations and inflation by improved efficiency.
4. Systematically build in reliability.

It was Winston Churchill who said, during the Second World War, that it was no use having perfect plans unless they could be modified to take account of the actions of the enemy. He was clearly preaching flexibility in the planning process, that most desirable of attributes, and one often muddled with an inability to maintain the selected aim; the first principle of war.

Business charters

A business charter is a way of defining the boundaries within which a business may operate and, by default, those in which it may not. It is particularly useful in ensuring that different businesses in the same company avoid competing. The charter thus defines both the types of PPPs the business produces or plans to produce, as well as the markets in which it operates or plans to operate. The importance of well-defined charters is often under-estimated and, particularly in multi-divisional corporations, they can avoid duplication and waste.

An example showing the need for good business charters was the development by a single company of a new digital telephone exchange system at the same time as a new mobile trunk communications system. Whilst the implementation of the two systems in hardware terms did need to be different, due to the varying operating environmental conditions, the two system block diagrams were very similar. Unfortunately, the two solutions were developed in complete isolation, without any beneficial cross-fertilisation with consequent financial and resource savings.

There is still a school of thought that believes that in-fighting improves the breed, as if there were not enough external competition! While there may be some merit in this view, unless very carefully policed, which itself may undermine some of the advantages of de-centralisation, it can result in both parties spoiling the market for themselves.

Another problem that can arise is when a single business or division tries to operate in two disparate markets. A good example is the defence company trying to diversify into civil markets. Manufacture of both types of PPPs together in the same facility almost inevitably leads to overpriced civil ones, as they have to help cover the higher cost of the overhead for producing military equipment. Differential overhead rates can resolve this problem, but may be difficult to operate and are only a minute part of the necessary change in culture to suit the different markets.

There are occasions when subcontractors may be tempted to compete with customers. A decision to do so is a strategic one, since it will almost inevitably lead quickly to a loss of the existing customer base, as the buyers concerned recognise the move from supplier to competitor. It is, thus, essential to give careful thought to the relative merits and shortcomings of such a move.

Mission statements

It's a very competitive world and nowhere more so than in the PPP field. A mission statement can be useful for a company's customers, helpful to its employees and its shareholders. It needs to answer the basic questions "What business are we in and where is the Company going?" It should also address the internal standards the Company sets for itself.

It is clear from examination that not many mission statements help in business performance. The reasons for this lack of effectiveness vary.

1. They are seldom used by senior management in day to day decision making processes, so their credibility is rapidly eroded.

2. They are often thought up quickly, without sufficiently considering that they make commitments about the long term management methods of the Company.

3. They are neither publicised, nor are decisions explained in terms of them, to staff who can often make key suggestions and contributions.

4. They take on a life of their own, regardless of customers and market changes, rendering them obsolete and ineffective.

A Mission statement should certainly concentrate on four issues, while it may include a further two if considered appropriate.

1. Define the type of business in which the Company operates.

2. Define the type of core competencies where the Company will focus.

3. Be in terms which all employees can understand and be steered by in their work.

4. Embrace the role of the customer, enhancing their benefits from the relationship.

5. Possibly make statements about the management's attitude to:
   - Employees
   - Environmental issues

It should be clear that the creation of an effective mission statement centrally involves both the marketing function and marketing thinking, as it must reflect the external issues facing the Company.

There is a wide variety of differing forms in which mission statements are produced. A short sharp statement can easily be assimilated, but can also easily be misconstrued. NEC of Japan use "C & C (Communications and Computing) for human potential." Others will say something about the PPPs themselves, something about the Company and something about its employees. A cautionary note is appropriate. Those aiming at maximising the return to employees follow in the path of many such previous organisations that have gone bust. The focus is too internal and the rationale for their business survival disappears from view.

Others pick key issues such as increasing value for money, widening the customer base, PPP solutions and world class standards of quality, time and cost. In essence, the mission statement should be in terms that reflect the nature of the Company's business. If it contains too much detail no-one will remember it and it will not endure changing situations. Moreover and, most importantly, it should come with proper explanation, enabling people within the organisation to see how, through their role, they can contribute towards reaching it.

Many companies include in their mission statements words to the effect that they are going to be the best in their field. This type of statement shows little thought. Which company would wish to be second? A good mission statement makes a commitment that needs taking very seriously. Compiling such a statement normally takes six months of hard work. In practice, it often appears to have been drafted over a weekend executive retreat, whereas it merits much deeper and more extended thought.

Marketing and engineering cultures

By the very nature of PPPs and the great effort involved in their development and production, or alternatively design and construction, it is common to find that companies in the PPP sector are engineering led. This is not a healthy situation and, as was the case with Rolls Royce at the end of the nineteen seventies, led to bankruptcy of arguably the most famous engineering company in the world.

As competitive pressures grow, the need for companies to move to a market-driven culture is clear. The words have been carefully chosen to avoid the idea of PPP companies being market led. Market-driven implies the importance of what the market place needs, but does not ignore the import of the technical solution. A balance needs striking between the two functions with recognition, on any management team or board of directors, of the sales and marketing perspective as a key driver of the Company.

Routes to growth

The famous Ansoff matrix, named after its originator, provides a map of routes to growth for a company. It illustrates growth potential either through PPPs or their markets.

It shows that, staying with existing PPPs in existing markets, the only way to grow is by market penetration; that is increasing market share. This is never an easy proposition. Every single per cent of growth has to come from competitors' share; not usually without retaliation in one form or another. It may lead to the decision to try to push a smaller player into an uneconomic share of the market but, however tempting, rarely leads to the expected extinction. More usually, a small organisation will act in desperation to the detriment of all competitors. Typically, it eventually sells out to a larger concern, for which it represents a growth opportunity. Prepared to invest for growth, the resulting combination is likely to make life a lot more uncomfortable than did either predecessor.

The dominant share that a market will tolerate is very difficult to estimate. In turn, this makes the feasibility of using a penetration strategy highly suspect. The merger of Plessey Telecoms interests with those of GEC in the late eighties showed how the combined market share of some 70% quickly fell to less than 50%, as a result of British Telecom (BT) fears of facing a monopoly supplier. The customer response was to invite Northern Telecom of Canada to bid as a preferred supplier for many equipment ranges.

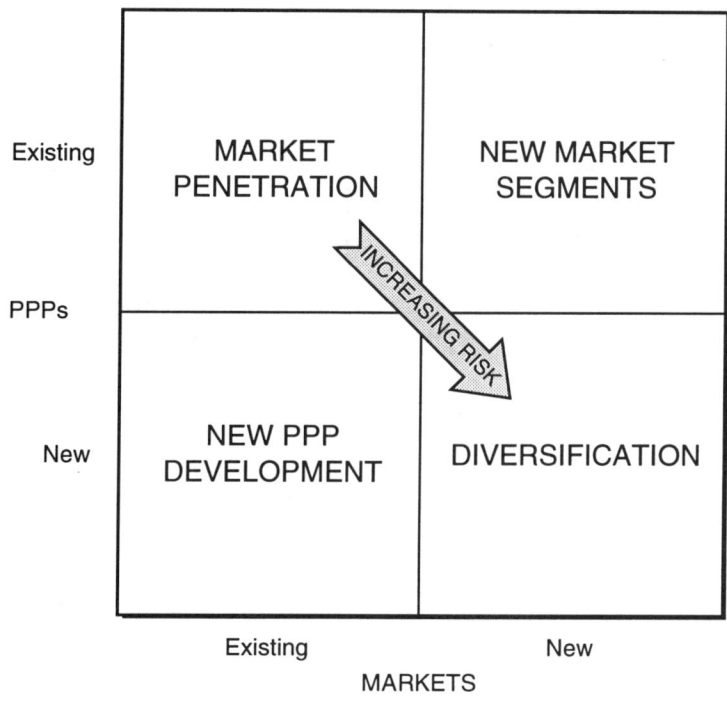

Figure 43. The Ansoff matrix shows four possible routes to growth, with an increasing risk in moving in the direction of diversification.

Entering new markets, or developing new PPPs are the classic ways to grow. The development of new PPPs to be sold in new markets, called diversification, is a route filled with risk and thus not recommended. If tried, then acquisition of a company already operating in the field is probably the preferred approach. However, the experience of a leading UK company's foray away from aerospace into finance and property was not one of the success stories of the 1980's.

When viewed as a map of routes to growth, the basic Ansoff matrix fails to identify two other possibilities and this leads to additions to the original matrix.

Of the other two ways of growing business, the first is to expand the market itself with an entirely novel product. Perhaps first tried by Henry Ford who, when asked who would be able to afford to buy his new mass produced Model T cars replied "The workers themselves." More recent examples include IBM's entry into the personal computer market, producing a powerful tool affordable to many in business and commerce at a fraction of the price of a full business computer installation. The low price of this new product at a stroke multiplied the size of the market many times over.

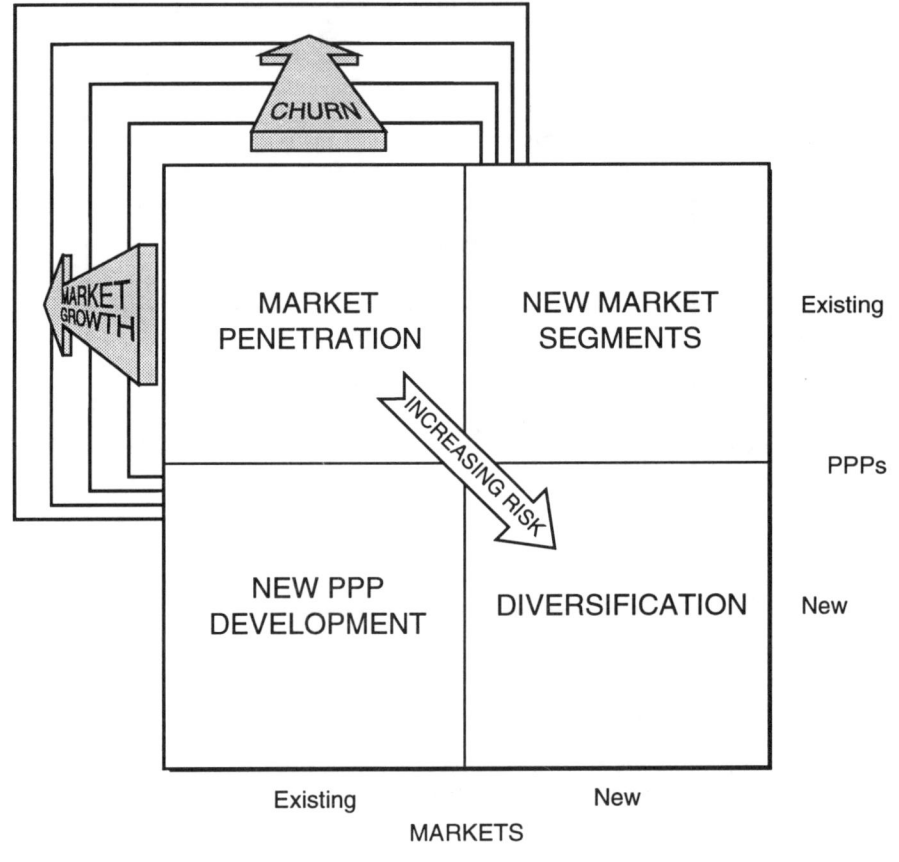

Figure 44. Two other opportunities for growth have been added in the Willson/Ansoff matrix

Churn

The other way of increasing the market size is through Churn. Using the interpretation of the replacement rate of a PPP, churn may utilise the characteristic of built-in obsolescence. This is delicate since, although it will cause customers to re-purchase, if they feel the life of the PPP is too short, they may well repurchase elsewhere. Churn is particularly common in the computer and software markets, with new items produced and launched on the market with alarming regularity. In PPP markets, technology drives churn and rapidly outdates new PPPs with its advances.

New legislation can also produce churn, by effectively making existing equipment obsolete if not illegal. Each time heavy lorry weight limits rise, it becomes uncompetitive for haulage companies to continue operating trucks with lower capacities. New environmental legislation is having a major impact, both on the chemical and water treatment industries. As a result, new PPPs to meet these tough requirements are being demanded from suppliers.

Customer bases can also be churned. The balance between existing and new customers is a good indication of this churn rate and for most healthy PPP suppliers, the churn rate should not be too high. However, with a new and complex PPP, it may only be suitable for the industrialised nations. As time progresses and the PPP moves towards obsolescence, the opportunity to change the customer base to the Third World may prove to be a very necessary move, albeit with mixed attractiveness and profitability.

Market segmentation

Of all the marketing concepts, segmentation is probably the most central and powerful yet, in the PPP environment, it is probably the most contentious both conceptually and in its exploitation.

Segmentation is essentially the grouping of customers that are similar in one way or another. The intention is subsequently to address them with a PPP offering that is the most attractive to them as a group, through channels that most readily access them. The reasons for segmentation are to determine the answers to the three fundamental questions.

- **Who** are the likely customers for a particular type of offering?
- **How** can the Company reach such customers?
- **What** specifically should be offered?

Obviously such issues are just as much of concern to a PPP company as they are in the consumer goods field, which universally accepts segmentation. Foremost amongst the reasons for this lack of acceptance is probably the much smaller number of PPP customers; each of which takes on much more importance to the supplier than is likely with consumer goods customers. This reluctance is understandable, given the lack of infrastructure in PPP markets, such as market research organisations and data, and the difficulty of analysis.

The lack of such analysis restricts companies to operating on a totally reactive basis. Often, they change the very nature of their business as a result of making case by case decisions of which opportunity to follow. This is not surprising since, although consumer and industrial product segmentation models are plentiful, they barely exist in the PPP environment. Indeed, what are suitable dimensions along which to segregate PPP markets?

It is worth reviewing a well-established model of segmentation before returning to the topic of whether segmentation applies to the PPP market and if so, how?

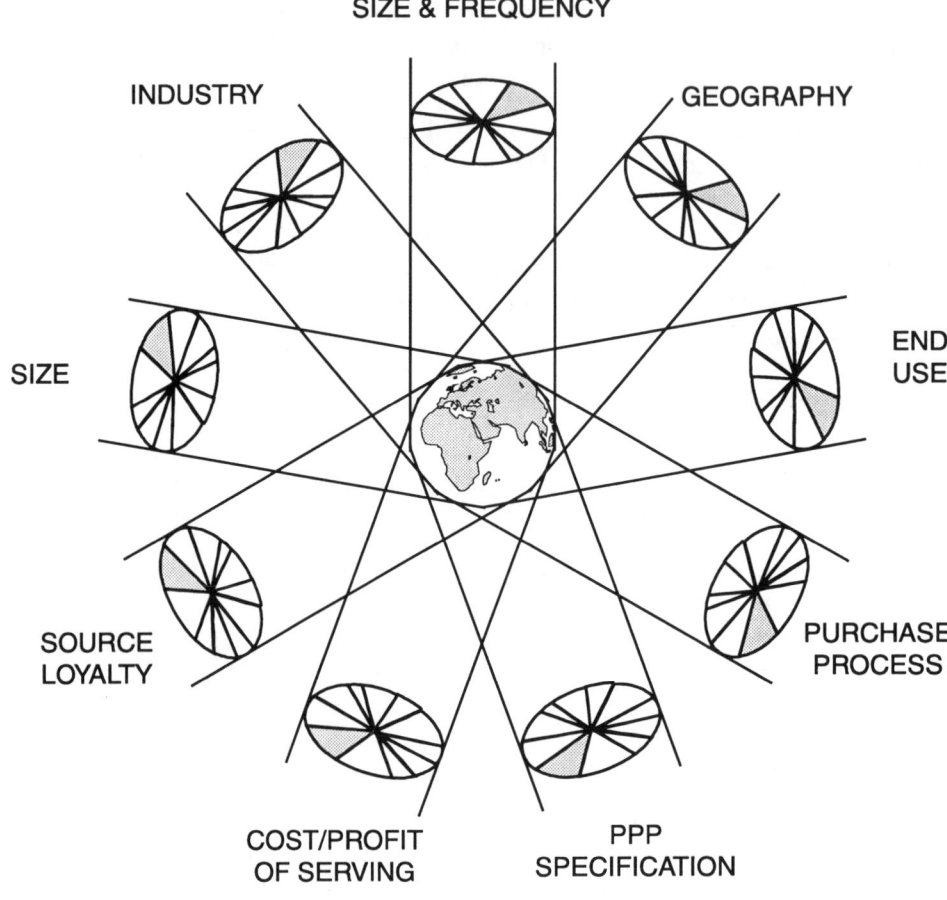

Figure 45. Nine potentially useful ways to segment PPP customers.

Geographical

One of the most commonly found methods of segmentation in the PPP sector, geographical segmentation is straightforward to apply. Possible divisions include by GNP, by region or by national credit rating. The trading model is important and includes things such as the use of hard currency, exchange rate variability, offset and counter-trade requirements. The availability of a support infrastructure is critical in the case of some types of PPP. What is important is that the particular geographical split suits the PPPs of the Company concerned. Chapter 6 gives more information on this particular topic.

PPP specification

Using the airliner as an example, long haul, medium haul, short haul, feeder and executive are obvious divisions. Similarly, segments might divide into jet and turbo-prop, by speed or by passenger load. The choice of divisions should readily be apparent to readers for their own industries and PPPs.

Industry

There is a Standard Industrial Classification system that uses two, four and six digit codes to define different industries. However, this is only a part of the industrial segmentation process. There are vertical markets and horizontal markets, shown in figure 46 overleaf.

Vertical markets define different processes within the same industry, or include all the various companies involved along the manufacturing process of a PPP. Horizontal markets refer to industries that, though different, share a particular process, such as the need for robotic welders.

A PPP distinction might be between end user industries and infrastructure suppliers. Typical of the latter are the public utilities. Fundamentally these organisations are not the end-users of water, gas, electricity or telecommunications, but are major and on occasions the only purchasers of the appropriate PPPs in any particular country. A manufacturer would probably make a similar classification when supplying equipment to a construction company building an airport. It is worth noting how rarely it is possible to achieve a consistent strategy within this structure in PPP markets.

Size

This does not refer to the magnitude of the segment itself, but rather to the size of the members of the customer community and their requirements. In construction, one might segment customer needs into long and short bridges, office blocks over and under 10,000 square metres, motorways, other trunk road, B-roads and urban roads. For manufacturing companies, the sizing would normally be by turnover.

Purchase size and frequency

The customer's perception of purchase size is influenced by whether it is a new type of purchase, the depth of implication for the business and the impact of a wrong decision. In the early nineties, there have been some classic failures in IT systems, of which the London Ambulance Service and Stock Exchange Share Dealing systems were both abandoned amid a blaze of press criticism. The implication of the failure in each case was close to catastrophic.

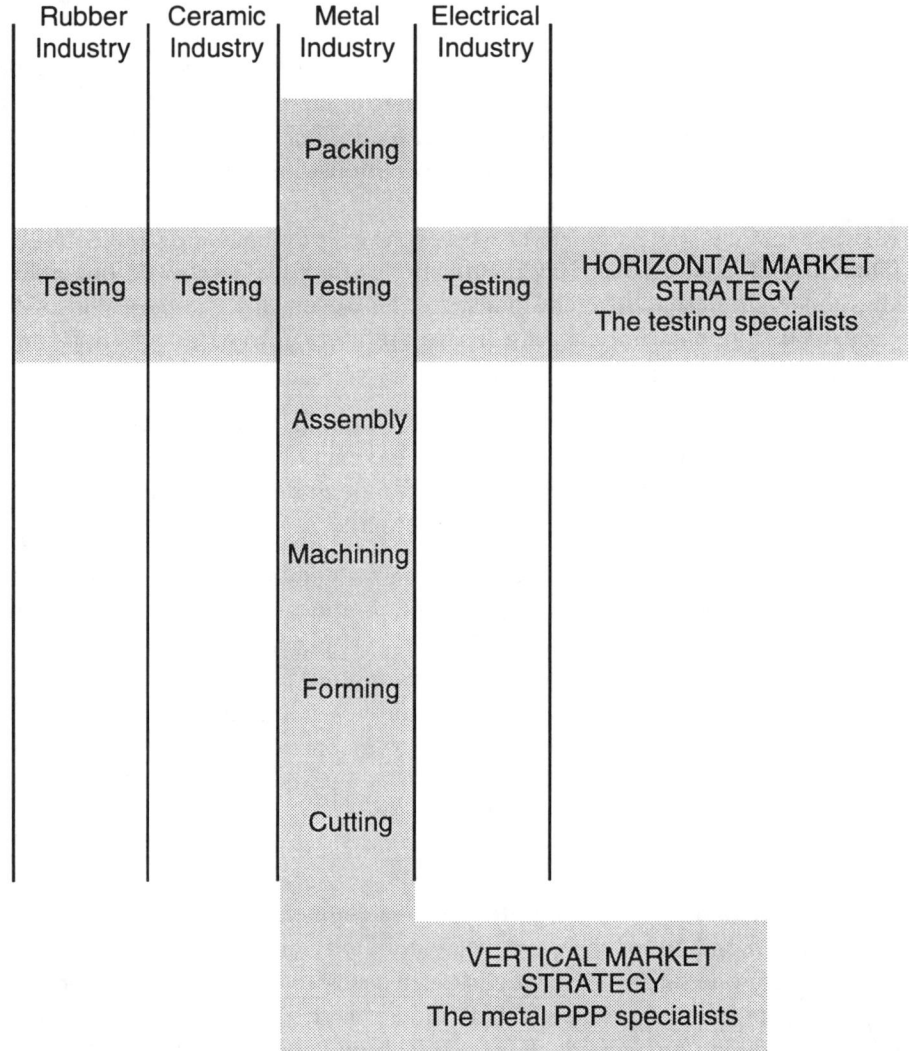

Figure 46. Segmentation and associated market strategies can be by vertical or horizontal sectors.

Frequency of use is also a part of this category and can vary from continuous for a flow process manufacturer to, hopefully, never for a fire warning and suppression system, even though availability might be considered a form of use.

There is also the world of difference, in terms of the buying processes and influencing the customer, between two clients purchasing, for example, a similar size of electricity generating plant. The first might be an electricity utility using the equipment for a local community in case of failure of the grid. The second could be a chemical manufacturer using the plant to supply a chlorine manufacturing facility.

For this latter customer, such a purchasing process might only occur once in twenty-five years. It will require a great deal of customer education in terms of what issues they should consider as well as help in analysing the offerings from alternative suppliers. It is also likely that the final purchase decision will take place at a much higher level within the organisation than might be the case in the electrical supply utility, which will be purchasing such plant on a regular basis.

End use

Where a PPP is supplied to a number of different users, the end use itself may be a suitable differentiator. A "day in the life" analysis can help in grouping customers for whom high value is available from purchase of a particular PPP. The tasks, who fulfil them and implications of delay or failure, are all distinct elements that may help in this segmentation. For example, power stations may be sold for base load, peak lopping, or directly to an industrial manufacturer. All involve different uses and have different failure rate requirements.

The actual application of the PPP may help, whether it will be critical to completion of the mission or merely undertaking a back-up role. Similarly there are different needs when comparing on-line and off-line procurements.

The complete opposite to a turnkey PPP is one where the offering has to interface into existing technology or civil works interfaces. These interface requirements provide a straightforward means of segmentation and thus many companies in the PPP arena put spares and support into a different segment from initial supply of their PPPs.

Purchase process members

Much of the "who" information sought in segmentation needs refining further than just "what organisations?" In particular, who are the key influencers? It is then essential to discover whether they are technically, commercially, operationally, financially or service oriented? Each will need reaching through different channels and with different messages.

Decision making varies enormously from customer to customer and from industry to industry. So do the people and their involvement in the purchase process. Influencers and users can have very varying impacts on the purchase process. Pilots usually have a major involvement in the purchase of new airliners, whilst lorry drivers may have little involvement in the purchase of a new fleet of trucks.

The influence of those outside the direct customer community, such as government policy makers, standards setters and engineering consultants, varies considerably. People's position in an organisation chart is often misleading, since the most common answer to the question "Who makes the purchase decision?" posed to people in institutional organisations, is "Me!"

Source loyalty

There is nothing better than a happy customer making a repeat purchase and single sourcing, or with special purchaser/supplier relationships that are becoming increasingly commonplace. Always remember, however, that source loyalty can be negative as well. This is especially so in terms of a customer's perception of an abused sole source, as a result of poor performance from a PPP or poor support for it.

By profit and cost to serve

Although this method of segmentation runs the risk of looking at company internal concerns rather than customer characteristics, it is important to review

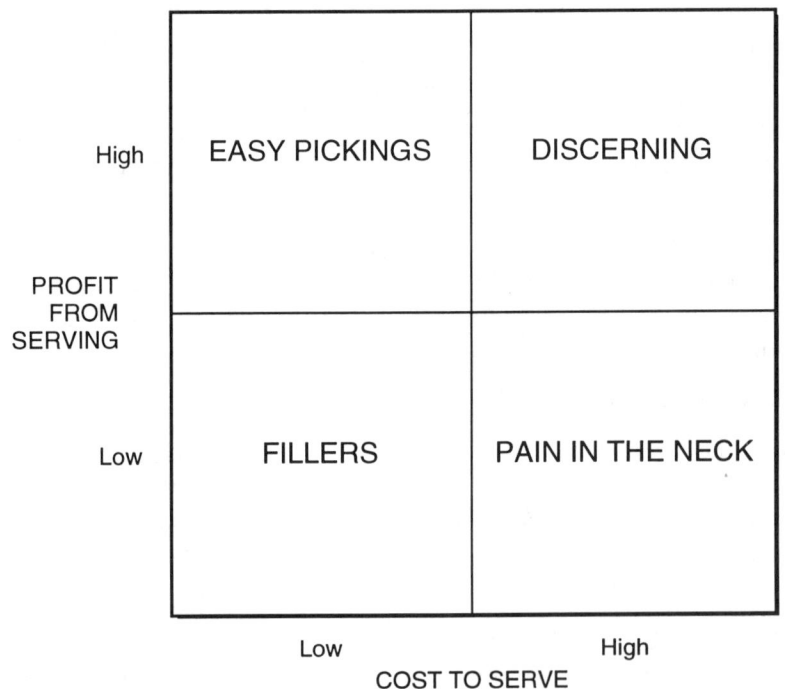

Figure 47. Segmentation by comparing the cost of serving and the profit from serving particular markets.

the complexion of various customer groups. The benefits are better resource allocation and prioritisation. The analysis needs fitting with the Ansoff/Willson matrix when considering routes to growth.

Unfortunately, most cost collection systems do not adequately gather the required cost to serve data. A system is needed which recognises such factors as the production of specials, small quantities, special procedures, the number of visits/meetings and customers changing their minds. A particular danger arises when production departments obtain work to fill gaps in their workload, since these fillers may end up taking priority over more attractive work.

Segmentation strategies

Often, companies in the PPP business unwittingly segment their markets, thus missing the full benefits through not putting sufficient thought into the process. Others prefer to segment on the basis of their own internal requirements; a very introverted approach that does not help to win business.

As an example, in the late eighties, THORN EMI divided its defence business by development and production requirements, with separate radar, electronic warfare, electro-optics and fuzing divisions. It was ideal from an internal point of view but far from helpful to the customers, almost all of whose needs crossed a number of divisions. A similar problem occurred with Siemens, that has a plethora of technology based business units, almost all with their own sales forces. To customers with diverse needs, this is confusing, frustrating and in the end costly to them, especially if such suppliers' divisional bidding policies and contracting terms and conditions differ.

When undertaking market segmentation, it is important to recognise that the segmentation is special to the particular company concerned. There are no universally right answers and anyway, answers will change with time. It is a fallacy to think that for a particular industry, one shared segmentation structure is correct. Segmentation also needs to reflect the disposition of the company concerned.

The nine levels of segmentation given in this book are not the only ones. They do however, indicate the level of current thinking in PPP markets. Having given a definition of market segmentation and proposed a number of possible ways of dividing markets, it is important to decide whether to employ a segmented approach and to what extent to use it.

There is, however, a common danger; the allure that "Everyone has good money." It is the direct parallel of the selling trap "If you don't tender you can't win." Any discussion on segmentation strategy should ignore it. It is, however, still disappointingly widespread and needs redressing with proper marketing analysis.

Segment strategies

A useful method gleaned from military thinking is to consider four possible scenarios; defensive, offensive, flanking and guerrilla. Each of them requires, not surprisingly, a different strategy.

Defensive

The strategy for a market leader is inevitably defensive, the more so as market share increases. There are five key considerations resulting from this strategy.

1. A market dominator can identify the easiest penetration routes, so called "loose bricks", and can block against the entry of new competitors.
2. Segment strategy can reduce the risk of being forced into a low price commodity approach through the penetration of new competitors.
3. It is necessary to keep revisiting the chosen segmentation method to avoid being put at a competitive disadvantage by a canny newcomer choosing a new and powerful segmentation strategy.
4. Segmentation forces a company closer to its customers. Early detection of trends may reduce the risk of erosion by a new and different segmentation.
5. Apply experience gained in specialist areas to strengthen stances in important segments.

Offensive

The classic strategy for the number two in a market is to go on the offensive against the market leader. It is likely to require an enormous expenditure of effort by the number two and can easily result in a bloody nose.

1. Often considered the blunderbuss, rather than the rifle approach, for example by cutting prices across the board.
2. It requires absolute superiority of investment and resources in a particular area to win market share or attempt to drive out the market leader.
3. It is considered a high cost, high risk strategy, which has largely been overtaken by the flanking strategy.

Flanking

This is the modern offensive approach to taking on the market leader and has the great benefit of avoiding a head on clash that can prove so costly. Japanese companies widely use this successful strategy in their overseas markets.

Strategic planning & segmentation

1. Penetrating a new market through a single segment comprises a low risk, limited resource approach. If it fails, the company can pull out with little smear to their reputation.

2. Careful selection of the entry segment can reduce the risk of retaliation from undifferentiated competitors, whether in terms of price, service or responsiveness. For the incumbent, it precipitates the classic forced choice of lose profit on every sale or lose market share.

3. By selecting marginally profitable entry segments, it is possible to force an established player into margin retreat, thus funding further penetration. Page 50 covers margin retreat in more detail.

Guerrilla

A small company or newcomer often has few resources and in such cases, the guerrilla approach is the only feasible one.

1. The opportunistic approach by the small player. Avoids any obvious segmentation and appears unexpectedly with very responsive bids.

2. Nurtures selected customers and builds key relationships.

Numbers of segments

When selecting one of the above four strategies, it is important to think about how many segments to tackle, to consider whether the Company is operating in a single or multiple segments and indeed whether it differentiates itself at all.

Single segment

1. Vulnerable to segment collapse. (The peace dividend effect on military suppliers.)

2. Often used as an entry point by small or newly formed companies.

Broadly targeted

1. Requires a breadth of resources.

2. Expensive, so worthwhile customer benefits must accrue from a specific segment offering.

3. Requires portfolio gains between segments served.

4. New technologies, such as flexible factories, are increasingly making this strategy feasible.

5. Enables growth of market share.

Undifferentiated

1. Danger of erosion by differentiated suppliers.

2. Tendency to degenerate into a cost leadership race.

3. Suits PPPs early in the life cycle, where customer reaction is unknown.

4. Probably appropriate when current position is protected by high barriers to entry.

5. Possibly suitable when short life cycle requires rapid acceptance to recoup investment.

In the first category, a good example is the railway supply industry, whilst a company, such as DEC in the computer industry, uses broadly targeted segments such as government, banking and industry. In the undifferentiated category come the traditional parts of the steel and coal companies of the world. Indeed, many PPP companies end up using an undifferentiated strategy because of the difficulties of segmenting their markets. This is an unsatisfactory situation and increases their vulnerability.

Strategies for competitive advantage

There are four possible strategies, which were first formulated by Kenichi Ohmae, that can each provide competitive advantage. Examining particular examples for each strategy helps to understand them.

Key success factors

Rolls Royce determined, in the period when turboprop airliners were taking over from older piston engined aircraft, that the key success factor was the reliability of these new aero engines. They developed their Dart engine progressively to a previously unheard of 5,000 hours time between overhauls and swept the market world-wide.

Relative superiority

Alcan, making commodity aluminium, needs to have the lowest costs for competitive advantage. The manufacturing process involves heavy consumption of electricity. This led to the decision to locate their factories in areas where they could negotiate extremely attractive electricity rates. A typical example is Canada's state of British Columbia, where hydro-electric power is cheap. The problem with this strategy is its vulnerability to movement of low cost areas. The cheapest electronic assembly areas in the Far East have moved with alarming regularity over the last few decades, from Japan first to Singapore, Taiwan and Korea, more recently to Malaysia and China.

Aggressive initiatives (changing the basis of the competition)

German gearbox manufacturer SEW Eurodrive wanted to expand into North America, a market cornered by local suppliers. These locals sold direct, at low margins, to the original equipment manufacturers, such as conveyer system suppliers. The associated repair business required rapid delivery and was served through extensive distributor networks, which demanded large commissions, again reducing the margins for the manufacturer.

SEW's first approach was to offer distribution agreements that provided low prices and good distributor margins. Gearboxes are subject to failure and SEW's were no exception. What became apparent was the unique facet they had designed into their product, such that all of the many hundreds of configurations could be built up from a minimal, shared kit list, enabling 24 hour supply from local SEW outlets. For gearbox users, this was a key selling point providing a competitive advantage. It took several years for the existing competition to emulate this in their own designs, local outlets and reputation.

Degrees of freedom

The builders of jet aero engines in the post World War 2 era hungrily eyed engine installations for naval warships, but their excessive fuel consumption ruled gas turbines out for normal applications. However, the manufacturers knew that their engines were very light weight and could go to full power immediately after starting; existing marine installations needing lengthy warm up times. They thus succeeded in selling their engines to give warships, with a modest top speed using marine diesels, a short term high speed dash capability by fitting gas turbines in addition to the diesels.

Know your competitors

A strategy cannot be selected in isolation, but needs to reflect what others are doing in the marketplace and be judged by performance against them. A powerful way of keeping abreast of the latest state of the art is through benchmarking. Here, the best in class is used as a goal for internal processes. There are several sources of competitor data and a number of factors about the companies that need to be known and understood. Sources of information require maintaining in competitor files and regularly updating.

Competitor data

- Annual reports
- Capability and PPP brochures
- Videos
- House journals

- Organisation charts
- Tender submissions

Having gathered the data, there are a number of factors that need regular monitoring. A sensible assessment of each major competitor demands a lot of work, but without it, the Company will fight in the dark. Page 187 further explores the topic of competitor information.

Required competitor analysis

- Market share
- PPP prices
- PPP deliveries and distribution channels
- PPP advantages and weaknesses
- Forward load
- Differential inflation and exchange rates

Retaliation

Retaliation is a fairly natural human instinct and its likelyhood in a PPP environment is very dependant on the attitudes and positions of the companies involved. Part of competitor assessment is to work out the expected response from the other players in the marketplace. It is essential to remember that provocative action is much more likely to induce retaliation than reasonable behaviour. The other factor to consider is that retaliation is almost invariably expensive to implement. Thus, the financial disposition and ability of any company considering such action are likely to be significant factors.

The fact that the incumbent is likely to hit back where it hurts most impacts on whether a predatory move is advisable. In fact, a move may push a competitor into desperate action, which could damage the prospects for both parties in years to come. When a particular company wins a key contract and similar ones are unlikely to materialise in the near future, there is a distinct possibility that a competitor will try to buy that company to gain access to the contract. While examination of monopoly considerations may delay this, trying to stop the sale of the company will inevitably prove expensive and may hamper the acquisition of new business in the intervening period.

Any response to retaliation should only follow careful analysis of the importance to the Company of the attacked area. As has been seen above, a particular segment may be more or less important to the long term future of the Company and also to its short term profitability. Thus, the response to any retaliation needs careful examination and a full understanding of the costs.

Chapter 8:

Market Research

Approaches to PPP market research · Market size · Estimating available market size · Who & what to ask · Gathering data · Desk research · DTI Statistics & Market Intelligence Library · Results

Approaches to PPP market research

Consumer market research is well established but almost exclusively focuses on individual or family purchase decisions. PPP procurement, on the other hand, is essentially an institutional process. Thus consumer goods market research organisations struggle when it comes to institutional procurement for a number of reasons.

1. The difficulty of identifying the appropriate target people and achieving an in depth dialogue with them.

2. Target audience size is mostly too small for statistical analysis, on which the results of much work is based.

3. The very small number of PPP suppliers will inevitably raise questions about who is asking.

4. Meaningful discussions with key people in the purchase process requires considerable depth of knowledge and understanding. It is unrealistic to expect a consumer goods research organisation to be able to glean this from a briefing.

Whether it is possible to overcome these drawbacks, and establish specialist PPP research agencies, is open to conjecture. The commoditisation of research in the consumer goods area may encourage the existing agencies to migrate in such a direction.

As a result, almost all PPP market research is conducted on a "do it yourself" basis. There are two methods in general use; individual opinion gathering and institutional customer data gathering. The first is preferable for gathering reaction to a new PPP design, but suffers from the intrinsic dangers of a customer's personal preference, bias, perspective or ulterior motive. In addition, it is necessary to gain the viewpoint from each of the key areas or functions within the institutional purchase process. Unfortunately, the wider the audience, the greater the danger of information about a new design, around which enquiries revolve, being transmitted to competitors either to ensure dual sourcing, or to retain an existing preferred supplier relationship if not with the questioner's company.

Institutional customer data gathering, on the other hand, generally focuses on library searches. It uses approaches such as gauging potential markets by looking at the size and growth rate of associated PPPs. For example the market size for pay phones can be estimated as a percentage of the number of fixed telephone lines. It may also involve talking to bodies such as industry associations and user groups.

PPP market research depends on probing sources of customer value and then measuring the number of such opportunities where the value/price ratio will prove to be attractive to the customer. The analysis may also need to take any switching costs into account. Without such depth, the findings are likely to fall into the "motherhood and applepie" category. These are findings that no one will disagree with but are unlikely to give useful insights. Worse, they are unlikely to be sufficiently resilient to support the significant investment of the time and funds normally required to replace or update PPP offerings.

As already mentioned, in the PPP arena the business is almost invariably very specialised, the sum total of units sold often small and few customers available. Thus, the use of a specialist market research company may be inappropriate. Take the example of market research for a new space shuttle. Probably, only the company proposing to supply the new shuttle can undertake the research.

- Number of customers: 3 (USA, Europe and Russian space agencies)
- Number of people in purchase process: Many
- Total market: About six units
- Number of existing suppliers: 2

Market research fundamentally addresses three questions:

1. What needs to be known?
2. What is the time scale for finding the answers?
3. What is the audience size and how can it be reached?

Market size

Clearly, growing a market that has become saturated may be a fruitless task, but is it possible to tell if a market has reached such a condition? A model is necessary to reflect the richness of the situation. It is obvious that there are several restrictions to increasing the volume of sales by a particular supplier in a saturated market. Focusing on overcoming the applicable limits is a much more useful approach.

There are a number of different way of looking at the size of a market.

1. The **total market** encompasses the total volume of PPPs required, accepting the limits of technology within the time frame of the PPP life, but without geographical constraints.

2. The **available market** is the total of all the individual segments of the market served by different applications of contemporary technology, limited by export restrictions and other constraints of trade.

3. The **accessible market** is the lesser part of the available market due to restrictions of company policy and resources, suitability of offerings and distribution networks.

4. The **actual market** is the number of sales made by a company into the market, as a result of such factors as capacity constraints and uncompetitiveness.

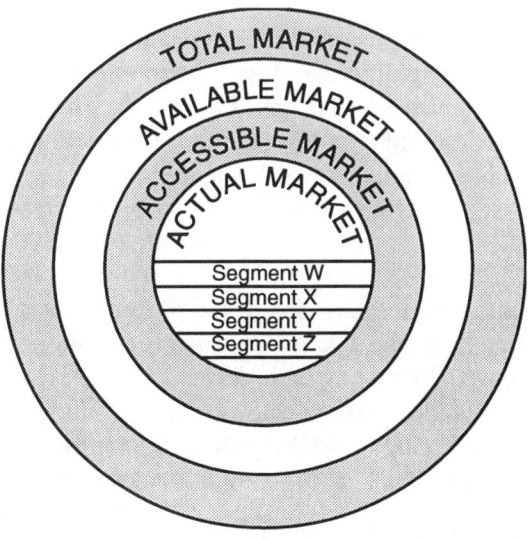

Figure 48. It is possible to define markets in a number of different ways.

Estimating available market size

Determining the size of the market is critical to deciding the scale of approach to an opportunity. Underestimating the available market size may negate the justification of funding entry into an important market and enable the larger scale entry of a "second to market" player. Overestimating causes over-capacity leading to increased costs and elevated prices that in turn reduce demand. There are a number of ways of approaching the problems of assessing available market size.

Volume of existing PPP sales

Unfortunately, divergence between the current and new PPP attributes and benefits will lead to error, particularly if the PPP is from the next technology/demand generation; a topic covered on page 197. Cellular phone volume projected for radio-telephone sales proved wrong, being underestimated by a factor of over 100. The error may be in the opposite direction if attention has not been paid to issues such as switching costs and backward compatibility with existing infrastructure.

Size of the target market segment

An effective segmentation analysis, as suggested in Chapter 7, will identify groups of potential customers for the offering in question. Enumerating these will depend on the specifics of the offering, in particular the value to price ratio and the target price levels.

Related segment sizes

In any particular market segment, there are usually closely related PPP areas and this relationship is useful in deriving the size of one segment if the size of the other has been established. It is possible to judge the potential for sales of sulphur dioxide (SO_2) scrubbers from the number of coal fired power stations. Similarly, the number of industrial solvent cleaning baths and paint spaying booths is a potential guide to the market size for solvent recovery systems.

Economic

Lower prices usually lead to increased demand. Economists call this elasticity of demand. In the era of the £2,000 personal computer, Amstrad chose to increase the market size by pricing their new PC at £499. However, to make the same turnover, they would have to achieve four times the volume of sales and, without making cost savings through value engineering and learning curve benefits, perhaps twenty times more to attain the same profit levels.

Previous PPP replacement rate (Churn)

Part of the available market consists of customers replacing existing equipment that has failed or is thought obsolete. The trend of changing PABX private telephone exchanges every seven years, down from thirteen years previously, has had the effect of increasing the available market. Again, there is the impact of switching costs to consider.

Who and what to ask

It is not easy to decide whom to target and it is the first issue that needs addressing. Individuals are rarely the answer in PPP market research and they are hard to identify. Institutional organisations can be difficult to penetrate and their structures obscure. This is why, in the PPP arena, such questioning usually falls to the sales executives. Even having ascertained who is accessible, it is necessary to decide if they can be probed for an opinion. Choosing a particular market segment can help to focus in on a particular group of customers.

The questions to be asked require framing with great care; there being two types of question, open and closed. A meaningful "Yes" or "No" can answer a closed question. A sliding scale (four graduations is usual) is also feasible; four yielding a forced choice. Open questions provide more information but are harder to answer and collate. The use of veiled questions, such as "People would say that…" is one way of couching awkward questions yet still obtaining the sought opinion. Similarly, questions often appear a second time, but inverted, to check for validity.

Having addressed rather more than half the questions to the subject of the research, the remainder of the questions are usually about the respondent. Without such information, it may be impossible to know whether the opinion is from the target audience and what cross-correlations exists. The feasible length of a survey questionnaire will be very dependant on the method of delivery; whether through the mail or part of a formal interview.

The strong sense of vested interest, commonly found in PPP customers, allows the use of longer questionnaires, but at all costs avoid the long or difficult to answer documents. The risk of the marketeers personal opinions also finding their way into the survey results is a perpetual danger that requires careful attention. A particular problem that faces the market researcher working in overseas markets is the cultural issue. Apart from the obvious language factor, phraseology and terminology may differ. Many cultures use "Yes" to mean "I hear you."

Most unsatisfactory research results from a poor brief to the researchers. Expect to spend a large proportion of time on getting the brief right. A traditional approach is to try the research on a small pilot audience and then further refine the brief before continuing with the full survey.

Gathering data

There are three basic ways of undertaking market surveys. These are the guided interview, by mail and, least applicable in the PPP market, the telephone interview.

The direct interview is suitable where the total size of the audience is small and thus requires a high percentage response rate to gather representative opinions. Problems may arise with a geographically widely distributed audience. The method is expensive and must not be used too often.

Surveys sent out by mail generally yield a low response, typically as low as 10% in the PPP market. They are vulnerable to bias arising from whether the sample represents the opinions of the total audience. The use of incentives is uncommon in the PPP market and can incur mischievous responses in order to gain the reward. Telephone interviews are susceptible to the "Go away" response. This is becoming more of a problem because telephone selling is tainting an otherwise effective channel, particularly with an increasing amount of consumer selling taking place under the guise of market research.

Desk research

The desire to undertake market research internally is generally true of companies in the PPP business, where there may be a reluctance to use an outside agency, regardless of the expertise and anonymity they offer. Desk research is one area where there is a stronger case for in house effort since this should, in any case, be an ongoing endeavour. There is an increasingly wide range of sources of useful information shown in figure 49 opposite.

DTI Statistics and Market Intelligence Library

The Statistics and Market Intelligence library, housed in the Department of Trade and Industry's London headquarters, is available for public use by exporters and potential exporters. It contains collections of statistics, as well as UK and foreign directories and development plans. Its services divide into six parts.

1. Foreign statistics

Published statistics for all foreign countries including trade imports and exports, production, prices, employment and transport.

2. UK statistics

Statistical publications relevant to exporters covering trade, industrial production and general economic indicators.

3. Market research

Some less expensive commercially produced market surveys are available to supplement official statistics.

4. Directories

Foreign trade directories, telephone directories for most countries and specialised industry sector directories.

SOURCE	APPLICATION
LIBRARIES	An easily overlooked source, which, in the case of business, university or large city libraries can be well-informed and offer useful assistance.
ON-LINE DATABASES	Library staff experienced with the search process can save on the hourly cost and connection charges (£60 per hour in 1994).
CD-ROM DIRECTORIES	These are becoming increasingly available at business libraries, are low-priced, generally fairly up to date, and quickly and cheaply accessed. It looks as if they will supersede on-line services, not least because there are no connection charges.
SPECIALIST REPORTS	Some companies such as Frost and Sullivan produce reports on specialist subjects, sometimes even by region; for example, 'The market for security systems in Europe over the next five years.'
ULRICH'S, WILLINGS	These publications list international journals and their publishers. They are a short-cut to circulation lists for use as mailing lists although the Data Protection Act limits their sale. Audited circulation analyses are available as a check to audience relevance and as a guide to the number of readers in the industry in question.
NEWSPAPER CLIPPINGS	These are available from clipping services as directories or as sponsored searches and can be used in the same ways as on-line databases. With the texts of several mainstream newpapers now available on CD-ROM, this specialist area must be considered under threat.
GOVERNMENT BUREAUX	Always out of date but a mine of useful information, cross-referenced information is available from the Central Statistics Office, the US Bureau of Census and the publications of HMSO as well as many trade associations. Import statistics can illuminate market shares held by overseas competitors, though these may be disguised under the heading of spare parts.
COMPLAINTS	After sales support and service functions, which also deal with complaints, should be able to provide valuable information about current purchasers' opinions.

Figure 49. There are numerous different sources of written and computer compatible data, which can yield useful information to PPP researchers.

5. Development plans

These plans provide the earliest indication of export potential and provide a useful indication of the current and predicted economic situation.

6. Bibliographical abstracts and indexing services.

Results

When, at last, the results of the survey are finally to hand, three things need watching.

Cross-correlation

Of the correspondents who claimed to be...and...75% said this. The use of computer packages, such as SPSS, can find such cross-correlation's. Without them, the limit of research findings is the first level number of "Yes" and "No" responses.

Tolerance limits

Most research is presented to a misleading number of significant figures. Bought in research, in particular, suffers from wide tolerances and dubious credibility. The traditional expectations are plus or minus fifty per cent for desk research. Consequently, a common practice is to find two different sources of information to allow corroboration, although it is notoriously difficult at times to find genuinely independent sources.

Bias

Bias is the bane of all researchers' lives, since it is incredibly difficult to isolate and remove. It arrives at every level.

- In selecting the audience
- In responses only from people who have the time
- In people saying what they think the answer should be
- In go-away responses
- In mischievous answers
- Through interpreter bias
- Through self-fulfilling prophesies

Finally, thought needs giving to the integration of the resultant data into the marketing IT system.

Chapter 9:

PPP Strategy

Strategic issues · PPP issues · Keeping factories full · Positioning analysis · Perceptual mapping · Competitive analysis · Competitor changes over time · How companies compete in markets · Life cycles · The four phases of a life cycle · Market growth & market share · Mid life updates · Market life cycles · Barriers to entry · Switching costs · Barriers to new entrants · Relationships between value, price & cost · Cost & differentiation strategies · Customer constraints

Strategic issues

PPPs are not bought for what they are but for what they do for the customers. These, often hidden, justifications for purchase are referred to as benefits. Strictly to be a benefit, the customer must express a need, say for revenue generation. If the need is unexpressed, then it is only an advantage. Other aspects and characteristics of PPPs are features. These three facets, benefits, advantages and features are, in descending order of importance, able to influence a purchase to a greater or lesser extent. An effective PPP strategy will allow the use of examples of each type, readily understandable to the influencers of the purchase decision.

Reviewing all the aspects of a PPP offering raises many more issues than might normally be considered. Attending to any shortfall is a route to increased competitiveness. First, those aspects that are features need distinguishing from those which enable customers to reap value. The latter obviously need more prominence, based on their superior ability to influence customer purchase decisions. Second, those elements that are intrinsic to the PPP and add value, or more usually worth, require isolation through the so called PPP augmentation concept described on the next page. Thirdly, aspects of the total package need consideration.

One aspect of PPP strategy is bundling. This refers to the associated elements of the offering supplied within the basic price of a PPP. It is mostly found in new PPPs, particularly where such additions are intangible. Bundling can act as a useful differentiator and may be necessary for those aspects that are difficult to price out separately.

One of the great benefits of bundling is its appeal to different players in the purchase process, providing more features for users while avoiding any apparent increase in the price seen by accountants. Bundling is the norm in some areas and customers grow accustomed to purchasing such bundles.

As an example, it is not uncommon with equipment to include spares, test equipment, installation and commissioning within the basic price. Bundling is also becoming increasingly common in offerings of company and office telecommunications systems; particularly since the installed base is still rapidly growing. These offerings might comprise central office telecommunications equipment, pre-loaded with software containing a certain number of features, together with some ancillary items of hardware.

Once the growth rate in the market slows, the pressures will mount towards unbundling, in order to sustain a steady income stream for at least some parts of the bundle. Managing such a transition can be quite a challenge where customers have grown accustomed to purchasing the bundle. Their accountants may, for example, need to adopt new practices to handle usage based software pricing in contrast to outright purchase.

The augmented PPP concept refers to the characteristic of customers to view an offering in its entirety, rather than just the physical PPP itself. They would consider status implications and possible association with a well-respected supplier. In this way, the company name, country of origin and reputation are all significant aspects. Typical of this augmented concept are the views of companies in getting prestigious headquarters designed by a famous architect. Increasingly, it is the intangible aspects of an offering that are dominant. Field service, software and long-term supportability are typical examples. Indeed, the supply of PPPs has, in this sense, many of the attributes of the provision of services.

PPPs require tailoring to the characteristics of their target market, in terms of customer behaviour and usage. Such purchasers may have sophisticated or naive operators and maintainers, already have established systems or be starting from scratch, and located in regions where ease of service is likely to be critical, for example when exporting to Russia.

Several important issues surround the structure of a complete line of PPPs. Traditionally, there is one accepted entry point for first time customers in the market. A particular price point may constrain the beginner and support the use of cross-subsidisation between PPPs in the range to attract initial purchasers. Thereafter, an easy upgrade path, inertia and switching costs all help to retain customers. Ranges of offerings also often include complementary PPPs. These can provide easy profit contribution and suit less sophisticated buyers who prefer a turnkey supplier. Perhaps more importantly, they can slow the ingress of competitors.

PPP issues

When preparing a PPP implementation plan, it is very easy to concentrate on the PPP itself and forget a whole range of important ancillary factors, not to mention the likely need for alternative bids and optional additions. During the development phase, the way of implementing the operator/machine interfaces can be of paramount importance; the design of the safety systems in a control centre for a nuclear power station being a classic example. System modelling can be equally important for complex PPPs and can significantly reduce problems in the field, as hydraulic modelling in the water management field has shown.

Moving to the manufacturing stage, computer aided design and manufacturing processes need careful consideration as does prime responsibility over major subcontractors. The use of the same protocols and standards by both prime and subcontractors can give significant market advantage, whether the Company is operating in a prime or sub role. Logistic support is a critical area. Both time and effort will need allocating to cover the preparation of handbooks, spares and test equipment lists, setting up training courses and a field support service, as well as looking at the range of applications and installation configurations.

Finally, the ability to bring sources of finance for the potential customer community can make all the difference between winning business and a contract never being placed. There are opportunities to fund the development of new PPP's from sources other the Company and its customers. Government and United Nations grants can be obtained and the availability of venture capital from the money markets also needs careful consideration. See also page 250.

Keeping factories full

A key driver for many companies in the manufacturing field is the need to keep the workload in their factories at an economic level. It is, therefore important to consider what steps need taking to achieve this essential aim.

- Plan for a full factory, realistically sized and equipped
- Make the sales department responsible for achieving orders
- Ensure sufficient back up prospects as a fall back
- Sustain a realistic investment in sales resources
- Maintain an ongoing review of long term trends

The possibility of biasing make or buy decisions more in favour of internal manufacture to help maintain factory utilisation also requires consideration. A further issue arises when licensing out designs. There is a danger of the licencee improving the design and, working from a lower cost base, competing aggressively. The pressures of keeping factories full are leading many companies, facing rapidly shrinking markets, to consider diversification. Page 161 gives a warning against making such a move across the Ansoff matrix.

Positioning analysis

Misleadingly, there are three distinct marketing concepts each masquerading under the same title of positioning.
- Company positioning
- Positioning an offering
- Positioning as customer perception

Company positioning results from strategic choices, such as whether to be a specialist or volume producer, first to market or "me too", broadly targeted or differentiated, regional or international, core or peripheral to the business. These policies often come from addressing the classic question "What business are we in and is it an effective one?" The Company's mission statement should give the answer. Akin to a statement of strategic intent, it should contain items that are meaningful throughout the organisation and reflect its core competencies. There is more information on mission statements on page 158.

Positioning a PPP is about assembling an offering, coherently and cost effectively, to address the wants, needs and structures of particular target markets. It requires a clear understanding of the type of customer purchases and the rules and outlooks of each of the parties involved in the purchase process.

Positioning as a perception is how customers rate an offering in relation to other propositions, in ways that influence their purchase decisions. In contrast with the first two definitions, this is a result, rather than a choice. Consequently, its determination involves difficult issues arising from the underlying area of market research. Not the least of these problems are bias and interpretation.

Perceptual mapping

Consumer marketing widely and effectively uses positioning as customer perception. Its adoption in the PPP field is dramatically less common. The reasons for this probably include reduced numbers of potential purchasers and complexity of the customer's purchase process as well as lack of market research expertise and infrastructure. The perceptual map is the usual manifestation of such a positioning analysis and is a plot of the results from large scale market research.

It is still worth considering the customers' perception of a PPP and the example of aircraft makes this easy to understand. Comparing the prestige of an aeroplane against its flexibility, whether single or multi function, gives a useful insight into positioning for PPPs. Concorde is a high prestige, single function aeroplane, whilst

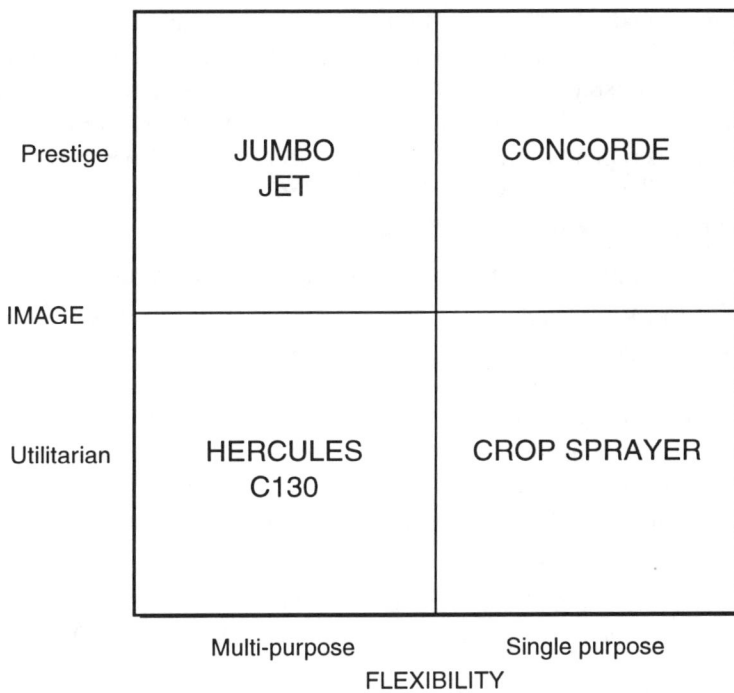

Figure 50. The positioning of different types of transport aircraft is an easy concept to grasp in this well-understood field.

a crop spraying aircraft is utilitarian but dedicated to a single function. These examples contrast with the jumbo jet, which combines prestige with flexibility since it may carry passengers, freight or a mixture of both. Finally, the C130 Hercules air force workhorse provides similar flexibility but at a utilitarian level. Interestingly, the various members of selection committees may perceive the same PPP in different quadrants of the chart, posing quite a challenge for the selling team.

Competitive analysis

Competitive analysis should be an ongoing process. Such analysis relies on competitor information, which must be gathered and continuously available across the organisation in the form, for example, of files on each of the competitors and free-form data-bases. Such information should also include the results of lost tender debriefs by customers and recent recruit debriefs. Competitor analysis involves examining a competitor's positioning in each of the interpretations of that term. What is the position of each competitive company?

Looking again at an aircraft analogy, is the company making and selling relatively small aeroplanes for the commuter airlines or fulfilling most of the major airlines' needs for wide bodied airliners. Alternatively, are manufacturers specialising in the business jet sector or, as was the case with British Aerospace and Aerospatiale, developing a supersonic transport? Such an analysis should also consider their resources, both currently to hand and readily accessible. Regrettably, the same failure to embrace positioning analysis also occurs with competitive analysis in the PPP field. The results extend from a reduced bid success rate to failure to maintain competitive advantage and core competencies.

In essence several items of information should be sought about each competitor.
- Range of PPPs offered
- Scope of responsibility accepted with PPP offerings
- Service arrangements
- Pricing strategy and tactics
- Promotion push and pull
- Distribution channels used
- Political influence; how used and where powerful?

Market research along key dimensions is the best way of determining customer perception of competitors, by undertaking customer satisfaction surveys, interacting with customers and in some cases by looking at press feedback.

Competitor changes over time
- What business are they in?
- What is their segment strategy?
- What is their stance in terms of vertical and horizontal markets?
- How do they create competitive advantage?
- What are their core competencies?
- What is their strategic intent?

The analysis should incorporate the manner in which the companies compete. For example, are they opportunistic, short or long term, co-existing or cut throat? These variations often occur because of differences in the strategic importance of a particular market to the competitors. Such diversity might arise through the market being an avenue to growth or a target for reference customers/installations. Do not imagine that trying to eliminate a competitor is always desirable. This sentiment can often apply when a competitor is experiencing a difficult period. As has been mentioned, the dangers are that the competitor will start to act desperately, or may even be taken over by another company, presenting an even worse threat.

A matrix, comparing the size of the competitor with the number of PPPs/market segments in which they are involved, is useful in assessing competing companies. In figure 51, most new companies start in the bottom left hand corner and eventually end back there through decline until they finally disappear. Some small companies prefer to stay there, and may be recognised and respected for what they are.

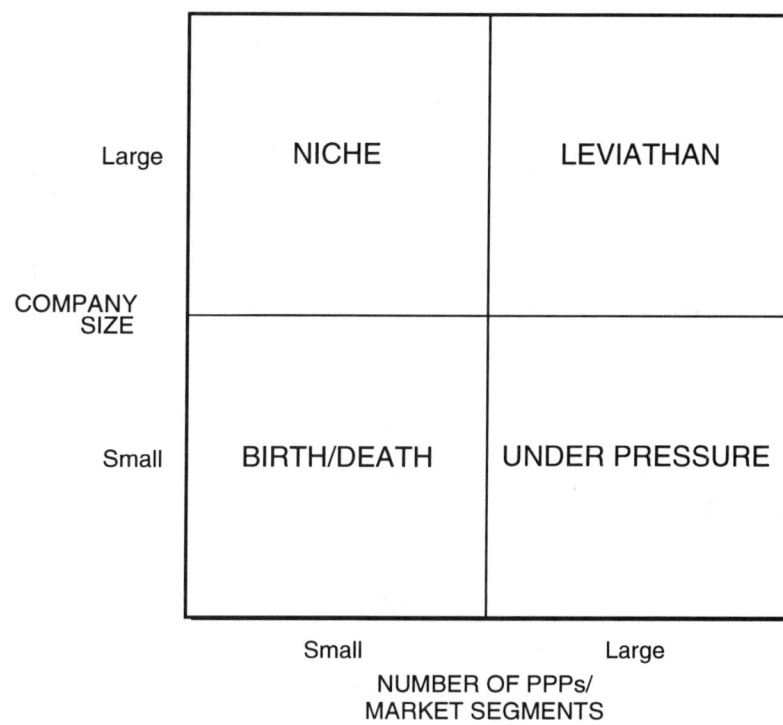

Figure 51. Comparative assessment of competitors and their direction of movement with time is a useful and worthwhile exercise.

Success as a niche supplier or leviathan is common. It is surprising how many companies with too large a portfolio for their size end up under pressure and in trouble, moving rapidly to a death position.

One way of assessing the relative competitiveness of individual PPPs against competitors' offerings is by plotting their position on a price/performance graph and noting their relative direction of movement. This should be an ongoing process as both the Company's and competitors' PPPs are updated and eventually become obsolete, with new PPPs then being launched. This is shown overleaf in figure 52.

Benchmarking

Competitor analysis often has parallels with benchmarking. This latter involves comparing the performance of a company, in certain key areas, with the performance of the relevant best in class performers. It shows up key and critical weaknesses in actual rather than in absolute terms and is essential to the successful management of all companies in the PPP business.

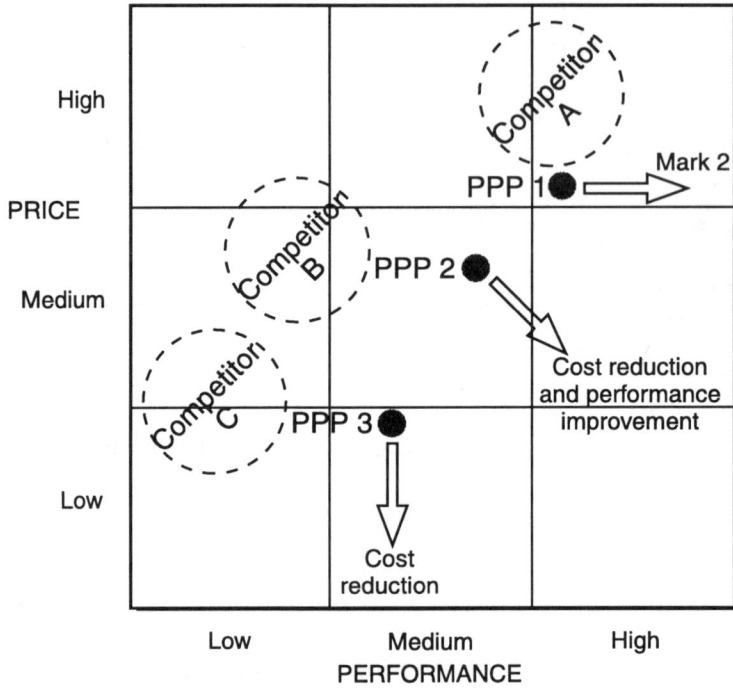

Figure 52. Compare individual PPP attractiveness with other PPPs available in the marketplace.

An example is that of Ford's 25% equity share in Mazda that enabled them to take a view of why their own manufacturing costs were out of line. Mazda used electronic funds transfer and bar coding of goods inwards from suppliers to do away with the 1.5% cost of invoicing; an approach which must consider any VAT requirements. Although there were many other aspects of Ford's equity purchase, such as outsourcing, it does demonstrate the importance and the difficulty of gaining such information.

Use of Strawmen

Over and above this strategic outlook, a view is needed of how potential competitors are likely to bid on specific tenders. At such times, the construction of a so called Strawman can provide rewards beyond the effort invested. Page 71 details this method. Its use involves second guessing the approach taken by any particular competitor and undermining the strengths anticipated as being the basis of their offer. The opposition's likely costs and the technologies expected to form the basis of their offer are also key aspects. While avoiding the pitfalls of openly criticising the opposition, it re-inforces the Company's position by undermining the supporting arguments made in the expected competitive offering. Producing good Strawmen relies on well documented competitor files.

Fortunately, such a technique is fail-safe. If the Strawman was incorrect, then such counters appear merely as supporting rationale for the approach taken. It needs high quality, dedicated staff, familiar with the competition, to produce an effective Strawman. It will require assessment of the technical, financial and commercial offerings of the competitor as well as presentation of the most likely scenario in the Strawman. The Strawman's final impact on the proposal for a particular bid must be decided, however, by the bid team.

How companies compete in markets

Most companies in the PPP business will look at competing from two points of view. First, they will examine other companies competing in the market and analyse their skills and attitudes. This analysis then leads to a further set of questions about the ways companies compete in a particular marketplace.

The result of such analysis is particularly important for a company thinking of moving into a new market place, where the old adage "The grass is always greener on the other side of the fence" can often prove to be almost irresistible.

COMPETITOR ANALYSIS	COMPETITIVE ANALYSIS
What are their capabilities?	What are the relative sizes and numbers of competitors?
What resources do they have?	Do they act in allegiance or in a cut throat manner?
What are their key markets and PPPs (life cycle audit)	Are customers dealt with direct, through distributors or both?
What was their historic response to predatorial newcomers?	What is the basis of competition? Is it price, differentiation or application?
Are they a short or long term player?	What is the level and type of predominant media usage?
What is their corporate ethos? Is it strategically planned or financially controlled?	Is the industry nationally protected? Are there import duties, powerful lobby groups or national standards?
What is their cost base? Is it correlated to location, size or process technology?	Is a price list in use, are discount levels static or is it a free for all?
What is their perceived credibility in the market place?	Are there a lot of small players or a few dominant players?
How responsive are they to change?	What are the predominant ways of influencing the purchase process for their PPP? e.g. backhanders, free trial installations, entertainment?
Are they reputable or players of dirty tricks?	

Life cycles

An appealing concept from the product and consumer goods areas is that of life cycles. When a PPP is first launched on the market, its initial sales rate is slow, increasing with customer experience until it reaches some peak, following which sales decline until the withdrawal of the PPP from the market. The causes of the initial sales resistance are not difficult to understand. Customers will always be wary of a new PPP and see an early purchase as a high risk. There may even be a lack of awareness of the new PPP.

For a number of reasons, the initial price of any PPP is likely to be high, reducing as production experience increases and any initial one time costs are amortised. With PPPs, the life cycle profile will be clear for a major product, such as a bulk carrier. It may be more difficult to visualise for some categories of projects or programmes. However, providing there is a sufficient volume of sales, even these will follow the characteristic profile.

Many PPP's are customised for each purchaser and are frequently purpose built. In today's competitive world, it is likely that such PPPs will rely on standard modules or system components, which will then have their own life cycles. Life cycle trends are being influenced by the rising pace of technology, which is allowing development cycles to shorten. Improvements in global communications and distribution support this trend, which facilitates rapid acceptance of new PPPs. Flexible production processes reduce the risk of non-acceptance and a failure by an organisation to accelerate its learning rate will make life increasingly difficult for such laggards.

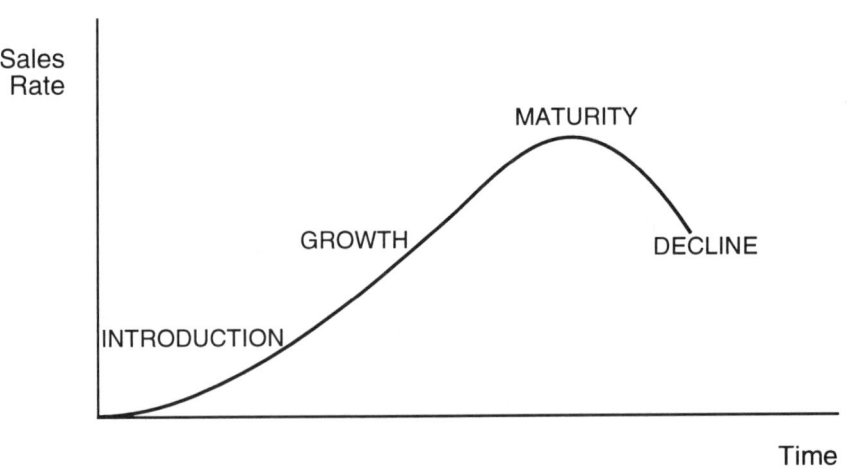

Figure 53. Most PPPs follow the classic life cycle sales pattern.

Regardless, predicting the point of inflection on the life cycle curve is difficult with any degree of accuracy and, when it occurs, overproduction and an industry shakeout are the almost certain consequence. There is a spread of success rates for newly developed PPPs, with a small number that are either total failures or incredible successes. The vast majority lie in the mediocre category.

The four phases of a life cycle

Let us now consider in more detail the four main phases of the life cycle; introduction, growth, maturity and decline. The introductory phase is undoubtedly the most difficult and the one where most PPPs come to a sticky end. Delivered PPPs in this phase will generally experience a high level of problems and require a great deal of support. Market resistance will vary from "I don't want to be the first customer and suffer the teething problems!" to "I've never heard of this new system or equipment!" In the latter case, even the standing of the Company may be of little help.

A GEC company used its experience in demanding environments to develop a sophisticated alignment system for use with coal face cutting machines. Having proved the system at the UK National demonstration coal mine, GEC asked British Coal how many they would like to buy. "Oh no," was the response "now you have to convince the local operations staff at every mine." The prospect of such a costly and protracted process resulted in their dropping the whole opportunity.

In the early stages, demand can fluctuate dramatically; for volume PPPs by as much as 100% in consecutive periods. What is clear is that after making the first delivery and the entry of the PPP into service, that first customer needs managing to become the best seller of that PPP. Indeed, often the deal struck in the provision of such trial PPPs trades a very low price together with twenty-four hour technical support in return for subsequent access to the PPP for promotional purposes.

The identification of such trial installations needs to take account of their accessibility, value/price ratio and the purchaser's leadership role in determining the procurement policies of the rest of their industry. It is usual to sell new PPPs to current customers with whom a good relationship exists, since the proving path may be far from smooth. Site visits by potential customers are the way of overcoming their sales resistance; not so easy for a new line where the first customer is far afield. This aspect and the high level of support required predicates against selling to a remote launch customer and it is therefore much better to find a launch site on the doorstep.

Second to market players reduce their risk by waiting to see whether the market accepts a new offering. If so, they can achieve a superior cost base to the first to market by taking advantage of experience within the industry, used to manufacture sub-systems. They are also likely to face a shorter gestation period with a consequent speedier recoup of their investment. Each of these factors makes life precarious and painful for first to market players, detracting from the understandable appeal of controlling an emergent market.

By far the most significant problem in the growth phase is keeping up with demand. Everyone involved in the company making the PPP will become overloaded and cash resources will be stretched to the limit. Despite market acceptance and reasonable quality, with the resulting reduction in support cost and associated resources, life is difficult in this ever changing phase. A premium price can be charged, with associated benefits to those in the distribution channels and bundling is a common technique employed at this stage. However, the honeymoon will not last for ever and competitors will start to appear with enticing new offerings, particularly as saturation approaches.

Maturity is the most important phase for any company, providing financial strength and the ability to fund new developments. Not all PPPs reach this stage. They may need withdrawing from the fight at an earlier stage as a result of changing technology and competitive action. The aim is to get any new PPP to this phase as rapidly as possible with production matching requirements. Competition is likely to be fierce, both on the grounds of price, which can never be as high as in the previous phase, and on PPP differentiation. This is also the time to launch life cycle extensions on the market, with added features hopefully allied to new markets, new users and even novel PPP uses.

Finally, the decline of the successful PPP is inevitable and this is the time to milk it. Minimal investment is key and marginal costing together with dumping are useful techniques to employ. This is also the time to launch life cycle extensions, with added features, on the existing market, hopefully allied to new markets and users, or even new PPP uses. It is important to be positive about the decline phase and aim to be either the first company to drop the PPP, or alternatively, the last.

Market growth and market share

The widely used Boston Consulting Group matrix effectively contrasts market growth against relative market share; the latter expressed as the percentage of the largest share. Traditionally, the matrix illustrates a portfolio of offerings, denoting their size by the diameter of a circle centred on their position in the matrix. The concept is beguiling, though evidence of it making large contributions to the success of organisations has been sparse and it has somewhat fallen from favour. One benefit, however, has been the recognition that today's businesses cannot be managed purely on the basis of a single diagram. What has endured is the useful descriptions of PPPs within the Boston model.

The "rising star" is a PPP in a fast growing market which, with a relatively high market share, will have a voracious appetite for investment to keep it there. The

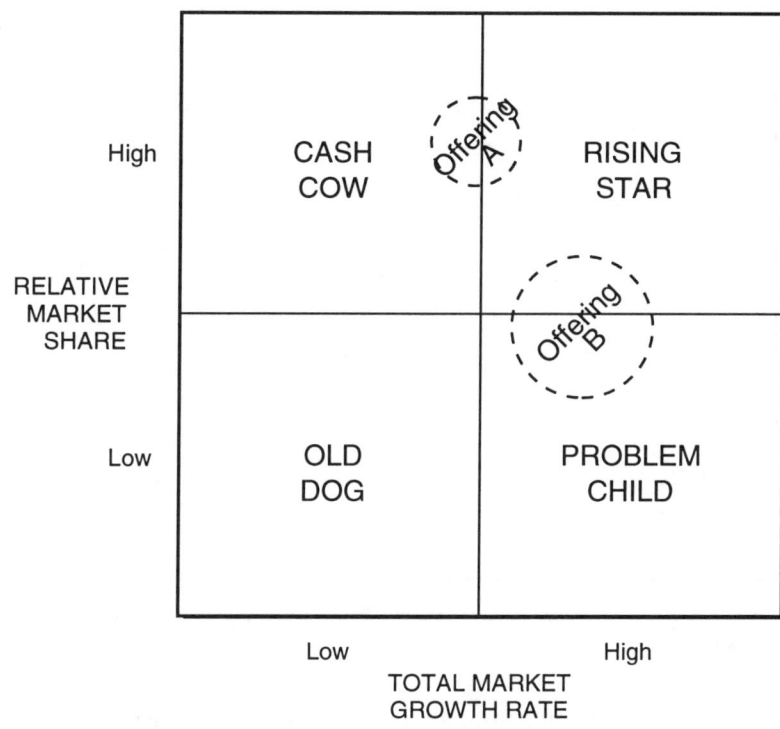

Figure 54. The classic Boston matrix compares PPP attractiveness, in terms of its market share, with growth rate in the market.

necessary cash for this "star" can, perhaps, best come from the "cash cow"; the market leader in a static market that can be "milked" for profit.

The "problem child" is a PPP in a high growth market area, but with only a low share of the market and is normally up against competitors' "rising stars." The achievement of an increase in market share for the "problem child" is necessary for success but, equally, a lack of acceptance eventually leads to failure. Finally, the "old dog" is in a static market with a low market share, not a position of any attraction. Inevitably, most companies will have a mix of categories amongst their PPPs, due both to their position in their life cycles and to their respective market life cycle.

Mid life updates

The classic mid-life update can modify the life cycle of a PPP and may be repeated more than once, further delaying the decline. Its appeal is reduced investment and uncertainty together with visibility of the justification, though it can be seductive

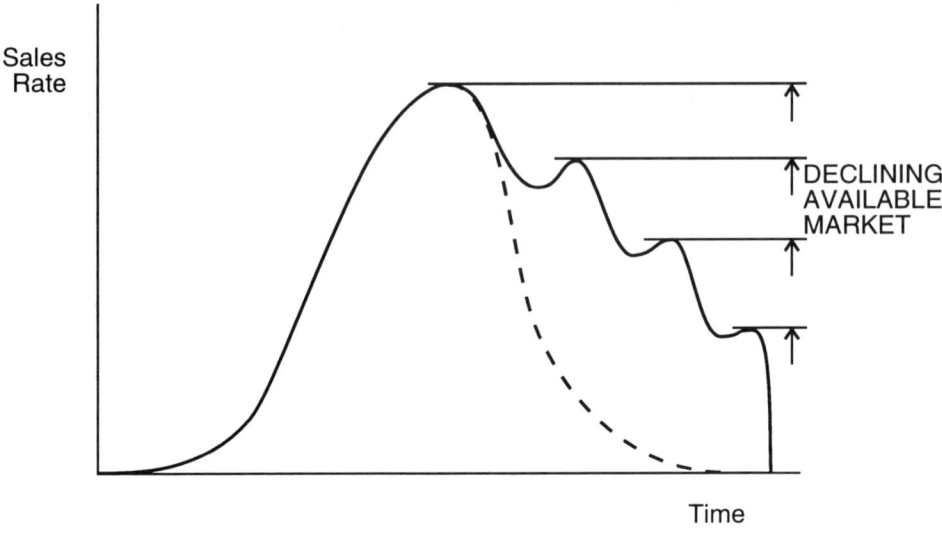

Figure 55. The extension of the life of a PPP by one or more mid life updates is a common practice.

as will shortly be seen. Such a strategy may also appeal to customers wishing to improve PPP performance and resenting premature obsolescence of equipment with long remaining service life.

Having successively extended the life of the original PPP, its appeal becomes restricted to a reducing number of customers. There is, however, a major problem with repeating this strategy. When, after several updates, the PPP finally does become obsolete, the drop off in sales is very dramatic. This leaves the company concerned in a difficult predicament, with a real break in production. Worse still, there are no existing sales to fund the development of the next generation of PPP, the approval of such work having been adversely affected by the expediency and success of each update to the previous PPP. Furthermore, it is virtually impossible to leapfrog the competition, having missed out on several intervening interim PPP generations.

A classic example of life cycles is that of the jet airliners of the Boeing Aircraft Company. Starting with the long haul 707 aircraft in the nineteen sixties, the company then followed with the medium/short haul 727. The next generation comprised the 747, wide bodied long haul, which first flew in 1969 and the 737 short haul. The latter used a large proportion of the fuselage and other components of the 707, and was later stretched to undertake the medium haul role in addition. Both the 747 and the 737 have gone through the -100, -200, -300 and -400 updates; the 737 a -500 one as well and the 747 an extended range SP variant. The

Company's latest offerings are the 757 short/medium haul aircraft and the 767 wide bodied medium haul aeroplane.

The question that arises is what will happen to 747 sales with the arrival of the new and competing Airbus A340 long haul wide bodied airliner, which entered service in the early nineteen nineties? The design of the 747 was at that time 23 years old and the aircraft had gone through three updates and a major variant; the 777 not being available until the late nineties.

It is also clear that the actual life of a PPP, before it becomes unfit for purpose, and the availability of a better PPP will affect the length of a life cycle. A key factor is an unacceptable rise in the cost of ownership, compared with competitive offerings, even after switching costs are considered. Efforts to reduce the life of a PPP and thus increase the size of the market is one interpretation of the term "churn." This is common in the computer market, with the continual update of both hardware and software with new features that quickly make the old versions obsolete. Currently, in the mid nineties, new software releases are being made every eighteen months. The other interpretation of churn refers to the degree to which a company's base of customers is stable or in a state of flux.

Market life cycles

Individual PPP life cycles collectively form a market life cycle, or demand/technology curve. The life of industries and companies also fit into this life cycle pattern; the disappearance of the steam engine and the passenger sea transport industries are good examples of demand/technology curves.

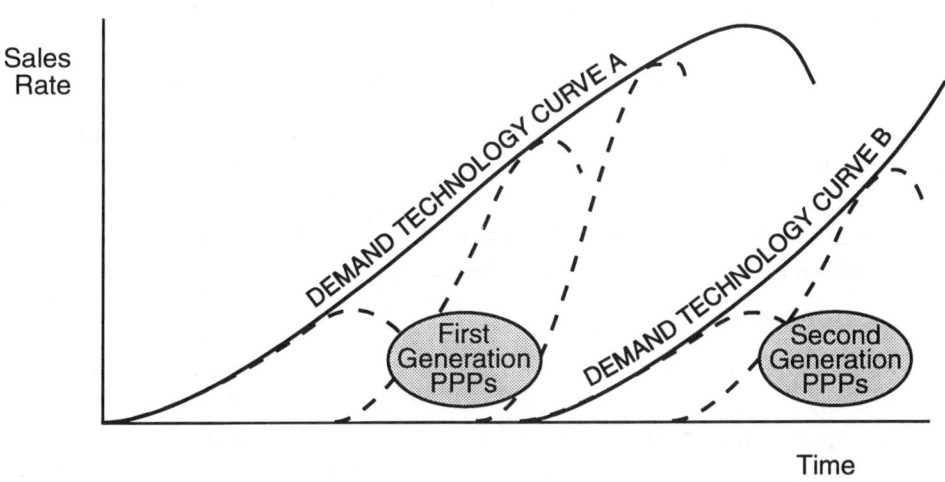

Figure 56. The demand/technology curve is an amalgam of a number of PPP life cycles.

P&O, the pre-war doyen of passenger shipping to Africa, the Middle and Far East, saw the imminent demise of passenger shipping and managed to extend their market through a move to cruise liners. Ideally, any company will have a number of PPPs, the life cycles of which are out of phase, aiming to give the steadiest possible workload. Forecasting sales of an offering into a new market cycle is obviously more prone to error than predicting within the same market life cycle.

Barriers to entry

Having made a large investment in a new PPP, no company wants to be overwhelmed shortly after the launch by a competitor with a copy of the new PPP, particularly due to the generally extended acceptance period for PPP offerings. The erections of barriers to entry are critical in deterring others. There are basically three types of barrier; those inherent within the PPP, process intrinsic barriers and market based ones.

Barriers inherent within PPPs

Patents, granted for 17 years, are the classic barrier preventing others from selling PPPs using the same principle of working. They offer only limited protection and are expensive to obtain on a world-wide basis, since the whole process of application and approval needs completing in every case. Not all countries recognise intellectual property rights and shrewd companies will regularly scrutinise technically explicit patent applications looking for ways to design around new patents. There is a saying in the electronics industry that there are always at least two entirely different ways of solving a problem using electronics.

Protection, in the form of copyright, applies to written material and more recently to software. Sadly, in this field, piracy is a major problem, not to mention customers copying things themselves. Worse still, it seems that no sooner has an anti-copying measure been introduced than an antidote appears.

The sheer size of investment in a new PPP development may in itself act as a barrier to entry. Examples include the expenditure of around one billion dollars to develop the next generation of digital telephone exchange, the same for a new car like the Ford Mondeo (cars are sold like PPPs to fleet buyers) and tens of billions of dollars for the Eurofighter 2000.

Process barriers

The first company to market will always benefit from being further down the learning curve than its competitors, with cost benefits not necessarily reflected in its prices. Some of these benefits may be the result of a large scale manufacturer strongly influencing the prices from materials suppliers, or even from owning the lowest cost sources. Usually, initial prices are set artificially high to recoup the investment in the PPP as soon as possible. A high price is sometimes a temptation to the competition, which may be in for a nasty shock as the market leader drops prices further than expected. A newcomer's use of optimum facilities with the latest, most productive equipment or processes may negate this superior cost position to some extent.

Secret production processes can be the most effective barriers. Used in the consumer field in products such as GoreTex and Clingfilm, with the process itself isolated in the factory, the few employees in the know are tied with "golden handcuffs." Examples in the PPP field include the IBM PS/2, with its micro channel architecture, produced to prevent cloning and the design of 'g' tolerant electronics for use in penetrating bombs and munitions, which prove extremely difficult to emulate or reverse engineer.

Market barriers

The first manufacturer to market often has the first choice of distribution channels. Success in becoming the market leader, with its volume implications, can also help to deny access to the newcomer, both through learning curve benefits and through the setting of standards that are costly for the newcomer to meet or challenge. Where customer technological experience is low and perceived risks are high, large organisations can sometimes use their reputation as a barrier to entry.

Temporary barriers are useful tactical tools for use as short term weapons. Examples include blocking attractive reference opportunities to a newcomer in order to slow their proving process. This appears to be the case with DEC's Alpha processor computers. Political pressures, too, can usefully create hurdles for the newcomer. Limited holding of previous year end prices, particularly during periods of high inflation, can also be an attractive incentive to order placement early in the following year. Industry cartels are another way of excluding the newcomer, with the diamond industry a prime example. It does not, however, endear the industry to the customer and long term damage to the participants is often apparent, since tightly associated groups of customers can bring in an outside supplier with preferred status if they feel they are being squeezed too hard.

Switching costs

Many, apparently highly justifiable, customer purchases never proceed because of so called switching costs. These costs result from the disruption to the existing supply arrangement. The increase in cost may arise from many sources, a typical example being new software that, though offering significantly benefits, won't run on the customer's computer system. There are large numbers of other situations where switching costs arise.

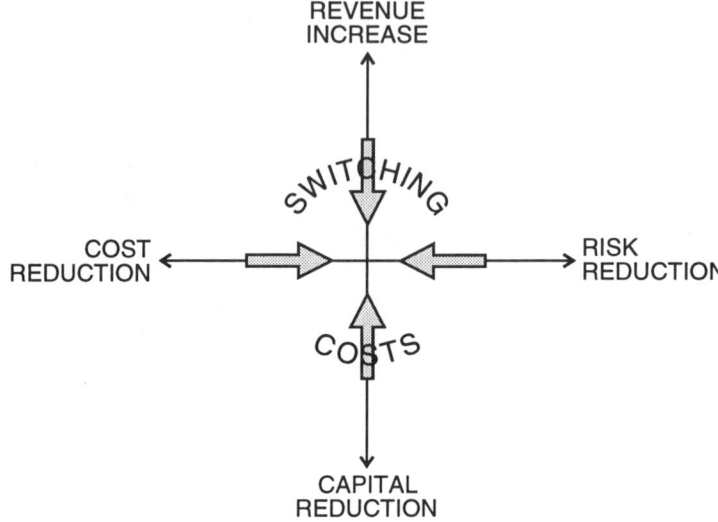

Figure 57. Switching costs can have a major negative impact during the tender evaluation of a potential new supplier's PPP.

- Requirement for new spares and test equipment holdings
- Retraining operators and maintenance staff
- Lost production during changes to the manufacturing process
- Incompatible interfaces to existing equipment
- Revising drawings and/or changing catalogues
- New purchase procedures
- Qualification of the new supplier

A further consideration is that of opportunity cost. This economists' term refers to the value of the alternatives not chosen. A supplier of mercury arc rectifiers, wishing to leave that business because of the age of the technology, doubled prices several years running. There was a negligible effect on the volume of units sold but not on the profits made! The opportunity cost was that of replacing the whole power pack, since solid state rectifiers were not directly interchangeable. Until that price point was approached, it was still cheaper for customers to purchase the exorbitantly priced replacement mercury arc rectifiers.

The potential for loss resulting from changing supplier is a further factor. For a chemical supplier to the plating industry, resistance to a change of supplier is high, since a performance shortfall in the plating process, resulting from the change, could result in the expensive scrapping of customer work in progress. A further twist is that established suppliers may retaliate to the prospect of losing one component within their supply by threatening to increase the price of other proprietary items to maintain the same revenue level.

In essence, switching costs are sources of "un-value." That is to say that they will lead to reduced revenue and increased costs, capital and risks. Any value case must recognise these and take them into account to generate the net value impact.

Barriers to new entrants

Looking at the subject from the opposite point of view, the current supplier possesses a number of advantages compared with a newcomer. Although at times these may seem to be insurmountable, this is not always the case. Incumbents, as with every other form of monopoly, tend to get lazy and careless. It is surprising how often a customer will welcome a newcomer to give genuine competition to the well-established supplier. Furthermore, purchasers recognise the dangers of having all their eggs in one basket.

FINANCIAL FACTORS	**CONTRACT WINNING FACTORS**
Switching costs	Insider knowledge of the purchase process
Learning curve cost advantages	Nationalistic sentiments

Elevated costs for a newcomer second source due to:
  Inaccuracies of the incumbent's drawings
  Proprietary processes
  Intangibles not included on the drawings
	Ability to influence the evaluation in their favour
	
	Exclusive agreement with the most suitable representative

Import tariffs and non-tariff barriers that may:
  Already exist
  Be raised by pressure from the incumbent
	Established incumbent reputation
	
	Knowledge of how to use the political process and influence

Private venture funding probably already recovered	Requirement for locally-owned representation
Retaliatory pricing of parallel proprietary PPPs	Ability to influence spec. writing in their favour
Restrictions on profit repatriation	Requirement for local manufacture
Established incumbent service infrastructure	
Certification and standards benefitting local suppliers	
Potential to block distribution channels and easiest entry points	

The barriers to entry conveniently divide into two groups; those which have a direct financial impact and those which affect the chances of the newcomer winning a contract.

Relationships between value, price and cost

In considering value, price and cost, value needs thinking of as a vector. In other words, unlike temperature, which is just a number (scalar), it is more like velocity, which involves both speed and direction. It is dependant on such factors as the source and members of the customer community, as well as the economic conditions, particularly interest rates. For value, the main aspects are the amount in financial terms and to whom is it tangible? It is likely, for example, that maintenance personnel will obtain a differing amount of value, for different reasons, from that gained by operations staff. Nuclear power had a higher value at its inception in the nineteen fifties, with its promise of clean efficient power, than it does today,

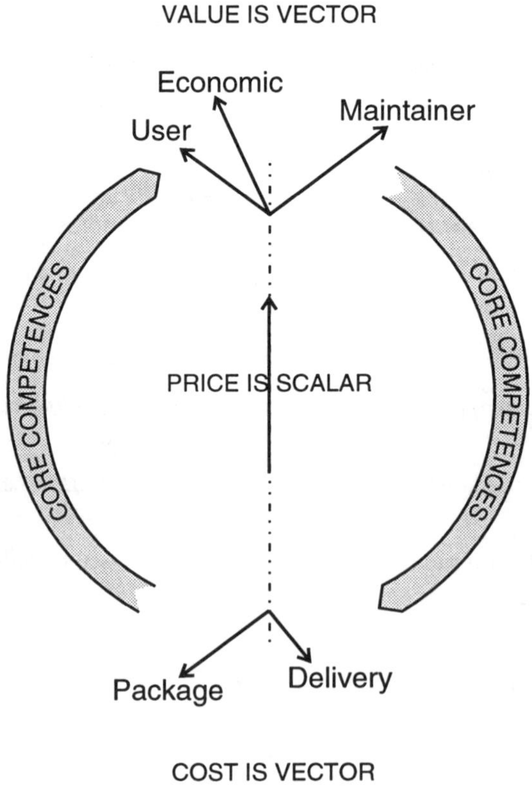

VALUE IS VECTOR

Economic
User   Maintainer

PRICE IS SCALAR

CORE COMPETENCES   CORE COMPETENCES

Package   Delivery

COST IS VECTOR

Figure 58. Value, price and cost all need comparing and relating to core competencies.

with its high costs and unpopularity with the Green community. Price, on the other hand, is clearly a scalar dimension. Cost is also a vector, where considerations such as the package and its delivery period need consideration.

It is revealing to examine the relationship between value to the customer and cost to the supplier. In the same way that value accrues to different members of the purchasing organisation, depending on their functional background and responsibilities, so costs accrue to the supplier for incorporating such value added features. For instance, modular design may provide significant value to customers. It can reduce the cost and complexity of fulfilling their responsibility. By holding modules as spare parts, rather than complete items, they can reduce costs without increasing the risk of not being able to diagnose and repair a fault in the available time. Providing a modular design is very likely to increase the supplier's cost; certainly in terms of the number of interfaces and possibly in the need for increased system stability, given the range of possible module operating characteristics.

It is the relationship between the extra customer value and the extra supplier cost that is interesting. Obviously the greater the leverage a supplier has, the more margin that will be available with an attractive value to price ratio for the customer. The internal processes that generate this leverage are the core competencies of the business. This established term for those things that a company is good at doing now becomes enormously more powerful, first conceptually and second as something quantifiable and systematically improvable. The result will be better competitiveness in the marketplace and more profitability, establishing a virtuous circle when the extra profits are re-invested to augment these core competencies.

Cost and differentiation strategies

There are two mechanisms for increasing the value to a customer of a supplier's offering.

1. Increase the external value to the customer by, for example, increasing their revenues, perhaps by increasing their available market size.
2. Improve the internal value to the customer, for example through customer cost savings or reduced capital cost.

The customers' strategy in terms of cost reduction and differentiation will influence a supplier's choice and potential use of such mechanisms.

Customer constraints

Customers can only receive value through overcoming their constraints, whether met through an increase in revenues or a reduction in risk, cost or capital expenditure. However, not all customers' evaluation processes will take such extra value

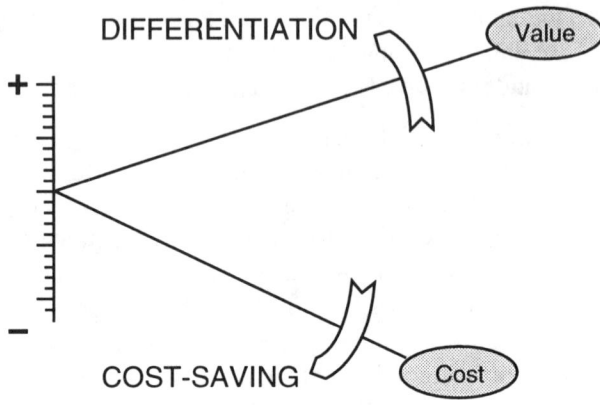

Figure 59. Cost saving and differentiation are both attractive to customers.

into consideration. Life cycle costing, for example, looks at through life costs, but ignores extra revenue that an offering may provide.

In such cases, the appropriate competitive stance is to provide only the precise level of value stipulated and drive the costs down of providing this level. Such an approach has parallels with the traditional competition on the basis of best price and delivery, ignoring attractive alternatives. The ultimate competitive stance is to increase value to the customer and systematically drive down costs through enhancement of core competencies.

Chapter 10:

PPP Planning & Development

PPP planning · SWOT analysis · PPP plan outlines · The diffusion of innovation · New PPP development and PPP life cycles · Salami slicing · Development problems · The dangers of prototypes · Using life cycles as a tool · System products · High-tech PPP matrix · Options with innovations · Break even analysis · Managing private venture (PV) development · Winners & losers

PPP planning

For major products, the concept of a product plan is generally well understood. Projects and programmes usually require a similar document before authorisation of a new development. It is thus logical to refer to such a document as a PPP plan. In essence, the document quantifies the market for a new PPP with likely sales and earnings over its life. It also gives an outline description of the PPP itself, as well as looking at the relationship with competitive offerings.

Effective planning is vital in order to proceed from a PPP idea to launch and beyond in a controlled and profitable manner. Each PPP or family of PPPs needs a document and a number of points about it are particularly relevant.

1. It deals essentially with how the PPP is to be brought to market. Thorough evaluation of the market, competition and sources of competitive advantage are essential.

2. It is primarily about penetrating markets rather than concerning itself with engineering aspects. It should cover the technical aspects of the PPP in outline only.

3. It must cover the anticipated PPP life cycle. With such life cycles often exceeding ten years, it requires detailed planning for three to five years with an outline beyond this timescale.
4. It is not a long document. Ten pages should normally suffice. Include supporting information in appendices.
5. Each plan needs an internal company champion to sell the concept to management and achieve implementation of the plan.

SWOT analysis

One of the standard techniques in the sales and marketing field is the use of the SWOT analysis, where the **S**trengths, **W**eaknesses, **O**pportunities and **T**hreats of a situation are identified and used to help decide future action. Such analysis is particularly useful when considering the market potential for a proposed new PPP, but can be equally powerful when trying to make a bid/no-bid decision. SWOT analysis should not be over-employed to generate lists, nor used as a reference for the subsequent analysis. Each of the four points is considered in turn when carrying out a SWOT analysis.

Strengths

If the strengths are technology ones, the lead is fragile and easily replicated through staff moving to competitors, parallel breakthroughs or reverse engineering. If the strengths involve people, there are dangers of group-think and introversion.

Weaknesses

A significant weakness almost invariably demands some sort of teaming or strategic alliance. It also poses the question "How long will it take to amend the situation and what resources will be required?" It may call for a basic examination of the Company's strategy and a review of core competencies; this latter subject covered at the end of the last chapter.

Opportunities

Having identified the opportunities, the following questions need responses:

1. What resources are required?
2. How much time is needed to recoup the investment?
3. What are the risks?
4. How many opportunities can be pursued in parallel?
5. Is any retaliation likely, especially if action is predatorial?
6. What is the implication of organisational changes precipitated by growth?

Threats

Whether external or internal, what resources are available for mounting a successful defence and what is the strategic importance of such a move?

PPP plan outlines

A PPP plan can be fundamentally broken down into six parts, together with a financial summary.

1. User need

A simple statement is required, identifying the basic need and who has that need, in what type of customer organisations. It must indicate the degree to which this requirement can be met and how such needs might change in the future.

2. PPP solution

What is being proposed must meet the user need. The advantages require comparison with existing offerings as well as with likely new competitive ones. The solution should cover the total package provided to the customer, including such items as maintenance equipment, training and in-service support.

3. Specification

There are two interpretations. The first is the operational specification, which covers performance requirements to meet the users' needs, but does not pre-empt the design. The second is the technical specification, which covers detailed design aspects, including standards such as customer interfacing and approvals. The latter interpretation should either be a separate document or included as an appendix.

4. Market assessment

This is the marketing justification for developing the new PPP.

Size and growth Estimate the available market and the currently served or accessible market. Then consider growth trends and key characteristics, justifying both. (See page 177)

Competition Analyse how competitor's offerings and prices compare with what is being planned. Estimate their current market share. Identify strengths, weaknesses and likely strategies. What are the sources of competitive advantage of the Company's proposed new offering? How far behind is the development of a similar offering?

Market share In the light of the above analysis, estimates the market share achievable by the new PPP and how quickly it can win that share. This will need to encompass switching costs and value/price ratio considerations.

5. Timescales

It is essential to have a framework showing how the Company will proceed. It should cover development, production, support, upgrades and sales and marketing.

Development plan Summarises cost, resources and timescales, identifying key milestones and critical aspects. Reliability and maintainability need particular consideration.

Production plan This needs thinking about at an early stage. Reviews make or buy decisions. Considers start up costs and capital equipment requirements.

Launch plan Covers aspects such as a press launch, PPP demonstrations and exhibitions, audio-visual material and literature availability. Also considers pricing policy. Some PPPs get launched merely through being featured in a bid.

Support plan Outlines the provision of customer training, manuals, spares and support. This is a critical area which is often neglected.

Upgrade plan Address improvements, in the form of a mid life update, at an early stage in the context of the anticipated PPP life cycle. A logical update programme is an important part of extending PPP life and maintaining market share.

6. Sales/marketing plan

It is important to consider all aspects individually. One particularly effective approach is to bring the appropriate experts together to discuss each area.

PPP Consider what will be offered and when. The timing of the launch of various items in a series needs careful analysis, particularly for its potentially detrimental impact on any of the existing range of PPPs; so called cannibalisation.

Promotion How will this be done; internally or by employing an external agency? Consider a plan for technical articles and sales literature, press announcements, advertising, exhibitions and demonstrations. Be very wary of premature announcements that may generate unrealistic customer expectations and give competitors the opportunity to catch up.

Price A complex decision, dependant on what the customer will pay, needing to address the compromise of maximising the profit for the Company whilst not unnecessarily encouraging competition.

Proforma value cases need generation and, after considering switching costs, an abbreviated value/price ratio justification included. The price/volume

SALES AND PROFIT	YEAR 1	YEAR 2	YEAR 3	YEAR 4	YEAR 5
Unit Selling Price					
Number of Units					
ANNUAL SALES					
Materials					
Labour					
Overhead					
Inflation					
FACTORY COST					
GROSS PROFIT					
Materials					
Labour					
Overhead					
Inflation					
DEVELOPMENT					
SALES & MARKETING					
ADMINISTRATION					
NET PROFIT					
BALANCE SHEET	**YEAR 1**	**YEAR 2**	**YEAR 3**	**YEAR 4**	**YEAR 5**
Additional Plant					
Tooling					
Test Equipment					
PLANT & EQUIPMENT COST					
Less Depreciation					
PLANT & EQUIPMENT					
Stock/Work in Progress					
Debtors					
Creditors					
WORKING CAPITAL					
TOTAL CAPITAL EMPLOYED					
RETURN ON CAPITAL EMPLOYED					
CASH FLOW	**YEAR 1**	**YEAR 2**	**YEAR 3**	**YEAR 4**	**YEAR 5**
CASH IN					
CASH OUT					
NET CASH FLOW					

Figure 60. A proforma is an easy way of presenting the necessary financial information.

relationship also requires consideration as well as the policy on spares and support.

Distribution By what route will the customer be accessed? Will it be direct, to original equipment manufacturers (OEMs), via overseas representatives or even by licensed manufacture.

7. Financial summary

This provides the financial justification for developing the PPP. Figure 60 provides an assessment of basic profit and loss. The completion of the parts dealing with cash flow and capital employed are best left to the financial function. Discounted cash flow techniques may be applied when evaluating the plan.

Typical criteria applied to the financial position vary widely from industry to industry and likewise for different types of PPP. It is usual to consider each of the following factors.

MEASURE	CRITERION
Payback of investment	May vary from as little as 2-3 years to more than 10
Pre-tax return on investment	Accountants are likely to require at least 25%
Sales revenue	Twenty times the PV investment is a useful guide

Do not think that the PPP planning process ends with the production of the plan. The document will need regular updating to take into account changes in the market place, particularly the development of competitive offerings. Furthermore, even before the PPP launch onto the market, life cycle planning will need to take over from the PPP planning process. Finally, it is interesting that the process of obtaining approval of an investment decision is very analogous to the process of winning a contract from an institutional customer.

The diffusion of innovation

During the life cycle of any new PPP, the purchasers divide into five separate groups; innovators, opinion leaders, early adopters, late adopters and laggards. Take care when listening to innovators, who always want more features; more bells and whistles, more megahertz, megabytes, larger, wider or whatever. They may well not be representative of the whole market being addressed. These five categories tend to relate to the four phases of the life cycle itself; introduction, growth, maturity and decline.

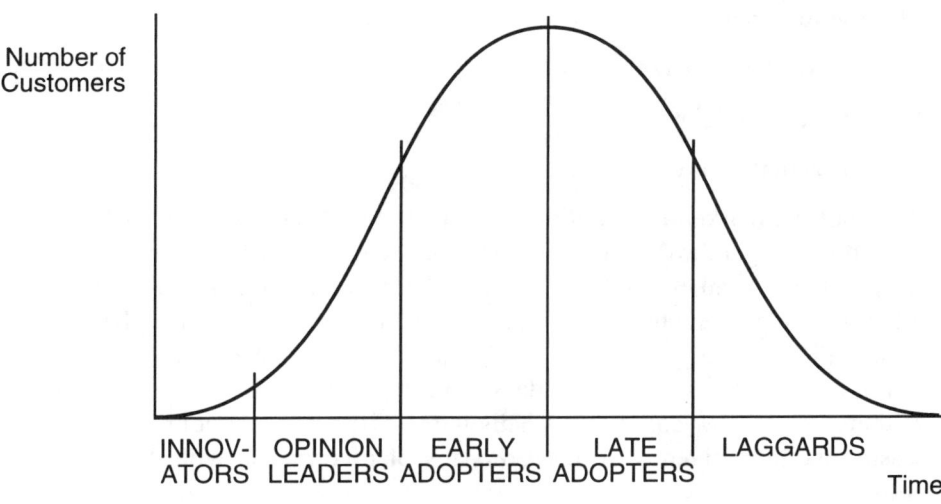

Figure 61. Purchasers fall into five different categories over the life of any PPP.

New PPP development and PPP life cycles

The problem with any new PPP development is that there is a significant delay before making any sales and achieving revenue. While in a few industries the customer may fund PPP development, and the defence market has historically been a leader here, shortage of customer funds, allied to growing competition has made even this an increasingly rare event.

The profitability of a new PPP is vitally dependant on the maximum sales rate and the time taken to reach that figure. In view of the significant negative cash flow at the beginning of a new development, the need for market research to obtain critical information is clear. A large amount of key data is required.

- Market size at saturation and its timing
- Timing of commencement of market uptake
- Prototype availability date
- Total investment in development and launch of the PPP
- PPP availability date
- Estimated time of availability of competitive offerings
- Interval to recoup the investment
- Viable price level (from company and market perspectives)
- Total return on investment

In addition, it is necessary to establish a number of factors about the market itself and page 177 gives more information about how to approach this.

1. The total market
2. The available market
3. The accessible market
4. The actual market

The size of the market at saturation is particularly difficult to establish. It is also clear that the longer the development time and the life cycle, the more difficult it is to forecast the numbers and the more vulnerable the information is to error. Furthermore, the acceptance of new proprietary standards, which may be intrinsic in a new PPP, is likely to reduce the speed of initial uptake. Consequently, any investment analysis should include sensitivity to alternative scenarios and a discounted cash flow calculation. This latter will provide a common basis for assessing the attractiveness to the Company of investments with different cash flow profiles.

In such sensitivity analysis, consider not just to what may happen, but the relative impact of the various scenarios. One straightforward way of doing this is to assemble a spreadsheet that reflects cost, price and volume data, year by year, in addition to the development data. Alter each variable to determine the overall impact of different changes on the financial result. Obviously, those factors that make the greatest impact will then require further investigation and justification.

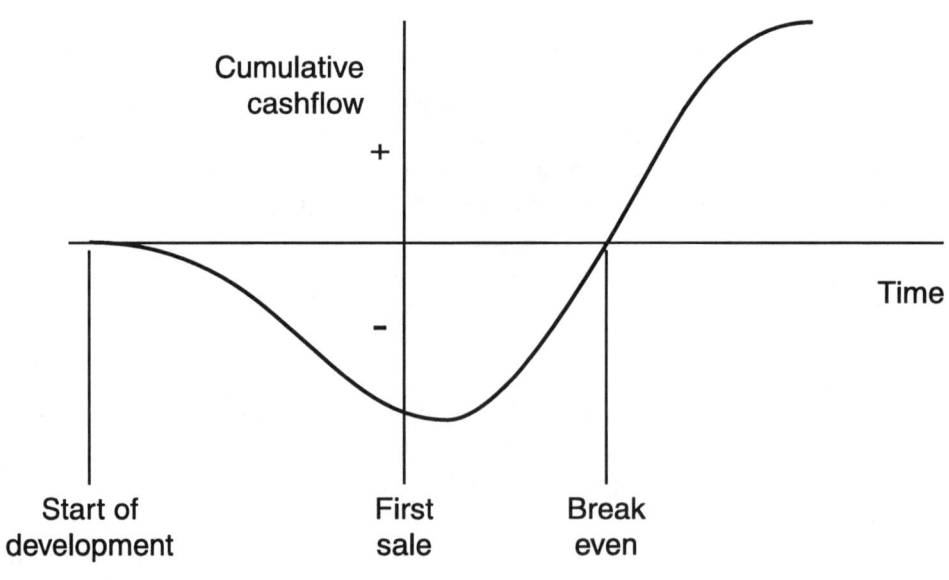

Figure 62. A visual presentation of sales and cash flow can be useful in supporting investment in a new PPP.

Salami slicing

There is a danger that individuals in a company will think that the cost of new PPP development is so large that they will salami slice by dividing the required investment into a number of small amounts, resulting in an unrealistically optimistic presentation of the return on the investment. When, as development progresses, the true investment becomes apparent, it takes strong management to cancel the work and "throw the money already spent down the drain." There is a strongly held view that previous investment is in the past and that an analysis of the return on merely the future investment is a better way of undertaking real-time management. Experienced managers may, however, be wise to this over-optimistic approach and so build in their own contingencies. The danger is that this will reduce open communication and the validity of the discussion over the real issues.

Development problems

The impact of problems in completing the development of a PPP to plan can be very serious. Apart from the obvious cost overrun caused by the unbudgeted expense of the "marching army" should development timescales slip, it will also adversely impact profit. Similar deterioration can result from the PPP exceeding its planned cost, being beset by compatibility or quality problems or, worst of all, by a delayed launch on the market. The following figure shows the relative impact of different scenarios on overall profitability for computer printers. In a number of studies, similar figures have now been found to apply to PPPs.

SITUATION	IMPACT ON TOTAL PROFIT
Development budget 30% overspent	-3%
PPP costs exceed goal by 10%	-4%
Compatibility problems reduce volume by 10%	-4%
Quality problems reduce price by 10%	-15%
PPP launch 6 months late	-30%

Figure 63. The impact of development problems has a serious effect on profitability.

The dangers of prototypes

Apart from the risks of prototype equipment failure during demonstrations, there are a number of other problems that may be less apparent. Customers seeing a prototype may end up saying they like it so much that they are going to cancel all their existing orders with the Company and wait for production versions of the new PPP. Almost as bad, they say that it is close to what they wanted, but they really must have a number of changes made. These, they say, shouldn't be a problem as the equipment is still at the prototype stage! What is almost certain is that they will appraise competitors of the development in the hope of attaining dual sourcing and consequent lower price levels.

Equally, members of the Company's management board may be very enthusiastic and order an immediate and premature launch on the market place. They may even demand immediate full scale production before resolution of all the usual prototype problems. Alternatively, they may be unimpressed and refuse to authorise further funding to take the new PPP into production.

Using life cycles as a tool

It should be clear that life cycles are an important tool in ensuring the future health of any company and that life cycle curves will differ from industry to industry, from market to market and from PPP to PPP. It is important that the development of new PPPs should make good use of these tools. Life cycle reviews of each PPP should take place from time to time as a standard company procedure. One such approach is for PPPs to have to pass a detailed phase review process before passing into the next stage of their life cycle. Current best practice is often sadly lacking in many companies. The use of a rigorous discipline is imperative to hold the competition at bay and nurture the long term health of the Company.

The main reasons for a first class procedure are to ensure fair comparison of all potential new developments, and the allocation of scarce resources to the most promising propositions. In addition, the reduction of investment risk through good control is also critical, particularly in terms of avoiding cost and time scale overruns, with their future adverse effect on profitability.

Companies involved in the PPP business are usually, by definition, large ones and the PPPs themselves complex and expensive. These factors put a premium on management and communication, both of which are assisted by the correct use of life cycle tools. One complicating factor is the construction of curves. Plotting data such as sales rate against time is totally inadequate, since many temporal factors will impact on the figures. Instead, market sizes need plotting and, with small numbers of customers and suppliers, this can be difficult, particularly since such data is usually confidential.

Far too many companies are still engineering-led and find it extremely difficult to move to a market driven culture. However, the dangers of neglecting market forces are clear. There is nothing to recommend following what is technologically interesting rather than that which is worthwhile for the target customer community. The result is loss of profit as a minimum and bankruptcy of the Company at its worst.

Rolls Royce, the cornerstone of British engineering for the first three quarters of the twentieth century, came to its knees and the bankruptcy courts because of time scale overruns on its new RB 211 aero engine; the problems being caused by pursuing a particularly interesting technical solution that carried with it an unacceptably high risk. As the classic engineering led company, Rolls Royce encountered not only the delays in getting its PPP to market, but also by the adverse cash effects on a classic life cycle cash flow/time scale graph.

System products

It is increasingly common to find the system product concept in PPPs. In this concept, individual sub-systems or modules of a PPP are standardised, treated as if they were products in their own right and grouped in a variety of ways to form customised PPPs. The approach can backfire, as with the elevator company, which felt it could offer more cost effective solutions to its customers by avoiding application specific designs.

What the company failed to recognise was that the deciders were the architects, who did not have to pay for the elevators, but for whom these items often heavily influenced the status and image of the finished building. Also, there are usually penalties involved with such an approach, in terms of cost, performance and the ability to achieve customised applications. Nevertheless, the system product approach is a powerful one that can bring significant benefits in terms of the reduction in one-time applications engineering needed to customise existing designs.

High-tech PPP matrix

Where a company has a range of PPPs, it is worth analysing the portfolio of PPPs in terms of the technical maturity of each one against the customer experience with that PPP. This is shown on the next page in figure 64.

Car drivers are unfamiliar with drive-by-wire systems, which are still "curiosities", although in aviation circles, glass cockpits and fly-by-wire are new but widely used and thus considered "distant cousins"; both technologies having only recently emerged. On the other hand, the hovercraft is an "under-achiever" and is an excellent example of a very mature technology where there are hardly any experienced customers. The "old friends", mature technologically with customers fully experienced, are so familiar that it is unnecessary to quote examples here. PPPs progress during their lives from "curiosities" to "old friends", often in a staircase type of progression. The real transitions occur where large available markets utilise PPPs with good value/price ratios without suffering high switching costs. Analysis should reveal the pattern of the Company's portfolio of PPPs, raising issues of growth potential, resource allocation, structure and culture.

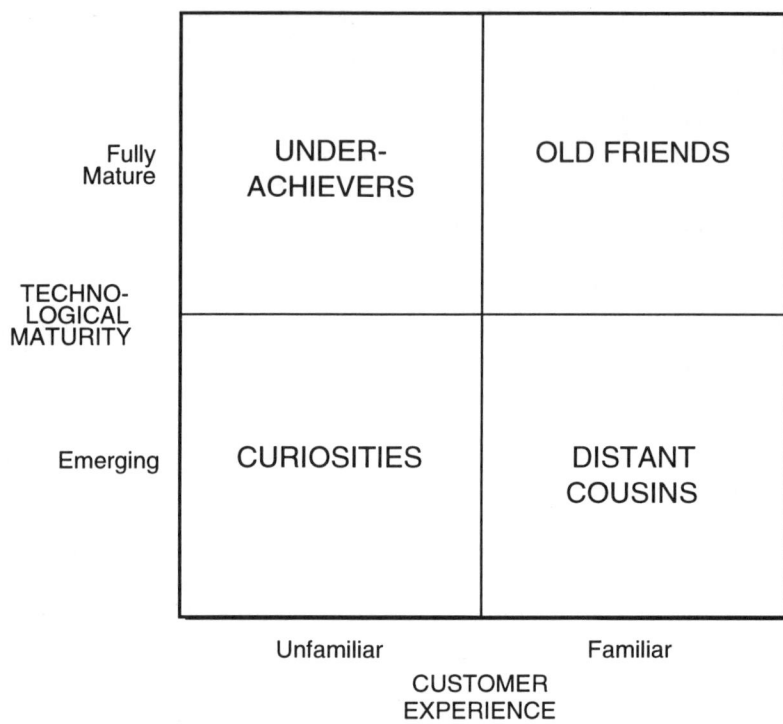

Figure 64. Four interesting categories arise from technical maturity/customer experience comparison.

Options with innovations

It is worth looking at complementary assets, that is those capabilities which fit well with the needs of innovation. These might be distribution channels, production technology or some other appropriate capability. It is interesting then to compare them with vulnerability to copying as shown in figure 65.

Clearly, with strong assets and low vulnerability, the preferred route of the vast majority of companies will be to try to monopolise the market. A typical example was Pilkington Glass during the seventies with its proprietary float glass process which it protected through the extensive use of process patents. Where it did not have distribution, that is where it was deficient in complementary assets, though vulnerability was also low, lucrative licence deals were the best solution; a stance which Pilkingtons took in such territories across the world.

Where the assets are strong, but vulnerability high, working to open standards is the norm and Sun Microsystems took this approach with their SPARC processor

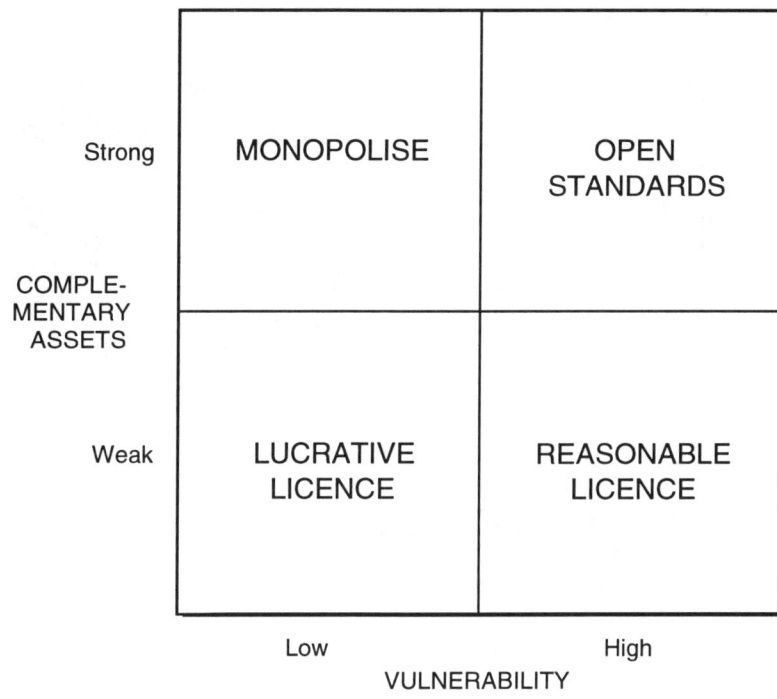

Figure 65. There are a number of different approaches to take with innovation.

design to increase the number of software applications available. Being market leader, they also had the most to gain from this strategy.

Where the complementary assets are weak, but the vulnerability is still high, a much more reasonable approach needs taking with licencing. The UK automobile industry has done just such deals over the years by in setting up car factories in the Third World with obsolescent generations of cars. Austin and Morris vehicles are still built in India!

Break even analysis

In this type of analysis for new PPPs, the break even point is reached when the total costs, both fixed and variable, of producing a given volume of PPPs are exactly equal to the revenue generated by sales at that production volume. Producing more than the break even volume results in an operating profit; less gives an operating loss.

Contribution pricing involves selling units for at least the unit variable costs, but at less than the sum of the variable and pro-rata fixed costs added together. Thus,

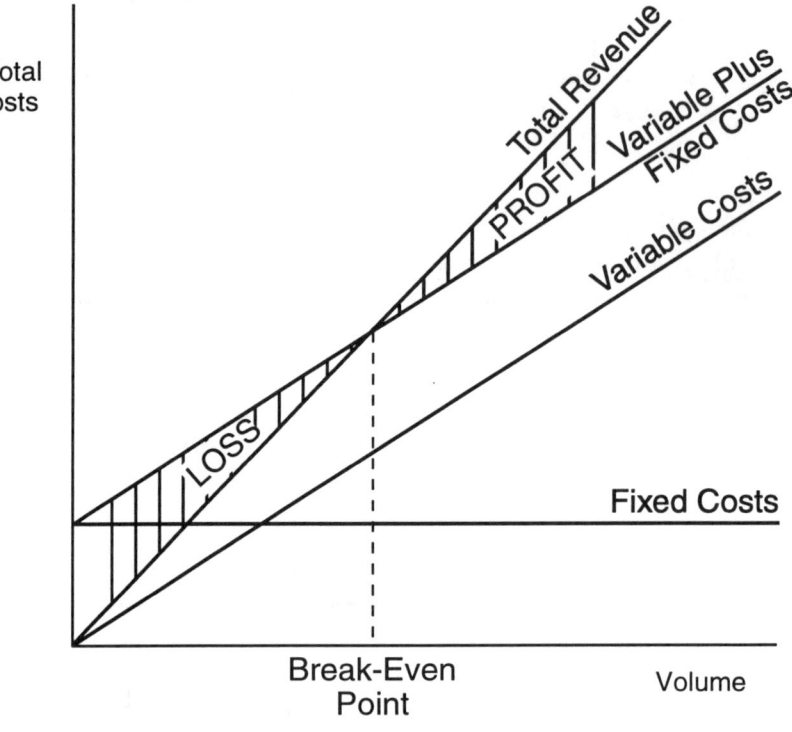

Figure 66. Not all break even graphs involve straight lines. Steps can occur at particular volume break points.

PPPs priced in this manners do not bear their full share of the fixed costs. The danger is of cannibalising existing sales at these lower prices, pushing up the break even point and reducing overall profitability. A classic tactic is to tailor the offerings for the separate markets to create a sense of distinctiveness; e.g. industrial specification versus commercial grade. Ideally this manufacturing process should utilise the same facilities and be at the same quality level, to avoid incurring additional costs. In practice, step increases in fixed costs, and reducing variable costs as volume increases, complicate real cost relationships. The amount to which these changes affect a particular situation is very dependant on the type of PPP, many of which never move beyond single figure production volumes.

Managing private venture (PV) development

Left to themselves, development engineers can quickly go wild when developing a new PPP. "Bells and whistles" get added, because they seem a good idea at the time, rather than because the market needs them, as discussed on page 66. Timescales can slip and expenditure overrun budget. Concessions are made to challenging and cost effective performance targets, and the final PPP can be much less competitive than was originally planned. It is the responsibility of the sales and marketing function to act as the "customer" for PV development programmes.

Monthly or quarterly review meetings need convening, when the development team presents details of their progress and highlights any problems. The "customer" should indicate any alterations to requirements in the market place, particularly those resulting from competitor activities. In this way, it is possible to have constructive discussions about modifications, and to document and approve any design changes. Furthermore, the development process does not end until the achievement of satisfactory and, where relevant, "bug free" in-service use, together with the definition of logistic support packages, including documentation, and the completion of any necessary value-engineering.

Winners and losers

It is a fact of life that, when a launching a new PPP on the market, it will impact on existing PPPs being offered to the same customers by competitors. With any new PPP development, it is important to examine existing winning offerings and quantify how much customers will pay for them. Likewise, losers must be identified and the pain of the loss to their suppliers estimated, together with their likely reaction and ability to spoil the market or even prevent the new PPP from succeeding.

Chapter 11:

Promotion Strategy & Public Relations

The roles & tools · The message · Promotional strategy · Press relations · Lobbying · Focused corporate initiatives · Exhibitions & conferences · Literature · Direct mail · Audio-visual · Presenting technical papers · Presentation skills · Advertising · House styles/visual identities · User groups

The roles and tools

A good definition of public relations in the PPP arena is "The planned and sustained effort to establish and maintain goodwill and mutual understanding between an organisation and its customers." This is a slightly modified version of the British Institute of Public Relations' 1987 definition.

There are three key functions which public relations (PR) has to fulfil in the PPP market place.

1. To project the Company as a reliable, progressive supplier with PPPs relevant to the market.

2. To inform potential customers and opinion leaders, imparting sufficient information on the key PPPs to arouse interest.

3. To develop the market, by publicising applications of key PPPs and their benefits to generate sales leads.

These functions include ensuring that invitations to tender are received from organisations that are rarely in the market, and damage limitation when allegations are made or faults arise. It is important to undertake scenario planning so that fallback campaigns are available.

Public relations is a service that has traditionally been provided within the sales and marketing function. In the past it has been confused with marketing in the PPP area. PR can only work given a proper marketing brief, together with the relevant PPP briefs which will vary through the life cycle of any PPP. It is thus important to prepare a PR plan to meet these briefs. Some companies prefer the option of using an agency rather than in house staff, particularly when working in overseas markets.

Public relations is not an end in itself. It is a means to an end. Many PR managers end up steering their ship onto the rocks because they haven't been given a course to steer. Imagination is essential in this field and has been important in getting greater public acceptance of PPPs such as waste recycling plants. The channel tunnel exhibition is helping to overcome user and neighbourhood uncertainties and fears. Public relations logically splits into six major parts or tools, each of which is applicable to the promotion of PPPs.

- Advertising
- Audio-visual
- Direct mail
- Exhibitions
- Literature
- Press relations

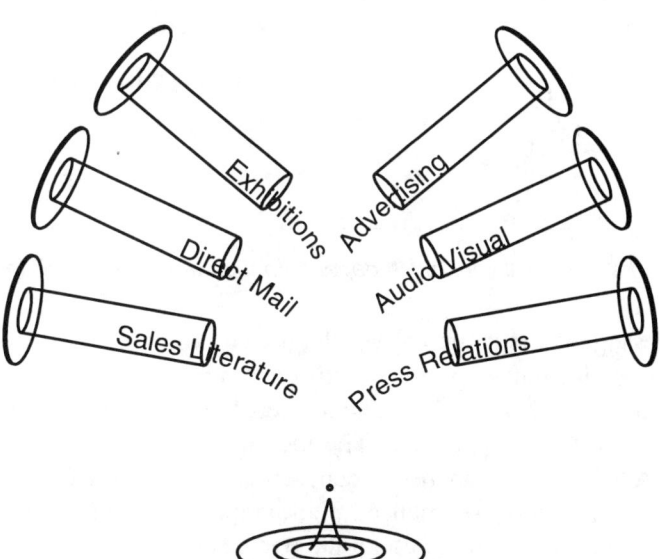

Figure 67. The key to successful public relations is getting the right mix.

Their use is very specialised in the PPP market place and, since each of these activities is costly, care is required to obtain the best value for money. A number of factors affect the use of public relations in this field.

First, the number of customers is generally fairly small. Second, the number of contracts for any particular PPP is usually not large and, finally, PPP customers object to the thought that someone is actually selling to them. Thus, the path taken needs treading with great care. In addition, the varying PR tools have differing importance during the life cycle both of a PPP and, additionally, of a company itself.

The message

The message to be communicated to potential customers is an area full of pitfalls, where a good PR department or agency should earn its keep. Difficulties often arise because of poor self-perception. "I know what I meant to say but, that's not how you understood the brief." The words should emphasise the benefits and advantages. Also, where appropriate, the message should allude to and build on the augmented PPP aspects, for example stressing that a new science park could become a technological showcase to attract overseas investment.

LIFE CYCLE PHASE	MESSAGE
Introductory phase	This is why you need it
Growth phase	This is where you can get it
Maturity phase	Ours is the best
Decline phase	Trade up with us

Figure 68. The message will very much depend on the stage of the PPP in its life cycle.

Part of the message is the choice of wording. One pitfall is that Americans don't speak English! Both countries use "Goes like a bomb" with diametrically opposite meanings. Americans also use shorter sentences; typically nine words long. A self check can be a salutary experience. The media itself can even give the wrong message. An A4 four hole punched brochure may not be welcome in 8½" x 11" three hole America. Poorly reproduced photographs in a corporate brochure can get a message over very clearly, but not the one desired.

Promotional strategy

The objectives of promotional strategy are many and varied. They can have a major impact on the way the market place views the Company and its offerings.

Promotion strategy & public relations

MARKET OBJECTIVES	PPP OBJECTIVES
Increase the size of the overall market	Create awareness of Company, capabilities and PPPs
Sway otherwise invisible or unreachable customer influencers	Generate interest in a PPP, enabling early involvement to influence the spec
Build credibility	Provide information e.g. a total breadth of capability
Generate invitations to tender	Alter perception of a PPP
Influence government policy formulation	Provide post-purchase justification
Alter company positioning	Nullify competitive compaigns (spend compared with competitors)

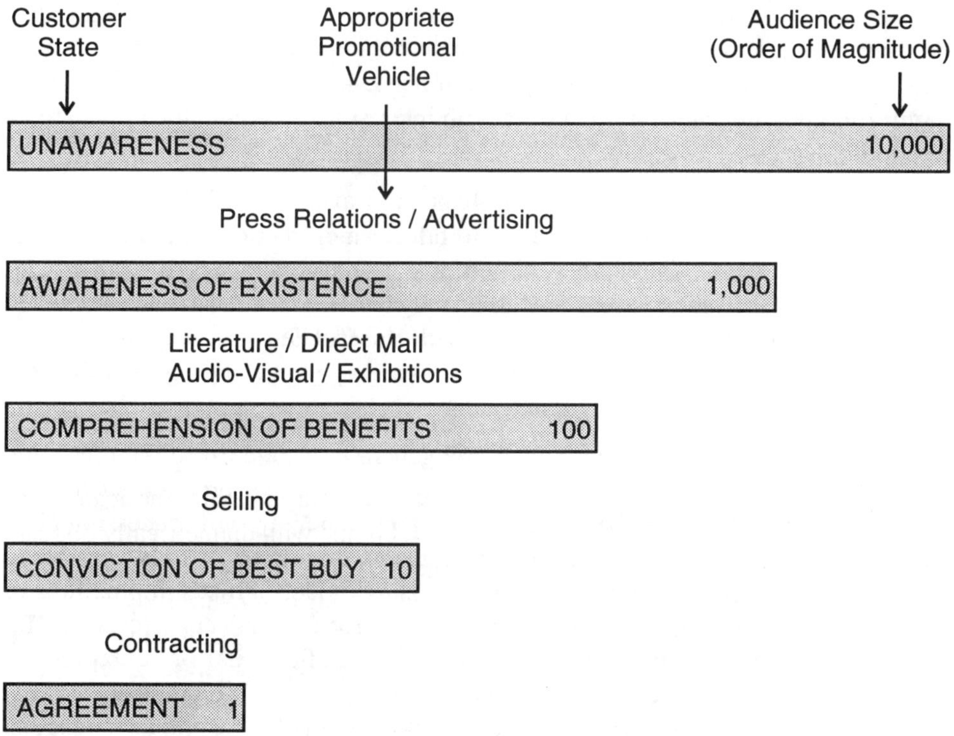

Customer State → Appropriate Promotional Vehicle → Audience Size (Order of Magnitude)

UNAWARENESS — 10,000

↓ Press Relations / Advertising

AWARENESS OF EXISTENCE — 1,000

Literature / Direct Mail
Audio-Visual / Exhibitions

COMPREHENSION OF BENEFITS — 100

Selling

CONVICTION OF BEST BUY — 10

Contracting

AGREEMENT — 1

Figure 69. The use of the various PR tools will depend on the level of customer awareness and interest.

The objectives conveniently divide into two groups; those concerned with the PPPs and their markets and those concerned with the Company.

Corporate promotional objectives may have little connection with the PPPs or their customers. They are, nevertheless, important functions of any corporate PR function, and tackle four groups which are not purchasers.

- Communicating with shareholders, actual and potential
- Communicating with employees
- Communicating with the local community
- Communicating with politicians

Press relations

Editorial articles are often considered to be worth countless advertisements and they are generally the result of press releases or press briefings. Carefully and interestingly written, together with an unusual and previously unused good quality photograph, most releases have a good chance of being featured by the trade press. If the news is of a contract, it is essential not to release too much information to the competition. Quantity or value, but never both is a good maxim. An individual briefing of one or a small number of journalists can have very rewarding results, with follow-up questions on the telephone if needed. The use of good visual aids, hardware if possible and a written brief with interesting photographic prints are all important aspects.

Providing there is a story, journalists are happy to travel to the Company or one of its installations, as they get the chance to talk to more people and even see the PPPs or parts of them. Another way of getting editorial coverage is to write articles targeted at specific trade journals or learned magazines. These can then be reprinted after publication, providing the Company with a useful and relatively inexpensive form of supporting sales literature that is enhanced by the third party endorsement acquired through publication by a magazine.

Briefings, at a new PPP market launch, are generally of interest to the press, but many PPPs are difficult to launch in this way. A new major product, such as an earth moving machine, may be straightforward, but a new type of processing plant may be less easy, unless a first sale has been made. It is probably only possible to launch a new design of steel mill in this way using models, artist's impressions or drawings; hardly the most inspiring or credible approach. Press conferences suffer from the same type of difficulties, though a good audio-visual presentation can often be successful in getting over a complex message. Two final points that always need watching are political and environmental issues. Companies neglect these at their peril and, wherever possible, take advantage of their benefits.

A considerate PR manager or director will hold an annual luncheon to thank the members of the press for their support over the year. This is a good opportunity to present a review of the Company's past year, unless by good fortune a hot news item just happens to be ready for release on the day. It is also a useful way of building relationships with the press and developing opportunities for future editorial coverage. In the PPP business, such a lunch needs support from the chief executive and the management team, as well as from relevant divisional managers and heads of sales and marketing.

Remember that in talking to the press, the conversation is always on the record. After a good lunch and a few drinks, it is easy to let the guard slip and make an unwise or indiscreet comment. Journalists are, by their very nature, inquisitive and on the lookout for a good (= bad) story. Never try to trick journalists. Always work to build a warm friendship with them, despite feeling very antagonistic at times. The friendship will always be rewarded, sometimes even by tip offs about what the government, customers or competition are doing.

One particularly difficult problem that falls into this area is that of disaster damage limitation. Clearly, any company may face a catastrophic failure of one of its PPPs. This can range from a collapsed bridge to a failed telephone exchange, from a nuclear power station reactor meltdown to a lost satellite. In all such circumstances, it is important that a well thought out crisis management plan has already been prepared and is ready for immediate implementation.

Lobbying

Political lobbying is a critical factor in winning major PPP business from the UK government and, for that matter, overseas governments. There are many facets to this subject. A good place to start is with the Company's constituency MP and there may be more than one if the Company operates from a number of sites. There are the specialist committees, both parliamentary and party ones. These have greater or lesser influence, often dependent on their membership and particularly who occupies the chair. It is important to establish the names of the members and which are most likely to be sympathetic to an approach by the Company. Ministers can be accessed, but are busy people protected by their staff. A letter of introduction from an MP is a good starting point, as is an approach through their parliamentary private secretary. The same general rules apply to MEPs and the commissioners of the European parliament.

It is no good commencing the political lobbying process at the last moment. MPs need cultivating through both the good and the bad times. Furthermore, they always appreciate thanks for their support. The top civil servants in the ministries also need winning over and warning them of the Company's forthcoming approach to politicians is a good way of ensuring their acceptance of an offer of a briefing. Reserve political lobbying for the largest PPPs and never use it too often lest it outlives its welcome.

Lobbying is not just something that applies to national and local government. There are many standards-setting agencies and regulators, such as those of the various United Nations organisations and the European Community, which require careful and often continuous lobbying. By their very nature, many of the large companies involved in the PPP sector will have representatives on the various standards setting committees. They will also be members of the various organisations that represent their industry; organisations that usually have good contacts with these agencies and regulators.

Focused corporate initiatives

The large financial commitments inherent within PPP purchases mean that it is often appropriate to mount a promotional campaign in support of an offering, particularly as part of the final win strategy. These campaigns are mostly slanted to influence the political process, containing appropriate messages, such as offset benefits, number of jobs created or retained and the building or retention of a national expertise.

In appearance, such initiatives often resemble corporate advertising, in that they may not include direct reference to the PPP performance benefits. Such information is, in any case, likely to be alien to the intended audience because of their unfamiliarity with the PPP's technical environment. Thus, the other aspects of the campaign assume even more importance. The choice of message, its presentation and the media must all be impeccable for this approach to be effective. The use by British Nuclear Fuels of a campaign to support the opening of its Thorp reprocessing plant at Sellafield was well thought out and effective in achieving its aim.

Timing, too, is likely to be critical. Too soon leaves room for a competitive counter. Too late means that the decision has already been made at the most senior levels and overturning it is an unlikely prospect. Of course, such campaigns rely heavily on the effective use of consultants and media specialists, such as corporate advertising agencies. It is probably a good thing that the expense and the high profile of such campaigns within a company limits their frequency of use.

Exhibitions and conferences

The cost of exhibiting can easily constitute the largest single part of any PR budget. Attendance at major trade fairs, particularly those held overseas, can be very expensive, particularly when staffing costs are included. Their number has grown alarmingly, as profit for the exhibition organiser is the key driver, rather than the provision of a service to the exhibitor or visitor interested in gathering information for a forthcoming purchase. Each company will need a PPP exhibition policy to take account of a number of factors.

The market segments being accessed, particularly from a geographical point of view, are important. Equally so is whether a particular industry or specialist customers are being targeted by the exhibition and where the latter lie in the vertical integration chain. For example, should a electrical generator manufacturer's attendance be at the "generator manufacturers' show" or the "power station builders show?" In the latter case, customers will be prominent on the stands and captive for the duration of the show, often feeling some camaraderie with fellow exhibitors.

Some critical questions need answering before making any commitment to exhibit.

- Why have we chosen to go to this exhibition?
- What message are we trying to put across?
- What are we going to exhibit?
- How will we present our PPPs?
- How are we going to judge the success of our stand?
- How large a budget can we afford?
- Which staff should attend?

Unfortunately, the answer to the first question is often "We can't afford not to be there." This form of moral blackmail needs serious questioning as, in fact, the negative aspects of not exhibiting are often far less than was first thought. Indeed, such drawbacks can be offset by thoroughly publicising the reasons for not attending beforehand. Exhibitions come large and small, as do companies in the PPP business. It is as well, when booking space, to take both factors into account. Bear in mind that a good stand location is often dependant on an early booking and that the stand design must be both attractive and effective from the customers' and the stand staff's points of view. Page 131 gives more information about exhibiting overseas.

Stand manning

Staff on stand duty at exhibitions need training for the role and there are some excellent books and videos available. Key factors are smart dress standards, a welcoming stance and avoiding the question "Can I help you?" which invites the response "No thank you." Far better to say " What is your particular interest in this PPP?" which forces a positive reply.

It is important not to baffle visitors with technicalities, unless they clearly signal a desire to discuss technical intricacies. As far as possible, discussions should not take place in a noisy environment. A well-designed stand will allocate space for sitting with visitors who wish to have a briefing. The Company has invested a great deal of time and money in its stand and a key decision maker may turn up right at the end of the day. Never shut down a stand before the official exhibition closing time.

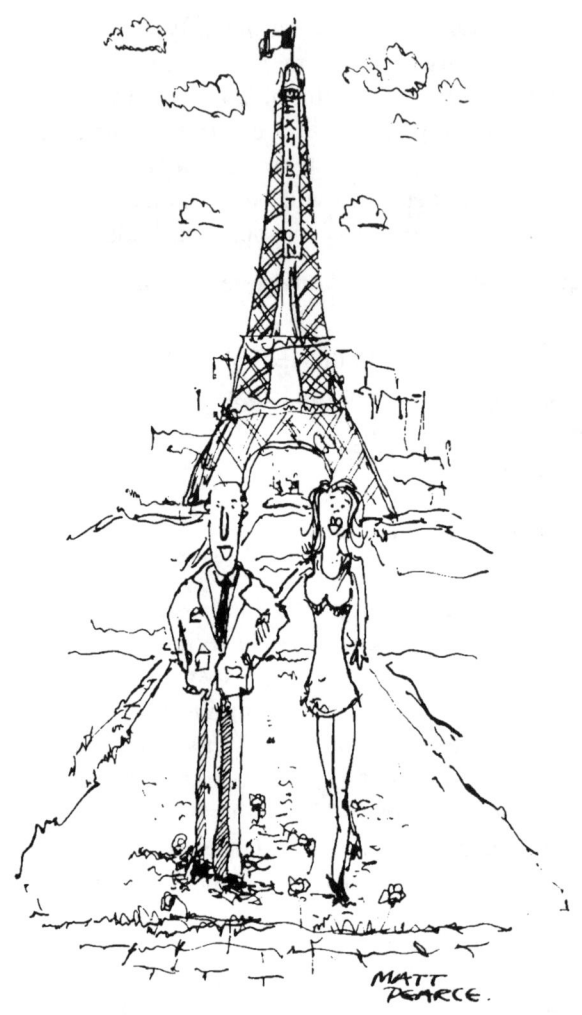

THE DECISION TO GO TO AN EXHIBITION SHOULD NOT JUST BE BASED ON THE GLAMOUR OF THE VENUE.

Smoking, as well as the smell of alcohol on an exhibitor's breath, can put off a potential customer. Stand manning is hard work and needs scheduling carefully to avoid total exhaustion. A half-day is the maximum time one person can effectively carry out this duty without a break. However, once someone is familiar with the stand, they are much more effective and should continue with the role for the length of the show. It is essential to appoint someone as stand manager and to have the senior sales or marketing member of the Company in charge overall, providing support to the stand manager as well as dealing with VIP visitors to the stand.

Never leave brochures and leaflets for visitors just to pick up. A display of available literature at the reception, together with exhibition enquiry forms, backed up by a literature store, can ensure that brochures are always exchanged for a business card (or name and address). This allows follow up of each enquiry after the show and also provides a qualitative as well as a quantitative tool for assessment of the worth of the visitors. It can also discourage competitors collecting literature.

Exhibitions are always a busy working ground for information gathering by competitors and staff need warning of the dangers of unwittingly briefing competitors of the Company's plans. This particularly applies to the young and enthusiastic members. Almost always, a competitor will make an approach, having filled in a badge at the entrance showing the name of some innocuous organisation. Remember to do the same and send company staff on a trawl of the competitors' stands, looking at their displays, collecting brochures and gathering information.

Staging a company exhibition

There may be occasions when a company wishes to hold a seminar or even stage its own exhibition. This is particularly relevant for some of the largest companies in the PPP business. Such events may be held in the UK or overseas, depending on the target audience, and are an excellent way of getting the attention of customers, providing they can be persuaded to attend.

Other events

Conferences, new PPP field demonstrations, inward visits by customers and corporate hospitality events all have something in common with exhibitions and the same PR staff can advantageously organise them. With a busy calendar, the department should always check for potential clashes with other events.

Many companies in the PPP business forget the importance of using their in-house conference rooms as a PR tool. Apart from good audio-visual facilities, illustrations of PPPs in service and new ones on offer provide excellent visual impact and can, for some industries, be supported by real hardware, often at the sub-system level. The same arrangements can be used at the main entrance hall of any building likely to be frequented by potential customers.

Invitations

Whatever the event, two golden rules are to send out the invitations early and to make sure that the mailing list is up to date and correct. A low acceptance rate is common if invitations are mailed late, as customers will generally have busy diaries and will invariably receive similar invitations from competitors. As far as up to date mailing lists are concerned, it is better to list people by function. Thus, when someone is promoted or moves job, the appointment still remains on the list, so that the newcomer is not missed. A mailing list with telephone numbers also allows a quick secretarial call to update the information.

Literature

The written word is one of the most important PR tools in the PPP business. This can range from company annual reports and capability brochures, often used during the first contact with customers, to descriptive PPP brochures, data sheets and catalogues. It is useful to reprint conference papers and trade press articles about the Company's PPPs as they provide a powerful soft selling tool.

House magazines, the ones designed for external consumption, are another useful soft sell. As well as providing PPP information and application reports, they are a means of giving news of recent company successes and organisational changes.

Design of literature

White space sells. At all costs avoid the temptation to cram as much information as possible onto each and every page. It can present the reader with an encyclopaedic impression of the document; enough to put anyone off. Good margins top and bottom, as well as on both sides, together with generous paragraph breaks can help to cheer up the reader considerably; improving information transfer. Illustrations confer similar advantages.

The use of colour requires careful consideration. While the benefits are very obvious, they have to be set against increased costs. It is surprising how effective it is to use two colours, black and one other, particularly when employing shades of each colour. Coloured or tinted papers can also provide an advantage far beyond their cost. Figure 22 gives further information on preferred sizes of paper.

When considering sales literature, there is a fairly natural progression, starting with the glossy leaflet or "flier." The aim of this document is to start the conversion path from opportunity to prospect. Do not distribute fliers until they are supported by the next level of documentation. A brochure must be ready for sending out with the response to requests, from the recipients of fliers, for more information about the offering. The technical proposal is the longest and most complex document in the literature hierarchy and page 71 deals with it in more detail.

Direct mail

Mailshots are generally under-used, yet with the number of customers in a PPP market usually quite small, they are a speedy and cost effective way of drawing attention to a new or updated offering. Electronic mail is one method of access, but more usual is a letter, often a personal one from the sales director, accompanied by a flier. Similar mailing of reprints of articles, those house journals designed for external consumption, and capability brochures can all help to keep existing customers, as well as potential new ones, up to date with company activities.

It is essential to involve the relevant sales executives in any mailshots to enable them to hold fruitful follow up discussions with the recipients. Note that there is a considerable body of evidence which supports sending a follow-up to the initial mail shot as a key method of increasing the response rate.

Audio-visual

Videos are a powerful and increasingly popular means of showing customers PPP offerings, particularly where it is impossible in the early stages to show an actual installation. Videos can describe the Company and its capabilities, or a particular PPP or range of PPPs. While expensive to produce, a good PPP video is worth its weight in gold and is one of the most successful aids available to sales staff. It can often overcome language barriers by means of a foreign "voice over" and reach those with a visual outlook on the world, as distinct from those who relate to facts, data and concepts.

Next in importance are 35mm slides and overhead projector (OHP) view graphs, transparencies or acetates. The term view graphs will be used to cover all three latter terms. Capable of projecting both photographs and textual information to large audiences, the quality advantage lies with 35mm slides. They are, however, less desirable in terms of cost and darkness of the auditorium, making it difficult for the audience to experience a close visual relationship with the speaker. An additional advantage of view graphs, and hard copy of them, is the ease with which textual view graphs can be produced using a PC and photocopier. Finally, the USA has standardised on view graphs and the projection of 35mm slides there may be difficult if not impossible.

Units are now available which plug into a personal computer, fit on top of an OHP and allow projection of the images from the computer directly onto a screen. With increasing complexity, it is essential to appoint a competent person to look after the audio-visual projection facilities as these do require regular maintenance, particularly the provision of spare bulbs and the cleaning of optics.

Photography

Black and white, as well as colour prints and transparencies are important for use in brochures, proposals, press releases and all other areas of public relations. Always hold a good stock. The importance of a "quality, interesting picture" cannot be overemphasised, and may result in its selection as a front cover illustration for a trade magazine. Colour prints can also be mounted in frames and used to brighten areas of the Company, such as conference rooms, as well as being given as gifts to customers and potential purchasers.

The relative pros and cons of the photographer being on the Company's payroll is likely to be influenced by the consideration of ownership of the intellectual property rights of photographs, which will stay with any independent photographer. This disadvantage, together with the lack of control of workload priorities have to be balanced against the outsider's greater chance of providing a fresh approach, improved creativity and a better standard of service.

Presenting technical papers

The preparation and presentation of technical papers have both advantages and snags. On the plus side is the publicity for the Company and the message that goes out to the customer community about the technical leadership of the Company. This can be a particular benefit in the PPP arena, where there are usually many key members of the customer community at seminars and there is often the opportunity to secure press coverage for the paper.

On the negative side is the fact that all the competition will also have access to the papers and be helped by them. In addition, when presenting the paper itself in open forum, answers to questions can often lead the presenter to give away more information than would be commercially sensible. Finally, the time involved in the preparatory work, as well as the cost of travel and accommodation, possibly overseas, are all factors that need weighing up.

Presentation skills

The whole subject of making presentations is sufficient to warrant a complete book on the subject and the bibliography lists a number. What is clear is that sales and marketing staff regularly have to make presentations to their customers and a high standard is essential.

It is worth starting off thinking about the way a sales executive should dress for a presentation. Smart, subdued dress is the order of the day. At one extreme, it isn't a fashion show. At the other, a scruffy appearance can lead the customer to wonder how well the Company is organised. One technical director in the electronics industry was reputed to own just one suit, which would be worn, under duress, only when presenting to customers!

It is a reasonable assumption that the speaker will have a thorough knowledge of the subject being presented and will have rehearsed the presentation a sufficient number of times to be fluent. However, it is often the case that presenters on one subject will have to field a question relating to the Company, but in a different area to their own. It is a wise precaution for all such executives to be able to talk for a short time about these other areas.

The world divides into those who prefer to read a text, or work from notes and those who have the confidence to speak unaided, though possibly with a small aide memoire card discretely to hand. The most important factor is that there is no correct approach and speakers should choose whichever is the most comfortable for them. Those who speak unaided will usually allow the visual material to guide them through their presentation. This is not an excuse for simply reading the words on the slide, as this habit can prove very irritating. What the speaker should be doing is amplifying such text.

A serious problem, which besets many speakers, is letting their voice fall at the end of a sentence, often to the point of in-audibility. This fault needs overcoming and a clear tone, with plenty of variation built in, will prevent a monotonous drone.

Visual aids

Much research has shown that neither speaking alone, nor solely providing visual information, allow an audience to remember significant amounts of the information presented. Clearly a mixture of the two is essential and the assumption is that all sales and marketing presentations will include view graphs, slides or, perhaps best of all, part or the whole of the PPP itself. When preparing visual aids, remember that, to an extent, they will compete for the attention of the audience. Ensure that they convey an effective message, but divert the audience's attention as little as possible, so that those listening can concentrate on what the presenter is saying.

The biggest benefit of using view graphs is that the room can have sufficient light for the speaker to maintain good eye contact with the audience, thus encouraging questions and improving communications. There is a great danger in trying to cram too much information onto a single view graph or slide. Research has indicated that the maximum content of one view graph should be six lines, each with a maximum content of six words; a rule for the guidance of wise people and the obedience of fools! A handout of hard copy after the presentation will act as an aide memoire to each attendee.

The use of pointers is a minefield. The telescopic ones are ideal from the presenter's point of view, but do provide an almost irresistible opportunity to fiddle with the telescopic mechanism, much to the irritation and distraction of the audience. A long wooden pointer gives similar opportunities to fiddle.

Laser ones, projecting a red marker, are sometimes heavy and awkward to manage; the small ones only projecting a tiny dot. Their novelty can also cause distraction. On the other hand, the worst situation of all is to be without any form of pointer.

Writing on a flip chart can be particularly helpful at less formal presentations, but requires skill and practice if the presenter is to provide a useful and legible written record. It also requires a pre-check that the marker pens are available in a sufficient range of colours and that they are not virtually out of ink. The use of short videos can be a great adjunct to any presentation. They should always come at the end of the presentation, due to the normally high standard of presentation skills found on videos and their high visual impact; a return to a live speaker then seeming an unacceptable anticlimax.

Presentation length

Generally, it is difficult to get anyone's undivided attention for more than twenty minutes, though with a generation that has grown up watching television programmes, an attention span of forty to forty-five minutes is becoming more common. This has a serious impact on the planned length of any presentation and two other factors also need consideration. First, attention span is much shorter if anyone in the audience is not interested in the subject matter; more common than might be supposed.

A second problem arises if the audience is listening to a presentation that is not in their mother tongue. In this case, the presenter must speak more slowly than normal, a skill that requires considerable practice. Furthermore, continual checks for comprehension are essential. Using an interpreter, any presentation will take at least twice as long as it would in English and the speaker will have to practice phrasing the presentation into translatable groups of words.

It is absolutely crucial to have a dry run with any presentation; the more so if it is an important one or if there is any new material involved. If it is possible to arrange an audience that will give feedback, so much the better. The audience can indicate what worked well and what did not, as well as giving some authenticity to the normal nervousness of the presenter.

The auditorium

Experienced presenters always keep monitoring the temperature of the auditorium and the efficiency of the ventilation. A build up of carbon dioxide will "knock out" any audience, no matter how compelling the presentation. The layout of the room, position of light switches and speaker audibility also need checking. Comfort breaks are an essential consideration in planning a presentation. Liquid and solid refreshments are welcome at the right time, but never too much of either. In fact, a light lunch is essential if the speaker who has the misfortune to cover the subsequent "graveyard slot" is to get any information across to the audience. Where equipment demonstrations are part of a programme, placing them immediately after lunch can assist the digestion process, to the benefit of all concerned.

Conclusion

The golden rules of presentations are first to "Tell them what you are going to tell them, tell them and then tell them what you've told them." Second, check that all the equipment works, including spare bulbs, and rehearse until fluent.

Advertising

This is an area where many in the PPP business seriously doubt whether they get value for money. Always expensive, there is no certainty of any advertisements actually being seen by customers. With a small number of people generally involved in the purchasing decisions, there are often other more effective ways of getting the message to them. Having said that, there are two occasions when advertising may be well worth considering.

The first is in getting the Company and its capabilities known in a new market segment. The other is in launching a new offering on the market. The message must be simple, the advertisement itself striking, and sufficient literature must be available to deal with the resulting enquiries. It is unfortunately still appropriate to recall that a single advertisement, even in the most prestigious media, will have zero impact such are the crowding and babble going on concurrently. A committed series of advertisements is the only valid approach.

Advertising can be a powerful tool in influencing shareholders at times when the Board needs either to raise further capital, or public confidence after a disaster with one of the company's PPPs. However, as with so many things, this type of advertising campaign needs good planning and running at the right time and in the right journals.

An annual review of advertising policy is always worthwhile and ensures the pattern of insertions matches the sales and marketing needs of the Company. In addition, it forms a useful reason for turning down the inevitable telephone call selling advertising space. A number of companies will carry out advertising effectiveness surveys. These are likely to provide useful feedback, both on the effectiveness of the campaign and perceptions of the Company and the PPPs being advertised. Key measures are assisted and unassisted recalls compared with the respondent's function within the customer community.

Editorial supplements (so called advertorials), published and distributed as part of some trade magazines, are a way of advertising a company's range of capabilities and PPPs at a surprisingly low cost. In many ways they are more acceptable to readers than straight advertisements and more useful to the Company when reprinted. Entries in yearbooks and directories are essential from a communication point of view, but the very use of these documents mitigates against the effectiveness of conventional advertisements in them.

Sponsorship and charity donations may be considered in this sector of PR, the former including the sponsorship of books, libraries, universities and colleges, research and even the Arts. Charity donations depend very much on the mission statement of the Company and the attitude of the main board. What is clear is that direct donations to charities give them better revenue than the purchase of advertising space in charity brochures. This is because a large percentage of the cost of a charity advertisement ends up going to the publisher.

Do not ignore free give away promotional items. By the very bureaucratic nature of the PPP business, there are many people involved in the purchasing chain who may appreciate a calendar, ball-point pen or similar item. These are particularly important when exporting to the Third World. However, it is essential to recognise a potential sensitivity to free give aways. As an example, for United States government employees, extra-territorial legislation means that all gifts must be declared and in the past, even buying guests a cup of coffee in the Company's restaurant has affronted their sensitivity. Fortunately, recent changes in the law have excluded such small items, but care is still needed.

House styles/visual identities

The name and visual identity can, to some extent, affect the whole feeling of the customer community about a company and its offerings. This close linkage with the perception aspect of positioning means giving it particular attention. Unfortunately, this is not always the case and there are still painful examples of company names that are unacceptable in certain countries. GPT, the name of the UK's leading telecoms manufacturer, translates into French as "I farted." Examples from the car industry include names like the Nova; in Spanish "Doesn't go" and the MR2, in French a most unpleasant swear word!

The identity will manifest itself in a wide range of areas.

- All types of stationary, including letterheads and forms
- Equipment labelling and drawings
- Audio visual standards
- Literature and publications
- Advertising
- Promotional gifts
- Building signs
- Vehicle liveries
- Uniforms and overalls
- Security passes

Unfortunately, careless and undisciplined implementation of the company's visual identity gives out important negative messages. Thus, serious consideration needs giving to the impact of a corporation's house style, and to the significant expense and time required to make any changes.

User groups

The formation of user groups can be beneficial, both to the supplier of a particular PPP and to the customers. More than just a marketing ploy, user groups can provide a channel for a useful interchange of information between the various users themselves and also back to the manufacturer. During the life of a PPP, user groups can organise the economic ordering of batches of spares and set up training courses with significant numbers of attendees. The user group may even exchange surplus spares and the knowledge imparted at such courses may be in the form of operational know-how even beyond that of the manufacturer. It is not uncommon for PR to become deeply involved in such groups, producing a user group journal and organising symposia.

PART 3:

SUPPORTING FUNCTIONS

Relating to the commercial function · Relating to the financial function · Relating to the project/programme management function

There are a number of functions, whose operations are closely interwoven with those of sales and marketing. The commercial function's involvement is in contracting and other forms of agreement, whilst the financial function's input is absolutely crucial to assembling the prices bid for PPPs in the marketplace. Finally, the project/programme manager's involvement in the selling of any PPP is a critical success factor. The aim of this part of the book is to deal only with those aspects of these three functions which are likely to impact on anyone working in the sales and marketing function.

Chapter 12:

Relating to the Commercial Function

Relationships between commercial & selling functions · Why contracts are needed · ITPs · PPP contracts · Contract signature · PPP contract documentation · Contract terms & conditions · Intellectual property rights (IPR) · Liquidated damages · Force majeure · International law · Export licences · Passage of title · INCOTERMS · Export finance · Bank guarantees · Insurance · Other types of contract

Relations between commercial and selling functions

It is rare in the PPP business, and even dangerous, for sales executives to be empowered to agree contract terms and conditions. The commercial department usually undertakes the application of commercial conscience, demanding a very close working relationship between the sales executive and the commercial executive trying to win any particular contract. This requires mutual respect, which takes time and experience to develop. A no less close working relationship is needed between the sales director and the commercial director. The combining of the two functions under a single director in the PPP arena is not recommended.

By their very nature, the two functions attract opposites. Sales staff tend to be of the "get up and go" mentality, unstoppable optimists used to brushing aside objections. Commercial staff, on the other hand, need to be thorough and painstaking even to the extent of appearing pedantic. The two types of personality do not work together easily, yet it is essential that they establish the best of working relationships. This does require some compromise on both sides. An understanding of the other's role is the best starting point. There are many examples of close personal friendships developing between executives from the two functions who have learned to work together.

In addition, the commercial department will have to protect the Company from unacceptable business risks, which may even make a PPP that is potentially an excellent new idea into a non-starter. A particularly common example is that of PPP liability. Consider the case of an air traffic control system where a problem could cause two jumbo jets to collide over London. The insurance cover needed for such an eventuality would amount to billions of pounds and, although the chances of such a failure are remote, the cost of the necessary insurance might be prohib-itive. Similar problems face potential suppliers of collision avoidance systems for all types of transportation.

Thus in summary, the role of a commercial function is to deal with all commercial and legal issues; mainly working on agreements, intellectual property rights,

A TYPICAL SALES EXECUTIVE'S VIEW OF THE COMMERCIAL FUNCTION.

government and banking documentation as well as obtaining export finance and not forgetting preparing and signing contracts. They are also normally responsible for submitting the final price and leading contractual negotiations with the customer. In addition, they usually deal with shipping PPPs to destination and obtaining payment from the customer. On occasions, they will have to provide parental guarantees from the overall corporation to an operating division.

Why contracts are needed

In an ideal world, contracts would not be required. In the normal, less than perfect situations and with the complexity of most PPP solutions, contracts are essential to define who is to do what work, in what period of time and for how much money. Hopefully, the words of the contract will rarely need quoting by either party, but they are there when things start to go wrong and, hopefully, will cover every eventuality. Such events may range from the destruction of the supplier's facility by fire, through major strike action to failure to deliver. The aim of any contract is to protect both parties from potential damage by the other. As well as contracts to provide a PPP, there are a number of other types of contracts, which impact on the sales and marketing function, and they are covered at the end of this chapter.

ITPs

A letter of intent to purchase is an advance notice by a customer of the intention to place a contract and has no legal status whatsoever. It is useful in getting a customer's commitment to the purchase of a particular PPP, but does nothing except giving a warm feeling to the sales executive. An instruction to proceed, on the other hand, when followed in good faith, results in a liability on the part of the purchaser to pay a reasonable amount for the work done. This can amount to the full contract value if no contract is ever agreed.

An agreed limit of liability is a contractually binding agreement, usually covering initial work of a loosely defined nature up to an agreed amount. It is actually a mini-contract! If and when the formal contract is eventually agreed, any work completed under the limit of liability is considered to have been executed under the terms of this contract.

PPP contracts

A contract is a legally enforceable promise. The key criteria used to judge the existence of such a promise are the "consideration" and the "agreement."

The consideration

The consideration is the price of the promise. It must be sufficient though it need not be adequate, as with peppercorn rent. Past consideration is not a factor in a new contractual commitment, but variations to existing contractual terms that are agreed do not require a new consideration. Likewise, it is possible to have promises made after the contract, which are enforceable, depending on factors such as the wording and intent. For example, a contract to deliver a truck in eight week's time at a price of £100,000 may be varied by agreement to an earlier delivery at the same price and these revised terms, once agreed, would be binding.

The agreement

The agreement requires an offer and an unqualified acceptance.

An offer

Offers may be written, verbal or established by practice, e.g. rights of way, strike of a gavel. Offers are either refused, subject to counter-offer, accepted or expire. Counter offers negate the original offer that can no longer be accepted unless re-offered. An offer must be comprehensive and contain the terms in a way that are clear, complete and certain.

Offers can be withdrawn at any time before acceptance unless there was consideration that the offer should be open for a specific period. Withdrawal is only effective when communicated to the offeree. In the PPP arena, there are often requests for extensions to the validity of offers and, in inflationary times, the granting of such extensions is tantamount to giving a discount on the price. There can also be a knock on effect where major sub-contracts are involved.

Requests for tenders are generally invitations to treat and invite offers. Note that unilateral offers are binding on the offeror but not on the offeree. In such circumstances, for a request for tender or enquiry to become a contract, it has to be an offer to buy and specifically directed to one supplier.

Price lists are generally not offers but invitations to treat. If a party reserves the right to negotiate further, then it is not an offer but an invitation to treat. Consequently, a letter of intent does not create legal intentions, it specifically identifies that negotiations are continuing.

An acceptance

An acceptance agrees to the offer under the conditions made in it. It must be unconditional otherwise it is a counter-offer. Once accepted, the contract binds both parties. Offerers can waive the right of notification of acceptance of an offer through their action, for example shipping goods in response to an order. If the goods are delivered with a shipping note containing the seller's terms and conditions and the goods are accepted, then those terms and conditions, providing that they are reasonable, would probably be deemed to have been accepted in what amounts to a counter-offer.

An agreement to agree is probably too uncertain about key terms to constitute a contract. Agreement, though silent on price, may be a contract with the expectation that the price will be reasonable.

Contract signature

A contract that leaves both parties with the feeling that they could have done better, is probably a reasonably fair one. Certainly, neither side should feel they have pulled a fast one on the other party. That is a formula for disaster in the PPP environment, both in terms of reputation and access to this customer for follow on business. After all, the contract is really only there in case things start to go wrong. In such an event, clarity and due process should be present, otherwise there is the risk of ending in court. A protracted and expensive struggle will result, with highly limited operating capabilities for both parties in the interim. If all goes well, there should be little need to resort to the clauses in the contract.

Sales executives should never allow the Company to take their customers to court, for whatever reason. If a dispute ends up there, this may limit the ability of the Company in the interim to chase new business because other customers will assume that there is no smoke without fire and that the Company is at fault.

Effective date of contract

A term, used mostly in export contracts, where signature alone is not sufficiently binding, legally and/or financially, to commence performance of the contract. The date may depend on such factors as the receipt of a letter of credit, issue of a performance bond or approval of an export licence.

PPP contract documentation

The contract for a PPP is likely to be quite a complex set of documents. There will certainly be the contract document itself, which will include the total price and payment terms, as well as other terms and conditions, the delivery time scale and a summary description of the PPP to be supplied. Normally, there will be a far more detailed description of the PPP with ancillary items such as its installation, setting to work, hand over, field support and priced spare parts for say the next ten years. This technically descriptive document or series of documents may include a significant number of drawings as well as the original proposal, though often the number and extent of amendments made during negotiations make a re-issue more satisfactory.

The main aim of the technical document is to enable compliance with the specification to be proved at handover of the PPP; something that is potentially much more difficult when the purchaser issues only a cardinal points specification. Inevitably, there will be other more detailed documents, such as spares lists detailing every single item, full syllabi for training courses and specifications for building interior decoration and furniture. The amount of paper can easily fill a four drawer filing cabinet and on the largest and most complex PPPs takes dramatically more space. Care needs taking as to which documents are part of the resulting contract, which are not, and to agree their order of precedence.

Contract terms and conditions

Purchasers usually propose contract terms and conditions in requests for tenders and these will normally have been prepared by their legal department. Some clauses are almost certain to be boilerplate ones taken from drafts prepared by some learned body. Since such a set of terms and conditions unilaterally represents the desires of the purchaser, the supplier's response will normally take exception to certain terms, offering replacements that reflect their concerns and reduce the risks they face. For the selected supplier, such clauses may be negotiated in an attempt to obtain a contract that addresses both parties' respective concerns and interests.

It is common to find that standard terms and conditions have been drawn up in the classic product companies, intended to reduce the cost of doing business. They are generally not relevant in a PPP environment, but are often printed on the reverse of a company's quotation paper. Standard models also exist which try to balance the obligations of the various parties. Examples include terms drawn up by organisations such as:

- British Electrical Allied Manufacturers Association.
- Joint Contracts Tribunal
- Institute of Mechanical Engineers/Electrical Engineers
- United Nations

Intellectual property rights (IPR)

All intangible rights including patents, registered designs, copyrights, trademarks, confidential know-how and trade secrets are generally defined as intellectual property rights. An increasing problem with PPPs, particularly but not exclusively those with a large software content, is the retention of IPR by the vendor. Recent public procurement policies have attempted to escape from proprietary solutions by gaining access, not only to intrinsic IPR, but also to background IPR.

This is a slippery slope for vendors, who may subsequently find themselves parting with manufacturing drawings to be bid on subsequently by competitors. The typical responses to such overtures by purchasers are the use of undetailed manufacturing drawings. A company that has invested significant funding in a new PPP will always need to protect its IPR. This single issue can take a disproportionately large amount of effort to negotiate to a satisfactory conclusion. IPR is also clearly a major consideration when dealing with licence agreements, a subject covered at the end of this chapter.

Liquidated damages

After price, probably the most important factor in a PPP contract is the delivery. The most common cause of breach of contract in the PPP arena is that of late delivery. Liquidated damages is the term used to define and limit the amount of money payable for this type of breach. These damages are intended to be a fair and reasonable constraint to the liability of the supplier. If the clause is penal, English contract law would not enforce it but would award unliquidated damages instead. There is no basis in English law for a penalty, though the term penalty clause is frequently misused, and it is often difficult to determine what is penal. Take care not to stray outside the clear definition of any liquidated damages clause and end up responsible for consequential loss or damages at large.

Force majeure

Force majeure is an unforeseen event causing excusable delay to or default of a contract. Such an occurrence would otherwise involve vendors in expensive, extended and sometimes international litigation with reduced chances of recovering funds. Since the law does not define the term, contracts should always include a definitive statement on the subject. It should include such problems as strikes, fires, outbreak of war, theft and the like.

International law

Ideally, any export contract should be governed by English law with arbitration, in the event of any dispute, in the United Kingdom. The rules of the arbitration process are those in use in the country where arbitration will take place. Thus UK arbitration does not involve the risks inherent in the use of another country's law. There are few legal systems regarded as reasonably safe but arbitration in Switzerland is a popular alternative, although more expensive for both parties should the process prove necessary. The choice of one of these "neutral" legal systems is always preferable to the other party's domestic law. Whilst on the subject of international matters, it is a sensible precaution to make any overseas customer responsible for the payment of any import duties or local in country taxes.

Export licences

All the governments of the industrialised nations have lists of restricted technologies and countries that require a special export licence as permission to export. Both the name of the customer and the country must be declared. Nations discuss the contents of these lists, with some imposition of views by the USA. If the customer is not the final user, then an end user certificate will always be needed. The list changes over time and high-technology exporters should monitor its contents regularly. Trade associations will lobby periodically for the removal of items from the list as technology marches forward. Authorisation by the Government to actually export goods, when the time comes, is in the form of the licence itself, issued just prior to shipment of the equipment.

The latest generation of mobile phones incorporates digital encryption and fell foul of these restrictions when attempting to export to Hong Kong; one of the largest mobile phone markets. The reason given was that the complex encryption is very difficult to decipher and, with the changing ownership of Hong Kong to a communist regime, such technology should not be released to them. The result was the development of a less secure encryption standard for that market, which then received a licence without problems.

Passage of title

The point of transfer of ownership of the goods is often a key element of what comprises the scope of supply. With most PPPs, the point of transfer is intrinsically far from clear unless carefully defined, and for software elements particularly so. Since there is no such thing as bug-free software, when is it regarded as delivered? A very few customers may be happy to accept their PPPs at the factory gates, but the vast majority will want the goods transported to site; often installed and commissioned there. In many cases, the PPPs will actually be built on site. A de facto standard has emerged defining each of the relevant terms. The International Chamber of Commerce publishes INCOTERMS and periodically updates them. They are generally recognised throughout the world.

INCOTERMS

Internationally used trade and delivery terms, INCOTERMS specify the respective rights and obligations of the buyer and seller in an international transaction. The most commonly used are:

Ex works

Title, along with risk and the cost of transporting the goods from the seller's works to the desired destination pass to the buyer when the purchaser accepts the goods that the seller has made available at the factory.

FOB

Free On Board is a widely used term signifying that the goods will be loaded onto a ship at a named port, the sellers' obligations being fulfilled when the goods pass over the ship's rail. From that point onwards, the buyer has to bear all the costs and risks of loss or damage to the goods.

The major exception to the international understanding of this INCOTERM is the use of FOB as a delivery term in much of North America. Here it is a catchall term signifying that the seller will supply the goods loaded into a vehicle at a certain location. E.g. FOB our trucks at our plant, FOB US Port or airport. At this point, title, risk and the cost of transporting the goods to the desired destination are the responsibility of the buyer. Typically, buyers will want the goods FOB site, whereas sellers want FOB their plant. Not only does the latter reduce costs, such as freight, but also passes on the risk of loss, which might also, for example, include consequential loss of revenue.

FCA

Free Carrier (*named place*). Title, risk and the cost of transporting the goods become the responsibility of the buyer when delivered into the care of the nominated carrier.

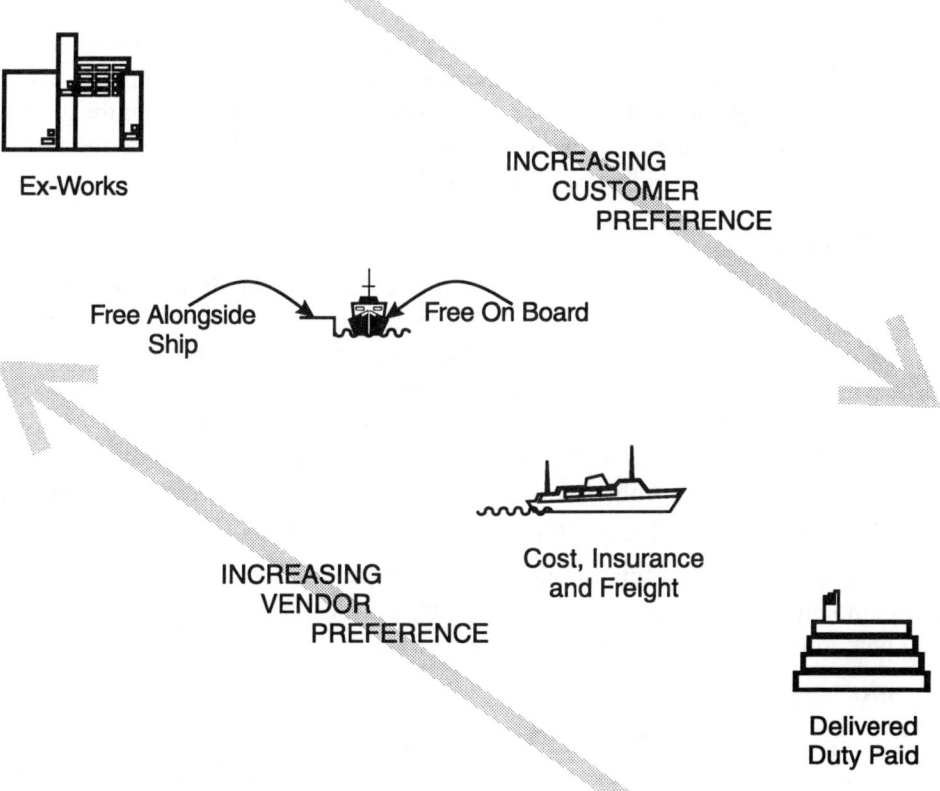

Figure 70. Some of the INCOTERMS (1990 edition), issued by the International Chamber of Commerce.

FAS

Free Alongside means the point of transfer of title is not on the ship but on the quay beside the ship. The other main difference in this term from FOB is that the buyer undertakes to clear the goods for export, obtaining and paying for all necessary documentation and licences.

CIF

Cost Insurance and Freight to a location is an alternative arrangement, in which the seller purchases and pays for the insurance and freight costs on behalf of the customer. Delivery is still effected when the goods are loaded, as with FOB, so that problems after this point will result in the buyer benefitting from any insurance claim settlement.

DDP

With Delivery Duty Paid, transfer of title occurs at the customer's site. Customers understandably prefer this arrangement, but it exposes the supplier to every type of vulnerability and shortfall of infrastructure required to deliver the goods. If the supplier is unable or unwilling to clear the goods for import, supplying on a DDP basis leaves that obligation with the buyer.

Export finance

Fundamentally, there are only two different classes of export finance worth considering. The first is credit, which deals with the loan of money to fund the PPP by a bank or similar financial institution, either to the buyer or to the supplier. This allows the customer to spread the pain of payment over a number of years. There are three different forms of credit. In the first two, there is normally an arrangement fee. This fee, together with likely interest payments, needs building into the PPP quotation before its submission. It is not unknown for a representative of the bank to form part of the negotiating team in these circumstances.

The other class of export finance includes all the various forms of counter-trade. It is incumbent on the sales executive to review all these options when it appears that any potential customer is unable to make a straight cash purchase.

Buyer credit

This is finance for high value (£2M minimum) export contracts, where a bank lends money directly to the overseas buyer to enable purchase of a specific PPP. The bank provides the customer with the cash who then pays the bank back over a fixed period, including interest payments. The ease with which this can be arranged depends on the credit worthiness of the buyer, itself related to the country in question. It is important for the sales team to remember that they may need to become heavily involved in helping the customer to obtain such credit. The seller also needs contractual safeguards to ensure the money is only used to pay for the PPP.

Supplier credit

In supplier credit, companies may approach their national pseudo-government body for preferential long-term financing to support their export performance. Britain's ECGD, America's Ex-Im Bank and Canada's EDC are examples and all have different policies on the way and the extent to which they will support their own industries. The best level of support subsidises exporters who can demonstrate that losing the contract will cause unemployment. The minimum support is so-called cosmetic financing, where low rates of interest are made available by levying finance and servicing charges. These costs are then hidden on top of the price of the supplier's PPP, to make up for the apparently low interest rate.

Alternatively, a commercial bank may operate on behalf of the supplier, making funding available, against which the supplier receives the full contracted payment when due. The loan value, principle and interest, are contained in the contract price and repaid by the buyer using Bills of Exchange or Promissory Notes, maturing every six months during the credit period. These bills or notes are purchased by the bank with no recourse to the exporter.

Many government sponsored supplier credit packages will only support PPPs with a high proportion of national content, eliminating such items as on-site civil works. As a result, such supplier credit is often used in conjunction with commercial financing. There is a framework of generally agreed consensus rates of interest which such bodies will quote, though some countries occasionally ignore them on PPPs they regard as important.

Tied aid

This type of financing may be available from the vendor's country, the Ministry of Overseas Development in the UK, from the European Community or even the United Nations. In the case of national aid, the expenditure is tied to industry in that country. Not all aid is available for any purpose. In many cases, aid is tied in terms of what can be supplied, often restricted to PPPs of a basic infrastructure nature, and the amount of foreign content permitted. Financing of local content may require special attention, as it may not be permissible to include it in the finance being provided for the prime contractor's content. Sales executives should examine all of these budgets to see if they can help finance the Company's PPPs and, if so, what conditions may be attached to the aid.

Counter-trade

Often and particularly in the Third World, the customer may look for counter-trade, where locally produced goods or commodities are provided in payment for the PPP. The Saudi Arabian Al Yamamah multi billion pound contract is paid for in oil. In fact, counter-trade is a financial deal where the seller agrees that, in return for the overseas buyer purchasing the PPP, the seller will exchange goods and services from the buyer's country. There are many different types including counter-purchase, barter, buy back, offset, switch-trading and evidence accounts.

There are counter-trade brokers who will purchase most items offered under counter-trade and quote a firm sterling price to the supplier, albeit with a discount for their services; usually around ten per cent. The main driver for the customer nation getting involved in counter-trade is that they are unable to sell the goods themselves. Access to suitable channels of distribution is essential before signature of any counter-trade deal. The use of brokers does, however, allow the supplying company to concentrate on what they are good at and not get involved in selling goods or commodities in unfamiliar markets.

Single project finance or project lines of credit are both common in the PPP arena. They involve acceptance of part or full payment in equity shares, buy back schemes or profit sharing.

Offset

Offset is one step back from direct counter-trade, where the customer demands that some work is placed locally, maybe a small percentage of the total contract value; on occasions over 100%. This offset involves finding local suppliers and can be fairly straightforward in terms, say, of building construction work for a new port complex, but more difficult in high-tech areas. However, the offset work does not necessarily have to be associated with the PPP itself and a company can build up credit in this area.

A UK company, needing to give offset work to Danish industry, put a local company on the bidders list for a new display for a PPP for a UK customer. The Danish company comfortably won the competition, on specification, price and delivery; a benefit in itself. It also met the offset requirement for a different PPP. The cold reality is that often the commitment by the vendor to ensure such offsetting arrangements is not honoured. The excuse has even been that local supplies of suitable quality could not match the price. Massaging of some figures is not impossible when local suppliers' workloads are at stake!

Bank guarantees

Contracts are all about managing risk. A particular and widely used protective measure is a bank guarantee, which is a guarantee or bond given by the seller's bank to the buyer, via the buyer's bank, as a surety for the seller's performance. If the seller fails to complete the contract, the buyer may cash or "call" the bond for its value at the bank or insurance company that issued it. Failure to perform may, or may not, require supporting evidence, such as an engineer's certificate.

In the event of disagreement over whether the call was rightful, the vendor's choices lie in arbitration or, finally, suing the purchaser. The vendor has no recourse to the issuer of the bond, providing the paperwork supporting the call is all in place. Sharp practices by certain countries have led to the availability of insurance against wrongful call.

Force majeure is probably the only acceptable reason for poor performance of a contract that doesn't warrant bonds being called by the purchaser. It is also worth noting the difficulty in getting bonds cancelled and returned after the performance of a contract, particularly an overseas one. The sales executive may need to play an important role in dealing this problem.

Guarantees are usually one of four types

Bid bonds

A guarantee that a quotation is serious and that the seller will accept a contract, if awarded on the terms of the quotation, or forfeit the bond. Its value is normally between 1% and 5% of the bid price. It is returned if the offer is unsuccessful and usually converted to a performance bond if a contract is signed.

Advance payment guarantee

An advance payment guarantee is one equal to the value of the advance payment. It offers security to the purchaser to offset the down-payment, made at the start of the contract, with nothing tangible to show for it. The value of the bond may reduce in proportion to deliveries made.

Performance bond

A performance bond is a guarantee to perform a contract in all its conditions. Usually 5% to 10% of the contract value, it is valid until completion of all contract activities.

Retention bonds

Buyers will often ask, during contract negotiations, for a cash retention. This is a percentage of the contract price, usually 5% to 10%, retained by the buyer until the seller completes performance of all contract obligations, including later tasks, such as warranty and in-country trials. Compared with holding back monies, a much better solution for vendors is to use a retention bond that guarantees that the seller will complete, in particular, these later obligations of a contract.

Insurance

There is a whole range of insurances that a company can take out. The ones of particular interest to those in sales and marketing functions include insurance during the carriage of goods, insurance against the unfair calling of bonds and against third party liability, as well as a government sponsored scheme against non payment by overseas customers.

ECGD and NCM

The government's Export Credits Guarantee Department offers one attractive form of export insurance that payment for PPPs supplied overseas will be made. The premiums depends on the amount of business insured and can be relatively inexpensive. The risk reduction for those using the insurance is the benefit. The availability of cover may be a deciding factor in whether to trade with a particularly difficult country. Cover is compulsory for PPPs supported by ECGD backed finance. For PPPs sold on credit terms of up to 180 days, NCM Credit Insurance, privatised from ECGD at the end of 1991, provides similar cover.

Other types of contract

In addition to the normal contracts for the purchase of PPPs, there are a number of other types of contract that are of importance to the sales and marketing function.

Confidentiality agreements

A substantial function of the commercial department is to protect company IPR as well as any other commercially sensitive information when holding discussions, for example, with potential teaming partners. Confidentiality agreements, between two or more companies that wish to exchange information of a sensitive nature to pursue a PPP, need signing by all parties to protect the information involved. Most companies have a standard form of agreement, which needs only the filling in of the names of the companies and a generic description of the PPP. Unfortunately, each company's form of agreement seems to vary, causing delays while the commercial departments of the participants agree changes to the wording.

Teaming agreements

Similar, but clearly much more comprehensive teaming agreements are needed, which require careful thought about the length of time and range of PPPs to be covered. Where joint ventures are set up, the parent companies will usually need to agree to provide guarantees. These allow passage of unfulfilled claims on the venture to the parent organisations, since the joint venture itself will often consist of little more than rented office space and furniture. "Joint and several liability" is also likely to arise, whereby both parties are responsible for claims, regardless of which of them caused the failure.

Overseas representatives' agreements

One particular type of agreement is that between a company and its overseas representatives. In the PPP arena, agents' agreements are more common than distributor agreements, though it is worth pointing out that overseas representatives do not act as agents in the legal sense of the word. Such agreements require careful thought, particularly in defining the timing and quantity of remuneration, as well as the circumstances under which the parties will terminate the agreement. Care is also needed in cases where governments prohibit the use of representatives and in any case to keep the amount of commission paid confidential.

Subcontracts

In the PPP arena, as has already been mentioned, subcontract values can be very significant percentages of total contract value. This means giving major commercial consideration to the letting of such sub-contracts. The very detailed examination of the Company's proposals means that, almost inevitably, the Company is committed to a nominated sub-contractor before placement of the prime contract. The sub-contractor will know this and wish to exploit the situation to advantage. A back-to-back contract is one way of dealing with the problem. This involves getting the sub-contractor to agree to any special terms and conditions imposed by the customer and also to match any percentage price reduction given by the prime contractor. Thus the sub-contractor agrees to share the risk equitably in return for a fair share of the profits. Such an agreement implies that the prime contractor will keep the sub-contractor advised of any changes during negotiations of the prime contract.

Licence agreements

A licence agreement is one where the owner of a design agrees that another party may build and sell it in return for payment. There are basically two forms of licensing; licensing in and licensing out. Licensing in may be desirable for the development or marketing of part or all of a new PPP. Any agreement should normally split the total market to avoid the licenser competing directly with the licencee; a no win area for the latter unless special market knowledge is available.

Licensing out is an alternative to a direct sale, particularly where the recipient country has or desires to have an indigenous capability in the particular PPP area. Technology transfer is a generic term covering the various methods of transferring a company's technical know-how to another party. It is important to think out how to control the licencee's use of the licensed technology. There are many past horror stories of overseas countries that did not recognise intellectual property rights; merely taking the expertise without further licence fees and using it widely thereafter.

Royalties are the payments made in the form of a percentage of the licencee's selling price, paid to the licenser under a licence agreement, and are really a much more satisfactory way of concluding a licence agreement than demanding a large initial payment.

Chapter 13:

Relating to the Financial Function

Financial goals · Profit · Cash · Determinants of profitability · Depreciation · Cost investigations · Overheads · Contract pricing · Standard price lists · Foreign currency · Buying forward

Financial goals

Different companies are driven by different financial goals to varying degrees. Most look for profit and many find it convenient to consider profit on sales. Shareholders' interest lies in return on investment (ROI) or return on capital employed, whilst the Company's financial director may well be driven as much by cash and cash flow. Whatever measures are used, and there are invariably more than one, it is essential to understand the chosen parameters as they will reflect in eventual offer prices and price negotiations. Better payment terms in exchange for a price reduction can be very attractive to a cash-hungry company.

Profit

Profit is the notional concept of the excess of revenue, generated by sales, over the costs associated with those sales. To reflect profit genuinely, the calculation must consider not only the PPP related costs, such as material costs per unit, but also an equitable share of time related costs, such as factory rent. Similarly, if stock levels have changed during the period, then the changed inventory value needs taking into account.

Cash

Cash is the funding available for expenditure. It is usual to add petty cash to deposits in those bank accounts that can be withdrawn without notice. The ease with which a resource can be converted to cash is termed liquidity. Liquidity crises have forced many small companies and not a few large ones, into bankruptcy, despite their being profitable.

Their problems have come about when their cash has run out and the banks have refused to increase their overdraft facilities. This is particularly common in a period of company growth, where the cost of fulfilling an increasing order book soaks up considerable amounts of cash before deliveries can be made and full payment received. A similar problem of funding work occurs in periods of high inflation.

Determinants of profitability

$$\frac{\text{Profit}}{\text{Capital employed}} = \frac{\text{Profit}}{\text{Sales}} \times \frac{\text{Sales}}{\text{Capital employed}}$$

i.e. ROI = Profit margin × Capital turnover

This equation illuminates the determinants of return on investment; usually abbreviated to ROI. The profit for a given capital employed is related to the return on sales and the ratio of sales to capital employed.

Consider two companies in the same business, with the same return on investment. One has a lower profit margin than the other but a faster capital turnover. Which is the better solution? There is no single right answer. Note, too, that the method that each uses to improve their profitability will vary according to their approach.

	RETURN ON INVESTMENT	PROFIT MARGIN	CAPITAL TURNOVER
COMPANY A	28%	14%	2
COMPANY B	28%	4%	7

Figure 71. Different approaches to profit margin and capital turnover can still result in the same return on investment.

Depreciation

Companies can, for their own purposes, calculate depreciation on any basis they want, provided it does not contravene good accounting practice. When it comes to the fiscal return, the government reverses the transaction and uses its own capital allowance tables to arrive at the actual amount of tax due. There are four different ways of viewing depreciation.

1. A way of taking into account the reduction in value of a capital item.
2. Part of the equitable distribution of costs to PPPs manufactured, in the calculation of profit.
3. A way of retaining value in the business, so that funds are available to help cover the cost of a replacement when a capital item wears out.
4. The mechanism used by the tax authorities to smooth tax revenue flows, regardless of whether purchases were made in the current tax year.

Cost investigation

Some industries and some customers within those industries may demand the right to investigate a supplier's costs. This usually merits separate data collection, analysis and presentation. Most common where the customer is a government department, the trend is now away from such practices towards firm fixed prices. However, where it does still exist, its importance in winning new business must be recognised and plans made for the consequences. Nevertheless, care needs taking to ensure that costs are collected and recorded in such a way that the customer can only gain access to the information specified in the contract and not other commercially sensitive data.

Overheads

It is useful to consider overheads in two categories:

1. The overheads directly associated with the production of the PPP.
2. The general or indirect overhead usually associated with the business' activities such as marketing, selling, commercial activities, accounts, human resources, company management, research and PPP development expenditure.

The finance function, in consultation with the board or management team, normally sets overhead recovery rates. They are calculated by dividing the predicted year's total overhead cost by the forecast annual turnover. Labour, materials and major sub-contract items may have different overhead rates, depending on the type of business of the Company. It is even possible to run differential overhead for different types of PPPs produced by the same company or division, though this approach does have several practical difficulties, see page 50.

Contract pricing

There are many adjectives used to define the various types of prices given in quotations and used in contracts. Never quote prices without an associated validity date. It is also important to ensure that everyone in the Company and the customer community agrees on the definitions. The following is a widely used list but the definition of the individual terms will vary from industry to industry. They are included to ensure that readers understand the various options and relate them to their own company practices.

Fixed or firm price

Firm price and fixed price are two particularly contentious terms, which are variously used to imply prices inclusive or exclusive of inflation.

Either   A selling price, inclusive of allowance for inflation made by the vendor, so that the purchaser can be sure of the amount to be paid before placing a contract.

Or   A selling price exclusive of inflation. Contracts containing such prices usually contain a contract price adjustment clause to cover inflation in the vendor's country and avoid the payment by the purchaser of any contingency, put on by the vendor, to cover the uncertainty of future inflation levels.

Fixed and firm price

Another possible description of a price inclusive of inflation.

Contract Price Adjustment (CPA)

Adjustment to a base price by means of an agreed formula to take account of inflation. Also known as VOP (Variation of Price).

Budgetary price

A price given to potential customers to enable them to put realistic figures into future budgets for planning purchases. It is essential to tie the budgetary figure to an order time scale, so that the customer can carry out any necessary escalation.

NTE (Not To Exceed) Price

This is similar to a budgetary price and needs to carry the same escalation caveats. As the name indicates, it is an attempt by the customer community to prevent sales executives quoting unrealistically low budgetary figures in order to get their company's PPP into a front running position.

Cost plus

Now a largely obsolete form of price, whereby the purchaser pays all the costs of doing the work plus an agreed profit rate. While it is clearly an encouragement for the supplier to do as much work as possible to maximise profit, it is still occasionally used when letting research contracts, where the amount of work to be undertaken is virtually impossible to estimate.

In the PPP business, with its lengthy timescales, it is normal practice to quote delivery timescales from the date of receipt of an effective order.

Standard price lists

Standard price lists may seem to be a long way from most PPP business but, though often controversial, they do have their uses. For major products, customers will expect to get an idea of price without necessarily asking for a quotation. The sales executive who has a price list handy is then at an advantage, particularly at budgeting time.

The real problem comes in export markets, where the amount of commission can and does vary from country to country. By grouping countries into high, medium and low commission territories, it is still possible to provide useful price lists, but the associated terms and conditions do need definition; for example FOB UK port, assuming a contract before the end of the calendar year, with or without a standard support package. These are price indications and it must be made unequivocally clear to customers that such is the case.

Foreign currency

Life becomes difficult from a revenue and expenditure point of view the moment a step is made overseas. Customers will want to pay in local currency while vendors will desire their home currency. Varying exchange rates, with no certainty as to the direction of movement, allied to the long implementation timescales of most PPPs, can cause significant problems. These can completely overshadow the potential profit on a contract. Unfortunately, buying forward may not be the end of such problems. In instances where the PPP is delayed, further expensive exchange deals may well need arranging.

More difficult is the period between bid submission and contract, when the Company will not wish to spend money buying forward, lest it fails to win the contract, yet will be giving an involuntary discount should the value of their currency rise during this period. Here, buying a forward option is the recommended solution.

An interesting alternative to the uncertainty is to provide a quotation, in the vendor's currency, but with a clause confirming that a fixed exchange rate with the purchaser's local currency will be agreed on the day the contract is signed. Behind this is the obvious need to arrange to exchange the local currency as it is paid, in a buying forward arrangement.

Buying forward

This is a way of getting around the problem of exchange rate variations in export contracts, where payment is in the customer's currency. It is quite feasible to buy forward foreign currency, once the contract has been signed. Though this is expensive, the cost can be built into the price. With the proviso that such currency is a hard one, for example US $ or French francs, arrangements can be made with a bank to buy forward given amounts of the supplier's currency, based on the purchaser's payment schedule.

Whilst there is a price to pay in exchange rate terms, PPP suppliers are guaranteed payment of fixed amounts of money in their own currency. A particular difficulty arises where the customer's currency is not convertible; a feature of many Third World countries run under communist regimes or dictatorships. In this case, the US dollar is the normal currency utilised, unless barter is acceptable. A useful option is to offset the risk by sub-contracting as much of the work as is feasible to local companies.

Chapter 14:

Relating to the Project/Programme Management Function

Project/programme management & managers · Sub-contracting · International teams · Collaborative assessments · Export contracts · Customer furnished equipment · Handing over orders · After sales support · Build to print

Project/programme management and managers

The stance adopted by PPP companies towards project/programme management and their strategy for such a function can be a critical success factor in a competitive market. PPP customers are trained to look at an organisation's management expertise in this area. Having cadres of suitable people available is an organisational challenge. The choice of project/programme manager (PM) designate and the Company's attitude to PPP management are certain to be examined. Most customers know from bitter experience that difficulties in this relationship will make the whole implementation process more cumbersome and risky.

There are likely to be three classes of PMs found in PPP companies. The first is the person who manages the development of a new PPP and the second is the individual responsible for a PPP production line. Finally, there may be a separate person who is answerable to the customer for the implementation of the contract. It is not the intention of this book to deal with the first two individuals, but rather to concentrate on whomsoever in the Company is executing the contract for the customer. That person is referred to as the PM and is often the bid manager for the PPP before contract award.

Sub-contracting

It is always important to ask why work should be sub-contracted, when in principle it could be done within the Company. There are three main reasons for giving work to sub-contractors. The first is to reduce the time to market for the PPP, the second is for peak-lopping purposes, when a company is overloaded with work and has a growing order book. The third reason is where the Company lacks the capability to carry out part of the work. This may be quite reasonable, as in the case of an engineering company sub-contracting civil works. In other instances, it may be necessary to question whether the Company itself should have the core competencies to do the work effectively. Employees often fail to be objective in this respect, particularly where it appears to them that the work involved may be interesting.

International teams

One of the major management challenges of the twentieth century has been the problem of running major international industrial teams. The problems facing the PM of an international programme are awkward, despite the partners working towards the same objectives. They demand political skill, tact, management of people and often the understanding of a foreign language and culture.

Collaborative assessments

When looking for a partner on a collaborative programme, it is important to be able to make an objective assessment of potential companies. A competitor analysis will beg appropriate questions as to whether some companies will be suitable partners. Page 187 further discusses this topic. In fact, it is quite common to collaborate on one contract and compete on another. The setting up of Chinese walls is a normal practice in such situations. The questionnaire opposite provides a good start to the assessment process and should help the PM designate and the sales executive to commence the evaluation process.

Further evaluation will follow from a short-list of organisations, which will be contacted and visited by a team from the Company. At the outset, it is important to consider how to resolve differences quickly and agreeably between the parties. To avoid bias, if at all possible the same individuals should make up the team visiting every company and the individuals should have the right mix of skills.

The sales executive can look at the attraction of the partner to the customer and assess the level of contact that already exists. The PM designate can look at the way the potential partner manages PPPs and examine possible incompatibilities or other difficulties in working together. Depending on the type of PPP, someone

TEAMING CHECKLIST				Commercial in Confidence
ASPECT	**WORST**			**BEST**
STATUS OF RELATIONSHIP	Nil contact	In contact with the Company	Collaborative work in progress	Previous collaborative partner
MANAGEMENT STRUCTURE	Unknown	Part known, with details attached		Known & diagram attached
HIGH LEVEL CONTACTS	None established	Sporadic contact with a few senior people		List attached (Name, known by whom, how well)
PERSONALITIES	Unknown	Part known, with details attached		List attached of those known (Name and position)
DETAILS OF COLLABORATIVE PPPs & VALUE TO COMPANY	Common areas of interest listed	Possible partnership for list of PPPs attached	List of current collaborative PPPs in progress	Past list of PPPs attached

Figure 72. A comprehensive check of all potential candidates should be made before any teaming agreement is reached.

from operations or engineering will need to assess capability and finally, though possibly at a later stage, a member of the commercial function will have to prepare a collaborative agreement.

Since such organisations are commonly competitors, either directly or remotely, discussions may need to be somewhat circumspect despite the existence of a confidentiality agreement. Those involved will need briefing on the appropriate degree of openness.

Export contracts

PMs need coaching the first time they deal with export customers who are in the process of purchasing or who have actually placed a contract for a PPP. They will have to learn to deal with a different culture and advice on this topic is best given by the appropriate sales executive, using the information contained in the second half of Chapter 6. In addition, the PM must ensure that the problems associated with foreign currency have been adequately covered, in order to avoid a shifting exchange rate turning a promising contract into a loss maker. There is information about how to achieve this at the end of Chapter 13.

Customer furnished equipment

The provision of customer furnished equipment or facilities can lead to more squabbles with the purchaser than almost any other topic. The problem is to ensure that the customer delivers what has been promised to time and quality. When, as happens from time to time, this fails to occur, then the supplier faces a time scale over run and consequential cost escalation. This is where the difficulties with the customer begin, with claim and counterclaim quickly souring what was a good working relationship. Tight definitions of interfaces and responsibilities are vital to avoid blame and counter blame should problems arise.

Handing over orders

By the very nature of the process, the sales executive has to hand over the main customer interface to the PM after the contract signature. This has a number of implications, not the least that the customer doesn't want to get to know someone else, particularly in Japan, the Middle East and, in fact, most Third World nations, where personal relationships with suppliers are often the most important rationale for their selection.

This difficulty is often exacerbated by the fact that customers see sales executives as sympathetic, helpful people, whereas they view PMs as aggressive demanding characters, who always seem to want more money and time to do the job. Despite this, one of the key roles of the PM is to win add on business. The sales executive should continue to support the PM in this, at times, difficult task that can be very rewarding for the supplier. Hanging on too long is likely to be a temptation for sales executives, particularly where they don't trust the rest of the organisation. Page 93 explores these and other issues.

After sales support

PPP support often lies within the project/programme management function, and can be a real Cinderella. Increasingly, companies are taking a far more positive view and it is not uncommon in the PPP market to find 25% of turnover and 50% of profit coming from this single area. The key need is for enthusiasts to run the PPP support business and enthusiastic sales executives to sell that support. However, customers are becoming much more aware of their needs in terms of logistics, spares and upgrades. They are including these costs in their life cycle cost analyses and often insisting on, for example, fixed prices for spare parts over a ten year operating life.

This professionalism is threatening the previous mechanism of winning the original contract at low margin and then bolstering it through captive spares sales mark-ups, as high as 300% to 400%. Technology is also arriving which enables "prototype" manufacture of spares in very short timescales, based on the original worn component. This is usually a much cheaper proposition than the spares quoted by the original equipment supplier. Large turbocharger rotors are a notable example. Care is essential, however, as some high-tech solutions still have components hand-picked during manufacture to ensure that they meet tight tolerance requirements, which may not be clear to the purchaser.

Build-to-print

Build-to-print is a specialised manufacturing business not normally associated with PPP companies. It can on occasions be a godsend to a well-managed company in the PPP arena, which will use such work to smooth out the almost inevitable peaks and troughs of the big brick type of business. Everyone in the management of the company needs to understand the difficulties of winning build-to-print work.

Most of the companies involved on a full time basis are lean and mean with minimal overheads. Thus, a large corporation will have to indulge in marginal costing to have much hope of winning. It will also need to have a very efficient manufacturing operation; as if such a thing is not an important factor in the PPP sector anyway. The other side of the coin is to be aware that every specified piece of work usually involves a customer who would like the next phase to evolve to a build-to-print basis. Thus the purchaser can gain directly equivalent quotations from multiple sources, trading one off against another; the intention being the general lowering of price levels.

Appendix A

Glossary of Terms

Advantage	An aspect of a PPP offering potential gain to the purchaser
ABC	Activity based costing
Augmented PPP concept	The characteristic of customers to view the total offering; the PPP itself as well as support, service & reputation
Available market	The total of all the individual market segments served by different applications of contemporary technology but limited by constraints of trade
BAFO	Best & final offer
Blue team	A group which concentrates on finding technical solutions for a proposal independently of the bid team, to see if a better way of meeting the requirement can be found. The group can also help to find alternative offerings to the main compliant solution
BIF	Bid initiation form
Boilerplate	Any commercial or technical clauses or paragraphs, which are found in many different proposals or contracts, and are thus frequently required in such documents
Bug	An operating situation which causes an unpredictable and undesirable system response
Bundling	The provision of related products or services within the offering e.g. "free" operator training, delivery, on-line support
Benefit	A gain through ownership for the purchaser which addresses a need they have already identified
Cannibalisation	The substitution of existing orders by orders for a new offering
Carnet	A document for the temporary export of equipment for a demonstration, trial or exhibition
Cash cow	A PPP with a dominant share of a static market
Cherry picking	A customer strategy of purchasing the cheapest items from a number of suppliers' quotations to assemble a total solution
Churn	The replacement cycle of a PPP or the rate of change of the customer base

Competitive advantage	The ability to beat a competitor whether using superior key success factors head on, changing the rules, or flexibly identifying and producing winning PPPs
Core competencies	Those company abilities which convert small amounts of cost into large amounts of customer value
Customer family tree	A chart showing all the people involved in arriving at a purchase decision, and their inter-relationships
CIF	Cost insurance and freight
CPA	Contract price adjustment
CPS	Cardinal points specification
Discounted cash flow	A method of converting the value of future cash flows into today's value using a discount rate
Dog	A PPP with a low growth rate in a static market
DTI	Department of Trade and Industry
DDP	Delivered duty paid
EC	European Community
Feature	An attribute of a PPP
FCA	Free carrier (named place)
FOB	Free on board
FOC	Free of charge
G & A	General & administrative overhead
Greenfield site	A un-developed site location where a PPP is to be built or located
Group think	A phenomenon whereby a group of people make a decision which the majority individually do not support
IPR	Intellectual property rights
ITP	Instruction to proceed, or intent to purchase
"-ilities"	Reliability, maintainability, quality etc.
Learning curve	A graphical representation of the reduction in the cost of manufacturing a PPP as the volume of uninterrupted production increases
Life cycle costing (LCC)	A financial method of assessing PPPs that accounts not only for the original purchase price but also spares, down-time & operating costs to arrive at the lifetime cost of ownership
Loose brick	A new market entry strategy relying on identifying relatively poorly served customers, selling to whom ideally should not lead to a competitive reaction
Margin retreat	A response to a competitive threat that has reduced the profitability of peripheral PPP offerings which are subsequently dropped. The resulting increase in overhead burden for the remaining PPPs precipitates another round of cuts

Niche	A specialised portion of a market, usually part of a segment
NPD	New product development
NPV	Net present value of a stream of cash flows
NRE	Non-recurring expenditure
Opportunity cost	The advantages foregone through not proceeding along a particular avenue
OEM	Original equipment manufacturer
PM	The project or programme manager who is answerable to the customer for implementing the contract to provide a PPP
PPP	A project, programme or major product
PV funding	Private venture funding. The use of the Company's own money, in contrast to a customer's, to fund the development of a new PPP
Penetration marketing	Attaining growth through greater market share i.e. of existing PPPs in existing markets
Positioning	a) Positioning a company through defining its business b) Positioning a PPP as an offering c) The customer's perception of an offering
Problem child	A new PPP with a low share of a high growth market. Increased share can lead to success; reduced share to failure
PPP segments	Market segments grouped by similarities typically in the PPP, buyer type or geography
Prime	Prime contractor
RD	Development funding recoverable from the customer
Red team	A group of company employees which acts as if it is the purchasing organisation carrying out the tender evaluation and giving a critique to the bid team
Reverse engineering	Producing a PPP by acquiring a competitor's solution and discovering how to build it
RFP	Request for proposals
RFQ	Request for quotation
RFT	Request for tender
Rising star	A PPP with a high growth rate in a rapidly growing market
ROI	Return on investment
Segment	A group of customers with a shared characteristic whether of type of benefit sought or geographic location
Sensitivity analysis	An analysis of those aspects of cost which, if increased, will have the greatest adverse impact on profitability
Spec	Specification
Specmanship	The ability fo influence the way in which a purchaser writes a requirement specification

Appendix B

Bibliography

Industrial Marketing	Reeder, Briety, Reeder	0-13-457482-6
The Mind of the Strategist	Kenichi Ohmae	0-14-009128-9
Marketing Plans	Malcomb McDonald	0-434-91230-1
Competitive Advantage	Michael Porter	0-02-925090-0
Strategic Selling	Miller & Heiman	1-8509-1951-8
Positioning to Win	Beveridge & Velton	0-8019-7112-8
101 Great Mission Statements	Timothy RV Foster	0-7494-0952-5
Negotiate: the Art of Winning	Harry R Mills	0-5560-7287-4
Negotiating Skills and Strategies	Alan Fowler	0-8529-2416-X
Successful Exhibiting	James W Dudley	1-8509-1798-1
The Exhibitor's Handbook	Barry Siskind	0-8890-8885-3
The Essentials of Public Relations	Sam Black	0-7494-1083-3
The Principals of Public Relations	Harold Oxley	1-8509-1984-4
Public Relations	Frank Jefkins	0-7121-1709-1
Effective presentations	Anthony Jay	0-2736-0037-0
Making Successful Presentations	Terry C Short	0-4715-2848-X
Making Effective Presentations	Peter Martin	0-9513-9602-1
Marketing Research	Peter M Chisnall	0-0770-7429-7
A Management Guide to Market Research	James M Livingstone	0-3332-2676-3

Index

A

activity based costing/ ABC, 51
advertising, 235
agent, 132, 255
agreements
 confidentiality, 254, 265
 licencing, 255
 overseas representatives', 255
air travel, 143
Alcan, 172
allocated budget, 17
alternative
 attractive, 28
 options &, viii, 28
Ansoff matrix, 160
audio visual, 231
available budget, 28
available market size, 178, 203

B

back up prospect, 185
BAFO, 58, 63, 69
best & final offer, 58, 63, 69
bank
 charges, 46
 guarantees, 252
 World, 126
barriers to entry, 198
barter, 252

bid
 initiation form, 101
 loss analysis, 107
 review, 80
 /no-bid decision, 98
 win analysis, 106
bidders list, 71, 99
 sub-contract, 69
BIF, 101
Blue team, 79
boiler plating, 76
bond
 bid, 98, 253
 performance, 54, 253
 retention, 253
Boston Consulting Group, 194
break even, 217
bribery, 57
British
 Aerospace, 20, 188
 Columbia, 172
 Coal, 193
 Electrical Allied Manufacturers Association, 246
 Institute of Public Relations, 220
 Nuclear Fuels, 226
 Overseas Trade Board, 131, 140
 Telecom, 160
budget(s)
 annual, 40
 approval limits, 11

budget *(continued)*
 available, 28
 bidding, 37, 119
 capital, 53
 customer's, 44, 47, 58, 64
 initial, 120
 internal, 97, 98
 knowledge of, 99, 104
 operating, 119
 order intake, 95, 108
 ownership, 18
 page, 76
 PR, 226
 PV, 120
 sales & marketing, 119
budgeting, 119
bundling, 184, 194
 software, 47
business
 charters, 157
 concept definition, x
 development, 14
 strategy, 153
 plans, 154
 PPP, 207
buyer credit, 250

C

cannibalisation, 30, 208
capital budget, 53
capital
 cost, 203
 expenditure, 203
capture plans, 35

cardinal point specification, 54
cartels, 43, 199
cash, 257
  cow, 195
  foreign exchange &, 124
  from a finance house, 52
  inflow, 41
  purchase, 250
  resources, 194
  retention, 253
  shortage of, 128
  unspent, 11
cash flow
  competitor's, 44
  driven by, 257
  helping, 93
  in PPP plans, 215
  negative, 211
  predictions, 53
  smoothing, 48
  unpredictable, 49
cashing a bond, 253
churn, 162
CIF, 250
cognitive dissonance, 63
collaborative programmes, 21, 264
commercial
  code, 149
  proposals, 80
commission
  as an incentive, 114
  European, 43
  representative's, 46, 91
  payments, 136
competitive
  analysis, 22, 187
  assessments, 71
  Strawmen, 71
  data-bases, 111
competitors
  know your, 173

compete
  how companies, 191
conferences, 226
  papers, 230
  press, 224
  representatives, 139
  rooms, 120, 229, 232
confidentiality, 20, 91
  agreements, 254, 265
  commercial, 91
consensus rate, 251
consultant, 11
contingency, 44, 213
  for inflation, 260
  on contingency, 12, 44, 53
  plan, 37
contract
  documentation, 245
  negotiating, 61
  other types of, 254
  PPP, 243
  signature, 245
  terms & conditions, 246
corporate advertising, 226
corruption, 57
cost(s)
  activity based/ABC, 51
  accounting, 50
  base, 22
  based pricing, 48
  benefit, 190
  build up, 47
  capital, 217
  collection, 169
  demonstration, 19, 119
  development, 52, 105
  differentiation strategies &, 203
  direct, 29, 42, 51, 105
  effective, 12
  elements, 46
  excessive, 32
  factory, 42

cost *(continued)*
  fixed, 33, 42, 217
  indirect, 29, 42
  investigation, 259
  labour, 50
  learning curve, 33, 122
  life cycle, 40
  manufacturing, 34, 190
  marginal, 50
  material, 257
  of ownership, 197, 232, 248
  opportunity, 200
  overrun, 213
  parametric, 45
  price & profit relationships, 49
  reduction, 29, 34, 203
  saving, 23, 178, 203
  shipping, 42, 46
  "should", 45
  start up, 208
  switching, 199
  target, 49
  to serve, 168
  value & competition, 32
  variable, 42, 217
counter-trade, 251
credit
  buyer, 250
  letters of, 130, 132, 245
  ratings, 164
  supplier, 251
cultural differences, 126
customer
  budgets, 44, 47, 58, 64
  furnished equipment, 266
  purchase process, 114
  training, 208
  visits, 95, 108, 131
customs & immigration, 143

D

danger signals, 90
data-bases, 84, 108
    competitor, 111
    free form, 187
DCF, 35, 210, 212
DDP, 250
deadlocks, 60
deciders, 27, 215
demand/technology, 197
demonstration, 18
    costs, 19, 119
    facility, 120
    of prototypes, 213
development
    funded, 26
    new, 211
    PPP, 211
    PV, 219
    recoverable, 99
differentiation, 70, 194, 203
discounted cash flow, 35, 210, 212
distributor, 7, 132, 255
Dutch auction, 63

E

ECGD, 254
end use, 167
end user, 11, 52, 131, 167
    certificate, 247
engineering consultant, 11
English law, 247
estimates, 44
European commissioners, 225
evaluation
    criteria, 26
    process, 40, 57, 73, 203
    scoring, 86
    team, 29, 75, 76
    tender, 56

evaluation *(continued)*
    weighted scale, 23, 28, 56
executive approval, 82
executive summaries, 75
exhibitions, 226
expenditure
    approval, 11
    cut backs, 97
    capital, 203
    development, 259
    overruns, 218
    PV, 120
exploitation plans, 37
export
    drives, 123, 140
    finance, 250
    licences, 247
    rules & tools, 141
    quotations, 130
exporting, 121

F

FAS, 250
FCA, 249
feasibility studies, 18
female members of sales teams, 125
final win strategy, 39
financing, 251
FOB, 248
forecasting
    order intake, 108
    sales, 198
foreign
    currency, 261
    language, 147, 264
funding, 18
    bids & proposals, 35
    project, 99
    PV, 105
    international aid, 125

G

gatekeepers, 6

government purchasers, 6
greenfield sites, 18
growth
    routes to, 160
guarantees, 252

H

house styles, 236

I

incentives, 114
    in market research, 180
INCOTERMS, 248
influencers, 6
information system, 84, 107
information technology, vii, 57
initial win strategy, 26
innovations, 210, 216
institutional purchase process, 6, 176
insurance, 254
intellectual property rights, 246
inter-divisional, 12
internal budgets, 97
investment plans, xi
IPR, 246
Iraq, 98

K

Kenichi Ohmae, 172

L

law
    arbitration &, 99
    breaking the, 145
    international, 247
    local ownership, 133
learning curves, 33
letters of credit, 130, 132, 245

278 Index

licencing
  agreements, 255
  designs, 185
  export, 247
  PPPs, 52
  software, 47
life cycle(s), 192
  cost appraisals, 40
  market, 197
  using as a tool, 214
lines of credit, 252
liquidated damages, 247
literature, 230
lobbying, 225
local
  offices, 140
  representatives, 132
logistics
  staff, 64
  sales executive, 90
London Ambulance
  Service, vii, 165
long term prospects, 157

M

major banks, 127
major product(s), vii
  account management, 89
  distribution, 136
  life cycles, 192
  market based pricing, 49
  market launches, 224
  overseas demonstrations, 119
  standard price lists, 261
major sub-contract, 34, 44, 244, 259
make or buy, x, 185, 208
margin retreat, 51, 171
market
  growth, 194
  life cycles, 197

market *(continued)*
  research, 175
  segmentation, 163
  size, 177
marketing
  mix, ix
  planning, 154
  plans, xi, 208
medical care, 145
mid-life updates, 195
mission statements, 158

N

negotiating
  contracts, 61
  factors, 58
  stages, 60
  strategies, 58
new technology, 13, 64, 157
Northern Telecom, 160

O

OEMs, 11
offset, 252
Ohmae, Kenichi, 172
open standards, 216
options with innovation, 216
order intake, 104
original equipment manufacturers, 11
overheads, 259
overseas
  bid teams, 69
  public relations, 130
overseas representatives, 132
  agreements, 255
  appointing, 135
  conferences, 139
  managing, 137
  sacking, 139
  selecting, 133

P

page budget, 76
passage of title, 248
payback analysis, 35, 40
perceptual mapping, 186
planning
  & preparing for negotiations, 58
  marketing, 154
  PPP, 205
plans
  business, 154
  capture, 35
  exploitation, 37
  investment, xi
  marketing, xi, 208
  PPP, 207
  PR, 221
  project/programme management, 37
  sales, 35
PMs, viii, 263
positioning, 186
PPP
  development, 211
  life cycles, 192
  market research, 175
  planning, 205
  plans, 207
  second hand, 13
  strategy, 183
PR budgets, 226
presentations, 232
press
  conferences, 224
  relations, xi, 224
price(s)
  cost & profit relationship, 49
  customers will pay, 35, 42
  lists, 261
  presenting, 53
  strategy, ix
  variation, 53

Index

pricing
   approaches, 47
   contracts, 259
   final, 53
   new PPP, 52
   software, 46
   strategies, 34
private venture
   managing development, 218
   funding to support bids, 105
products
   major, vii
profit, 257
   centre, 31
   level, 82, 178
   margin, 49, 258
project/programme
   management, viii, 263
   managers, viii, 263
promotion strategy, ix, 220
proposal reviews, 79
prospect(s)
   data bases, 108
   management systems, 108
   qualifying, 15
   ratholing, 93
   sales funnel instability, 91
   in visit reports, 108
prototypes, 213
public relations, 220
   overseas, 130
purchase decision(s)
   based on perceived value, 43
   effect on, 40
   influencers of, 183, 186
   making the, 63
   sales executives influencing, 86

purchase decision *(continued)*
   selection authority, 57
   selection committee, 57
purchase process, 3
   stages of, 8
   involvement in, 167
purchase
   process members, 167
   roles, 3
   stages of process, 8
purchasers
   government, 6
   institutional, 6
PV budgets, 120

Q

qualifying
   & quantifying customers, 15
   opportunities, 15
quotation(s)
   bid bonds for, 253
   budgetary prices &, 86
   contract pricing &, 259
   export, 130
   foreign currency, 261
   including interest payments, 250
   paper, 246
   pricing sub-contract, 34, 53
   requests for, 23, 39
   specmanship &, 23
   standard price lists &, 261
   to other divisions, 12

R

ratholing, 94
recruiting, 111
Red teams, 80

reference installation(s)
   loss leaders &, 41
   pricing, 37, 52
   unusual bidding situations &, 55
reports
   annual, 88, 173, 230
   country, 127
   monthly, 98
   sales & marketing, 98
   sensitive, 148
   visit, 108
representatives, 132
   appointing, 135
   conferences, 139
   local, 132
   managing, 137
   selecting, 133
   sacking, 139
request for quotation, 23, 39
resignations, 117
retaliation, 174
reviews
   bid, 80
   Blue team, 79
   launch, 79
   proposal, 79
   Red team, 79
   storyboard, 79
RFQ(s), 39
   bid teams &, 67
   constraints, 74
   bid/no bid, 98
road travel, 144
Rolls Royce, 66, 160, 172, 215
routes to growth, 160
royalties, 256

S

sales, xii, 83
   budgets, 119
   control meetings, 95
   export, 121

sales *(continued)*
  female members of teams, 125
  forecasting, 198
  funnel, 91
  literature, 230
  logistics executives, 90
  management, 90
  organisational structures, 119
  plans, 35
  reports, 98
  split from marketing, 84
  staff, 111
  teams, 129
  training for other staff, 117
sales executives
  customers view of, 85
  role of, 85
  tools of, 87
sales staff
  incentives, 114
  recruiting, 111
  resignations, 117
  training, 116
Santa Monica freeway, 55
second-hand PPPs, 13
security
  commercial, 147
  guards, 8, 10, 118
  of information, 146
  passes, 236
segment(s)
  number of, 171
  strategies, 170
segmentation
  of markets, 163
  strategies, 169
selection authority, 57
selection committees, 57
selling stances, 90
sensitivity analysis, 34, 40, 212

software
  barriers to entry, 198
  budgeting, 120
  bundling, 184
  churn, 162, 197
  IPR, 246
  licensing, 47
  passage of title, 248
  pricing, 46
  switching costs, 199
specmanship, 23
standard terms & conditions, 246
storyboards, 77
strategic
  alliances, 206
  intent, 156 186
  issues, 15, 183
  planning, 151
strategy (ies)
  business, 153
  corporate, 153
  cost & differentiation, 203
  final win, 39
  for competitive advantage, 172
  initial win, 26
  negotiating, 58
  penetration, 160
  PPP, 183
  price, ix
  pricing, 39
  promotion, ix, 222
  segment, 170
  segmentation, 169
  vendor, 65
Strawman, 71
Stock Exchange, vii, 165
sub-contract(s)
  bidders lists, 69
  commercial considerations, 255
  direct costs, 42
  estimates &, 44

sub-contract *(continued)*
  offsetting currency risks, 262
  overhead rates, 259
  quotations, 34, 35
sub-contractors, 70
  overseas representatives of, 134
sub-contracting, 264
submitting
  bids, 54
  prices, 243
  tenders, 54
supplier credit, 251
supply chain, 134
SWOT, 206
system products, 215

T

teaming, 20, 264
teams
  bid, 67
  international, 264
  overseas bid, 69
  sales, 129
technical papers, 38, 232
technology transfer, 133, 255
tender(s)
  evaluation, 56
  options & alternatives, viii
  process, 39
  sub-division of, 76
  submitting, 54
  terms & conditions, 246
  win/loss analysis, 106
training
  customer, 208
  other staff, 117
  sales staff, 116
transfer of title, 250
travel
  air, 143

travel *(continued)*
    costs, 69, 119, 232
    road, 144
turnkey, vii, 18, 167, 185

U

unusual bids, 55
user(s), 6
    ability, 7
    behaviour, 129
    buying influences, 89
    need, 207
    groups, 237
    wants & needs, 17
value
    based pricing, 47
    cases, 30
    cost & competition, 32
    customer sources of, 29
    engineering, 53, 219
    individual, 30
    purchase decisions &, 43
    relationships with price & cost, 202
    'un', 201
videos, 231
    as a tool, 87
    conferencing, 120
visit reports, 108
visual identity, 236

W

warranty,
    cognitive dissonance &, 63
    negotiating &, 58
    on second hand PPPs, 13
    retention &, 253
weighted points scale evaluation, 23, 28, 56
white papers, 22

Willson/Ansoff matrix, 162
win strategies, 26, 39
winning alternatives, 27
World bank, 126

To order further copies of this book

To obtain further copies of this book, complete and return the attached card, together with a cheque made out to Greenfield Publishing.

ORDER FORM

Please mail me...copies of **Winning Major Business** @ £30.00 each plus £5.00 postage and packing. Quantities of five or more post free.
I enclose a cheque for £........

Name: ....

Job Title: ....

Company: ....

Address: ....

....

Postcode: ....

Please tick box if a receipt is needed ☐

Greenfield Publishing
P.O. Box 12
KENILWORTH
Warwickshire
CV8 1ZS